WAR OR PEACE?

Contributors

James Finn is editor of *Worldview*.

J. Bryan Hehir is Associate Secretary for the Office of International Peace and Justice of the United States Catholic Conference.

James F. Childress is Professor of Religious Studies at the University of Virginia, Charlottesville.

Joseph Fahey is Director of the Peace Studies Institute and Associate Professor of Religious Studies at Manhattan College.

Paul K. Deats is Professor of Social Ethics at Boston University School of Theology.

Stephen E. Lammers is Associate Professor of Religious Studies at Lafayette College.

Michael True is Professor of English at Assumption College.

David J. O'Brien is Associate Professor of History at the College of Holy Cross.

Walter G. Muelder is Dean Emeritus of the Boston University School of Theology.

Eileen Egan is an Associate Editor of the *Catholic Worker* and on the staff of the Catholic Relief Services.

Paul Hanley Furfey is Emeritus Professor at Catholic University of America.

Thomas C. Cornell was Executive Secretary of the Catholic Peace Fellowship.

Thomas J. Gumbleton is Auxiliary Bishop of the Archdiocese of Detroit.

Gordon C. Zahn is Professor of Sociology at the University of Massachusetts.

Thomas A. Shannon is Associate Professor of Social Ethics at Worcester Polytechnic Institute.

WAR OR PEACE?

THE SEARCH FOR NEW ANSWERS

Edited by Thomas A. Shannon

ORBIS BOOKS
Maryknoll, New York 10545

Manufactured in the United States of America

Library of Congress Cataloging in Publication Data

Main entry under title:

War or peace?

Includes bibliographical references.
1. War and religion—Addresses, essays, lectures.
2. War and morals—Addresses, essays, lectures.
3. Just war doctrine—Addresses, essays, lectures.
4. Pacifism—Addresses, essays, lectures. 5. Peace (Theology)—Addresses, essays, lectures. 6. Zahn, Gordon Charles, 1918- —Addresses, essays, lectures.
I. Shannon, Thomas Anthony, 1940-
BT736.2.W346 261.8'73 80-15113
ISBN 0-88344-750-9 (pbk.)

For more decades than he may care to remember, Gordon C. Zahn has served the cause of peace through his personal witness, academic career, and writings. Although very unassuming and even shy, Gordon is the one who is almost totally responsible for the new status and respect that pacifism enjoys within American Catholicism. Rising above his personal dislike of meetings, Gordon serves on the boards of many organizations dedicated to the cause of peace and was one of those responsible for founding an American chapter of Pax Christi.

In recognition of his many contributions and to pay special homage to him, it is our pleasure to dedicate this volume of peace studies to Gordon C. Zahn, who has stood in constant witness to the cause of peace.

Contents

Introduction

Although we are technically at peace, the potential for a war is ever increasing and we continue to develop and stockpile weapons. Foreign policy is unclear, influenced as it is by oil diplomacy; energy resources are down, implying a rethinking of our relation to both oil-poor and oil-rich nations; U.S.A.– China relations are perceived as improving, but necessitate a re-evaluation of our relations with Russia; civil wars, guerrilla wars, and isolated instances of violence occur frequently and have the potential to bring the superpowers into nuclear confrontation. Discussion on SALT II progresses and disarmament is espoused; but how we remain sane in the face of such madness is a mystery that possibly not even the most skilled analyst could understand. We continue to say "peace, peace," but we know that there is no peace—only the absence of war.

Yet the quest for peace continues. Whether seen as an achievable political reality or a hope used to maintain sanity, a valiant band of men and women continue the search through political activity, education, community action, protest movements, and personal witness. Such efforts have focused on two major elements: peace as the priority, the *sine qua non* for all other activities, and the examination of the morality of contemporary warfare with special reference to nuclear warfare. Although often ignored, these loosely organized groups have gathered an equally loosely organized constituency and their impact is being felt in new ways. The somewhat fierce debate within the Roman Catholic community over whether or not to support the SALT II treaty is but one example of the newly found strength of the reborn peace movement.

This strength has not come because new questions are being raised; rather the questions are often the old ones, the traditional ones from the just-war tradition. This tradition, with its longstanding authority, has served as the framework for both evaluating the legitimacy of warfare and how wars are to be conducted (the *jus ad bellum* and the *jus in bello*). It has served as a constant reminder that violence must be justified and that war is a rule-governed activity. While obviously not able to prevent personal and national actions of immorality in the conduct of war, the just-war theory has served as a check on violence, a continued reminder that war or violence must be a last resort, and that politicians, soldiers, and citizens are morally accountable for how they conduct themselves in war.

Yet in spite of the value of this tradition and its authority, two factors are causing it to be seen in a new perspective and re-evaluated: nuclear weapons and a growing legitimacy of the pacifist tradition. Nuclear warfare, together with deterrence policies based on the possession of these weapons, has challenged the way many think about war. For some, the implications of nuclear warfare are so overwhelming and morally unacceptable that a new kind of pacifist has been born: the nuclear pacifist, one who could justify and participate in a conventional or traditional just-war, but who could do neither if nuclear weapons were used. For others, the use of nuclear weapons was the *coup de grace* for the just-war theory, for they showed its total inadequacy for analyzing contemporary warfare. The framework and theory of statecraft assumed by the just-war theory no longer addressed the modern world, it was argued, and new models for analysis would have to be found. Still others thought the categories of the just-war theory were adequate to handle nuclear warfare, especially when the primary issue was deterrence rather than the actual use of such weapons. The legitimacy of this position was further enhanced by the development of strategic nuclear weapons. Such varieties of positions have stimulated a new debate on the just-war theory, both formally and substantively.

The other factor is an enhanced legitimization of the minority, if not deviant, position of pacifism. Once restricted to the historic peace churches, political radicals, and anarchists, and to what Gordon Zahn has referred to as the "lunatic fringe," pacifism is enjoying a growing resurgence both numerically and, more importantly, theoretically and institutionally. Whether because of the unacceptability of nuclear warfare, the deep moral and political frustration over the futility of war, culminating in the Vietnam experience, or a genuine search for new alternatives, more and more people are turning to pacifism or a general philosophy of nonviolence as a way of life. While there is no dominant theory of or acceptance of a universal definition of pacifism, nevertheless, it is seen as a home or shelter for many convinced of the absurdity of war and violence. Also there is a new intellectual respect for pacifism and pacifists. Pacifists are no longer seen as those who already know the answer to the question. Rather there is a growing recognition of the value and validity of the foundations of pacifism and the significance of nonviolent defense strategies either growing out of or related to pacifism. The major institutional breakthrough came with the Roman Catholic Church's legitimization of pacifism and the call to evaluate war with entirely new attitudes in Vatican Council II. Other denominations have also made statements on pacifism which have been extremely important, but the Catholic statement is the most significant because it legitimized what had formerly been simultaneously tolerated but almost totally disapproved of. Additionally, Roman Catholicism was seen as the home, if not the parent, of the traditional just-war theory and for it to acknowledge the legitimacy of pacifism was truly to admit that the times were changing.

Such a situation gives rise to the theme of this volume: the search for peace as illuminated by the just-war theory and pacifism. The three major sections of this book—the just-war theory, pacifism, and the Church and the pacifist—address conceptual, institutional, and personal issues and dilemmas associated with both pacifism and the just-war theory. Such discussions provide a background to the issues being discussed, an analysis of the questions being raised, and examination of the social, political, and ethical dimensions of the question, as well as suggesting implications for the lifestyle of persons and institutions. Through this format, it is hoped that new answers will be provided for the old questions that are being wrestled with.

The just-war theory has been the dominant framework for the analysis of the morality of war. The two shifts in viewpoint previously mentioned make clear why the foundation and content of this theory must be evaluated. In his essay, James Finn points out that while it had been traditionally *assumed* that war could be justified, now this position must be *defended*. Such is the shift in the discussion of the morality of war. But Finn then goes on to pursue the problem of Vatican Council II's mandate to evaluate war with a new attitude. What does this mean? If I hold the just-war theory, must I become a pacifist *or* vice versa; or is there a third option, which is the correct option? The resolution of such issues will shape how one addresses three other issues Finn indicates as critical: the relation between superpowers which have nuclear weapons, between superpowers with nuclear weapons and smaller nations without nuclear weapons, and the problem of wars or uprisings of liberation. Such problems point to the need for a new theory of statecraft and new structures of international life. Bryan Hehir continues the analysis of the just-war theory by providing an overview of the historical development of the theory as well as its contemporary framework. Of particular significance in Hehir's essay is his setting out of the lines of the growing debate in Catholicism between the just-war theory and pacifism. Because of his sensitivity to official teachings within the Church as well as the development of the ethics of the just-war theory and pacifism, Hehir indicates that future areas of debate would include problems of theological pluralism and coherence of positions as they relate to the values of the community and the individual, as well as a re-evaluation of the role that the Church has within society.

A different dimension to the debate on the just-war theory is provided by James Childress, who looks at a rational reconstruction of the theory in relationship to the *prima facie* duty of nonmalfeasance. In providing this careful analysis, Childress provides both an analysis of the criteria and their logic, as well as an hierarchial structuring of the criteria for use in analyzing a particular war. Of particular importance in this essay is Childress' argument that because of changing historical and political situations the just-war theory functions primarily as a formal theory, which addresses the procedures for justifying war, rather than a substantive theory, which attempts to evaluate the morality of a particular war.

A final perspective on the just-war theory is provided by Joseph Fahey in his presentation of the analysis of that theory by both Pax Christi International and Pax Christi U.S.A. After providing a brief history of the development of Pax Christi, Fahey indicates that this organization began with an acceptance of the just-war theory, but eventually began to evaluate this in the light of the development of indiscriminate weapons of warfare and the call to evaluate war with a new attitude. Fahey's article also witnesses to the tensions between just-war theory and pacifism by indicating that Pax Christi on the one hand argues that the just-war theory is an inadequate basis for the conducting of national policy but, on the other hand, may be an appropriate means for an individual to resolve the question of participating in warfare. Fahey concludes this article with Pax Christi's position on deterrence, as exemplified by its rejection of SALT II.

The second major section—Pacifism—presents two religious ethical traditions on pacifism and two reflections on American experiences with pacifism, one literary, the other religious-political. Paul Deats begins his discussion of Protestant social ethics and pacifism by clearly stating the problematic of Protestant social ethics and the location of pacifism within that debate. Deats does this to provide a context in which individuals with different points of departure can begin to talk with one another in the hope of evolving a common framework for continuing discussions. To achieve this, Deats evaluates different definitions of pacifism and presuppositions on the nature of the state with respect to violence and justice, and clarifies the relationships between power, coercion, and violence. With this as background, Deats then engages in an analysis of Christian responsibility within an understanding of the relationship of the Church to society and the theory of statecraft. This article concludes with a statement of the mission of the Church in relationship to its higher loyalties and its obligation to members of its community as well as the body politic.

Stephen Lammers, in his analysis of Roman Catholic social ethics and pacifism, indicates the post-Reformation sources that coalesced to form a comprehensive social-ethical theory which saw pacifism as irreconcilable with Roman Catholic social ethics. However, as Lammers indicates, times and circumstances change and these have provided the background for his discussion of the reasons which made pacifism a legitimate option within Roman Catholic social ethics. These reasons are located in a re-evaluation of the nature of war, the increasing papal hesitation over justifying war, a new church-society relationship, a rethinking of the role of the individual, and a discussion of the implications of distributive justice with respect to human needs. Lammers concludes by suggesting that what will emerge in Roman Catholic social ethics is a pacifism of resistance which looks to justifying a legitimacy of selective conscientious objection to war as well as a clarification of the model of peace which is intended by such a pacifism. The major need is for a theory which can link together institutions which will provide order, an idea of justice that includes justice between nations as well as in nations, and new possibilities of conflict resolution.

In a highly original article, Michael True presents some of the sources for a nonviolent tradition in American literature. There are two frameworks which unify this article: first, an analysis of nonviolence as witness, as protest, and as a means of social reform; second, an historical framework in which the major actors and their writings are identified. Through his careful attention to both major literary figures and the songs and pamphlets of popular movements, True provides ample evidence for his thesis that nonviolence may also be as American as apple pie.

Another major source for evaluating pacifism is the way in which the American Catholic Church dealt with the Vietnam War. In this preliminary analysis, David O'Brien argues that two things occurred in the Catholic community: first, there was both a revival and a legitimization of the latent pacifist tradition within Catholicism; second, there was a continued use of just-war categories in public declarations both by the hierarchy and other commentators within the Church. O'Brien argues that the reason that the just-war categories won out over the pacifist revival was because of the need to obtain public support and to influence public policy. Consequently, O'Brien concludes that the current mission of the Church attempts to transcend both pacifism and the just-war theory by articulating the mission of the Church in terms of positive actions to eliminate the causes of injustice. Thus, the current strategy for achieving peace and justice focuses on practical action, rather than theoretical clarification of the ethical dilemmas.

The final section of this volume looks to the Church as a source for nourishing pacifism and nonviolence. The institutional dimension of this is provided in a clear overview by Walter Muelder's analysis of the World Council of Churches statements on pacifism. He argues that there is a potential peace principle within ecumenism, that religious liberty and conscientious objection are related, that nuclear weapons call into question a just-war ethic, and that the World Council of Churches statements involve the churches in a struggle against militarism and a recognition of the ambiguities of liberation movements. Muelder grounds these arguments in WCC documents and statements and concludes that, while not a pacifist organization, the WCC is closer to pacifism than at any time in its history and that the theory and ethics of nonviolence are being seriously debated as the distinctive Christian posture.

Eileen Egan continues a discussion of the role of the Church by looking at two critical elements of the Church's theology, the Beatitudes and the corporal works of mercy as a means of evaluating the conduct of war. In a searing analysis, Egan shows how the practice of war reverses traditional Christian morality and guarantees that the sins of one generation will be visited upon the next. Egan also uses this critique of the *jus in bello* to discredit the *jus ad bellum*. In doing this, she develops a strong vision of Christian pacifism that seeks reconciliation while avoiding war.

Paul Furfey shifts the focus of attention from the community to the individual, especially those individuals who are not obligated to military service. He focuses on individuals whom he calls civilian conscientious objectors and asks what their responsibilities are. Furfey raises two questions: What will be the fate of the country if there are no civilian conscientious objectors and why do Roman Catholics in particular often fail to examine the morality of war? After presenting his analysis of these questions, Furfey then provides a list of practical actions in which individuals can engage and, indeed, must if they evaluate a particular war as unjust.

The role of Catholics and Catholicism in witnessing against war is presented by Thomas Cornell. He traces the growth of Roman Catholic involvement in the peace movement, especially under the guidance of the Catholic Worker movement, and shows how this was a witness to the Church as well as of and for the Church.

Thomas Gumbleton provides a concluding meditation to this volume in which he reflects upon the role of the peacemaker in society. After beginning with the recognition that there is a need to allow the vocation to be a peacemaker to develop within oneself through careful nourishment by reflection upon the Scriptures and the example of others, Gumbleton describes peace as a gift to be shared with other individuals as well as with the community. Involved in this is a real dying to self and engaging in the resistance of evil wherever it is met. Gumbleton concludes that if one is serious in devoting oneself to a life of pacifism and nonviolence then personal and political strategies can be developed to achieve the social reconciliation that is one of the major goals of peace.

Many of the ideas expressed in these articles do not stand in easy harmony with each other. In many ways this is reflective of the current status of the debate on pacifism and just-war theory in the Christian community today. Nonetheless, the arguments and ideas expressed in these articles address substantive issues with respect to ethical theory, political strategy, and the responsibility of individuals and the community. Although many of the themes and questions in these articles are traditional, and indeed ancient, there are new seeds of hope expressed in them. And it is in the expectation of this harvest that we can draw courage in our search for peace.

Thomas A. Shannon
Worcester Polytechnic Institute
University of Massachusetts Medical Center

WAR OR PEACE?

PART I
THE JUST WAR

1
Pacifism and Justifiable War

James Finn

Peace is my parting gift to you, my own peace,
such as the world cannot give (John 14:27).

In the onion tower overhead
bells clash at the Elevation, calling
on Austria to change: whether the world has improved
is doubtful, but we believe it could
and the divine Tiberius didn't.

from Whitsunday in Kirchstetten, *W. H. Auden*

War has a bad name today, even among American Catholics. This was not always the case. In fact the change has taken place in such a relatively short time that we are only beginning to comprehend it. What has brought about this remarkable change? What does it mean for American Catholics? What does it portend for the future? To answer these questions we must first take a backward look down the path that has brought us to where we are.

The Problem: "What Is the New Attitude?"

On issues of war and peace there are today two principal positions that are legitimized within the Roman Catholic Church as acceptable applications of the gospel message—pacifism and justifiable war. Both positions start with generally pacifist presumptions: Peace is an attainment and an aspiration of a high order; war is an evil and is to be avoided; the fraternal order in which all humankind participates argues against the use of violence to resolve conflicts. But from there they diverge. The pacifist position states that the use of force to fend off or to overcome an evil is incompatible with the gospel. The other position states that some evils are so great and so threatening that the presumption against violence must be overridden; war under those conditions may be justifiable.

The determination that war is justifiable under certain conditions has been and remains the dominant tradition in the Church. If, in decades past, the allegiance of Catholics in the United States was occasionally held suspect, it was not because American Catholics failed to respond patriotically to the call of war. As late as World War II, most people regarded "Catholic pacifist" to be a contradiction in terms. A Catholic and a pacifist? Gordon Zahn, for example, has testified that when he applied for conscientious objector's classification during World War II, he was told by the local Catholic pastor, who also sat on the draft board, that it was absolutely impossible for a Catholic to be a conscientious objector. Only after that experience did he learn that there were other Catholic pacifists, some of whom published the *Catholic Worker* newspaper in New York.

In the closing decades of this century it would be almost impossible for a young American Catholic to repeat Gordon Zahn's experience. The years since World War II have wrought great changes. The Catholic Association for International Peace, solidly based on natural law and just-war principles, died a scarcely lamented death in the years of the Vietnam War to be superseded by many Peace and Justice offices shaped by the sometimes contradictory demands of peace, justice, and liberation. And, in spite of the fact that the doctrine of justifiable war remains dominant, in any large Catholic conference addressed to questions of war and peace today those who attempt to justify particular military conflicts under present circumstances are usually pressed very hard. What was once readily assumed must now be vigorously supported. This is something new on the American Catholic scene.

This increasingly skeptical attitude toward just-war principles has been accompanied by an impressive gain in pacifist sentiment and expression. During the 1960s and 1970s Catholic pacifists developed more clout in this country than they ever had previously. They were, during the war in Vietnam, a noticeable presence. Although still small in number, Catholic pacifists have produced highly articulate and very active leaders, gained national attention and praise, influenced school curricula and even statements of the United States Catholic Conference. A number of recommendations of the Detroit "Call to Action" conference show strong pacifist tendencies. This, too, is something new.

These new stirrings within the Church do not yet constitute a sea-change, but they are too insistent to ignore. What is necessary to pursue is what they mean and where they will carry us. No easy task.

In its finely balanced statements on war, the "Constitution on the Church in the Modern World" (1965) stated that although "war has not been rooted out of human affairs,"[1] we should attempt to evaluate it with "an entirely new attitude."[2] It has seemed to me ever since I first read that document that "attitude" is a peculiar and highly appropriate term in this context. Highly appropriate because it connotes *both* thinking and feeling in a way that indicates one's general disposition. What one thinks about war, or any considerable issue, should affect how one feels about it. The reverse is also true. Nevertheless there is a distinct gap between the question "What do you think about war (or the Vietnam War, the Cambodian slaughter, the Angolan revolution, etc.)" and "How do you feel about war (or the Vietnam War, etc.)?" That gap is narrowed when the question is "What is your attitude about war?"

I think that many people feel—without being able to account for the feeling—that something is happening in official Catholic statements about war that they cannot fully comprehend, that something is going on beneath the surface of the words. Take Pope John's *Pacem in Terris,* for example. Contrary to what many commentators have said, that encyclical is grounded solidly on principles of natural law and traditional just-war concepts. Nevertheless, *Pacem in Terris, Gaudium et Spes,* some subsequent papal statements, and some statements of the American bishops strike a tone that is new in Catholic discussions on war. It is removed at some distance from the coolly rational attitude that is fostered by most serious attention to just-war concepts. But if it is new, it is also uncertain. And this is why I have said that, if highly appropriate, "attitude" is also a peculiar term in this context. With the best will in the world, how does one develop "an entirely new attitude"? Does one who remains persuaded of the validity and utility of just-war concepts, as I do, desert them in favor of—of what, I ask myself? And pacifists? Are they to develop an entirely new attitude, or are they to believe that far from being addressed to them, the charge to develop "an entirely new attitude" merely confirms their stance and that the rest of us should now rally round their banner? Clearly, that will not do. If we are even to understand what it means to develop an entirely new attitude toward war, we must look, not first within ourselves with the intent of reshuffling our thoughts, feelings, and allegiances, but to that large outside world in which wars take place.

In his message to the special session of the U.N. General Assembly in the summer of 1978 devoted to disarmament Pope Paul said: "The question of war and peace, in fact, presents itself today in new terms." And there it is, the crucial statement on which all else turns. Not everyone agrees with that statement, certainly not those who insist that we must anticipate with dread a nuclear war but must prepare with resolute will to engage in such a war if it becomes "necessary." Nor those foolish people who regard the destructive weapons now at our disposal as simply another step in the continuum of powerful weapons that humankind has produced. But it is true nevertheless: *The question of war and peace presents itself today in new terms.* Pope Paul went on to say: "It is not that the principles have changed. . . . But today war has at its disposal means which have [quoting *Gaudium et Spes*] 'immeasurably magnified its horrors and wickedness.' "[3]

"An entirely new attitude" and "presents itself in new terms." Even a cursory exploration of these phrases will, I believe, bring us to the large, the overwhelming question: What should we do at this point in our history?

How should we respond to the questions of war and peace that are pressed upon us?

The Decline of the Hero Soldier

Dulce et decorum est pro patria mori. "It is a sweet and fitting thing," Horace wrote, "to die for one's country." And writers before and after him have echoed that theme, modifying it at times to suit their particular allegiance—to die for one's love, for one's honor, for one's principles, for one's faith. It was understood that this usually meant dying in combat. Although traditional education has changed and continues to change, it provides a long roster of heroes and heroines with whom one becomes acquainted in one's childhood and youth and who are then destined to dwell uneasily together in some more or less misty reaches of the memory: Hector, Achilles, David, Charlemagne, King Arthur, Joan of Arc, Robin Hood, Henry V of England, Philip II of Spain, Napoleon, Esther, Alexander, Hannibal, Lord Nelson, Robert E. Lee, Urban II, Richard the Lion-Hearted. The list, which could be extended indefinitely, is highly ecumenical, involving both secular and sacred history. The United States has contributed a sufficient number of worthies to this list, one of whom, Nathan Hale, produced a modern version of Horace: "I only regret that I have but one life to lose for my country."

What we were called upon to admire in those figures, and possibly emulate, is their dedication to their party, their country, their faith, and the willingness to risk their lives in that cause. Unchallenged because unremarked was the assumption that these individuals could, at least possibly, affect the outcome of the struggle. Assumed too was the belief that even if they did not change that outcome, they could die believing that their struggle, their sacrifice, was not in vain.

But as one approaches our own time and our own national conflicts one notices that the list of fighters who emerge as heroic exemplars dwindles. World War I remains a great watershed for all of the Western world, including Germany, France, England, Italy, and the United States. In World War I and the wars that followed there were, without doubt, individual acts of real heroism, acts of compassion and self-sacrifice. And individual names rose to moments of national attention and gratitude only to sink back into the great events that overwhelmed them. For World War I destroyed not only hundreds of thousands of "the nation's best"—as the undeviating phrase has it—but the high, heroic, and often foolish ideals that, like standard equipment, they carried into battle. "It's all great fun," Rupert Brooke wrote home in the first years of World War I.[4] Reflecting on that war, Ernest Hemingway said: "They wrote in the old days that it is sweet and fitting to die for one's country. But in modern war there is nothing sweet nor fitting in your dying. You will die like a dog for no good reason."[5]

One can trace this decline in the heroic fighter in the literature of many countries. In American literature, significant milestones along the way are Stephen Crane's *The Red Badge of Courage,* Hemingway's *Farewell to Arms,* Mailer's *The Naked and the Dead,* Joseph Heller's *Catch 22,* and Thomas Pynchon's *Gravity's Rainbow.* It is symbolically appropriate that the best-known American soldier to emerge from the Vietnam War was William Calley, whose targets—men, women, and children—were shot down for no good reason. The fictional transformation of the hero to the antihero was achieved in actual war with Calley.

This shift in attitude, which one can trace in various aspects of our culture, is profound and has multiple causes. It also has multiple effects, only one of which—and that not the most important—I will comment on here: the increasing legitimacy granted to pacifists by leading spokesmen within the Catholic Church in very recent years. Going back no further than the mid-1950s, I can find explicit rejection of conscientious objection as a valid option for Catholics. At that time there was a controversy in Europe about the placement of nuclear weapons in Germany as part of the defenses of NATO (North Atlantic Treaty Organization). Pope Pius XII, who considered modern warfare long and intensely, was impelled to reconsider and restate general principles concerning war in his Christmas message of 1956. His stated position provided little comfort to pacifists. Speaking to the Catholic Association for International Peace in 1959, John Courtney Murray said of that statement:

> Finally, the Pope of Peace disallowed the validity of conscientious objection. . . . The Pope's judgment was premised on the legitimacy of the government, the democratic openness of its decisions, and the extremity of the historical necessity for making such defense preparations as would be adequate in the circumstances. He concluded that such a government is "acting in a manner that is not immoral" and that a Catholic citizen may not make appeal to his own conscience as grounds for refusing to give his services and to fulfill duties fixed by law.[6]

In late 1967, when Pope Paul established January 1 of the following year as a "Day of Peace," the commemoration of which was to be repeated the first of each succeeding year, he made a number of statements concerning pacifism that deserve extensive quotation:

> Accordingly, in conclusion, it is to be hoped that the exaltation of the ideal of peace may not favor the cowardice of those who fear it may be their duty to give their life for the service of their own country and of their own brother, when these are engaged in the defense of justice and liberty, and who seek only a flight from their responsibility, from the risks that are necessarily involved in the accomplishment of great duties and generous exploits.
>
> Peace is not pacifism; it does not mask a base and slothful concept of life, but it proclaims the highest and most universal values of life: truth, justice, freedom, love.[7]

Again, no comfort for the pacifist. Yet attitudes were changing rapidly even at the time Pope Paul presented this address. The position of the Catholic pacifist was no longer what it was when Gordon Zahn presented himself to bewildered officials as a Catholic pacifist. Nevertheless, even into the early 1960s it was difficult for Catholics to buttress their position with supporting statements from recognized Catholic spokesmen or authoritative Church documents. It could be done, of course, and I remember consulting with Jim Forest when he was preparing a small pamphlet for the Catholic Peace Fellowship that would inform and support Catholic pacifists confronted with the war in Vietnam. It *could* be done; there *is* a clear pacifist strain in Catholicism. But compared to the long-developed and predominant just-war position, the tradition of Catholic pacifism, however strong theologically, is historically thin and insubstantial.

In the history of Catholic documents bearing on questions of war and peace, of warriors and pacifists, *Gaudium et Spes* holds a significant position. Not only did it call for the "new attitude" under discussion, but—even while it paid traditional respect to those in the armed forces—in a single sentence it acknowledged the existence of conscientious objectors to war and called for laws that would guarantee them humane treatment. At the time, Catholic pacifists regarded this rather limited official acknowledgment as a notable achievement. They were right to do so; there was nothing at that time to equal it. During the Vietnam War American Catholics assimilated and built on the position represented by this statement. When, in 1968, I edited *A Conflict of Loyalties: The Case for Selective Conscientious Objection,* I was able to include one of the last pieces John Courtney Murray prepared, an address in which he said he believed the provisions of our Selective Service should accommodate not only the absolute pacifist but the relative pacifist, the selective conscientious objector (SCO), as well. Some time later the bishops of this country publicly enunciated the same position. The enunciation of public support for *both* the CO and the SCO, positions generated by pacifism and the just-war doctrine respectively, represents a truly remarkable change, both in terms of general political discourse and of pastoral counseling to the Catholic community. Although there remain some lingering uncertainties, some concern that amounts to fear, and even some pockets of resistance to what is viewed as encroaching pacifism in a hostile world, the change seems to have been generally accepted and applauded by those who attend to what the Church does and teaches.

Continuing Dilemmas

It should be evident that these changes were initiated, not simply by the Church reflecting upon itself, but by many Catholics acknowledging and responding to the "new terms" in which questions of war and peace have presented themselves. Of the many ways these "new terms" have influenced relations between states and within states, I am going to select three, each of which poses particular problems to those who would arrive at sound moral/political judgments. First is the set of relations that exists between superpowers armed with nuclear weapons. Second is the set of relations that exists between superpowers and small countries. Third is the set of relations that arises within a country with a significant number of "liberation" forces. Each of these presents problems to both pacifists and others, the response to which may bring them, on occasion, into agreement and joint political action.

First: The U.S. and the U.S.S.R. have the ability to destroy each other and much of the rest of the world. Familiar to us for many years, this remains a terrifying truth almost beyond our imagination to grasp. All-out nuclear war would leave no victor, only a vast irradiated plain of victims. The alternatives are limited nuclear war, nuclear deterrence, nuclear disarmament, or general disarmament. For years the strategic policy of the United States has been a deterrent policy based on mutual assured destruction (MAD). Now there is a renewed move to adopt a posture that would allow limited nuclear war. The Soviets, it is argued, believe in and are developing a win-the-nuclear-war strategy. We must do the same. This is an attempt to achieve on a political/military level what John Courtney Murray asserted in 1959 as a moral imperative: "Since nuclear war may be a necessity, it must be made a possibility. Its possibility must be created." Many political leaders in high positions are working to create this possibility.

This public debate is shaping up at a time when Catholics represented by the Detroit "Call to Action" Conference recommended that the production, possession, and threatened use of nuclear weapons be condemned, and when, in a pastoral letter, the Catholic bishops of this country also advocate a position that would condemn, not only the *use* of nuclear weapons, but the *existence* of the deterrent (*To Live in Christ Jesus,* 1976). Clearly the Catholic community is receiving mixed signals on important ethical issues and is as uncertain in its collective response as is the American public. The American bishops, usually cautious to a fault, have in this instance spoken out precipitately. In spite of what one might infer from the Detroit Conference, the arguments concerning nuclear weapons systems have not been sufficiently advanced within the Catholic community to allow consensus or concerted action. To condemn the possession of nuclear weapons as a deterrent without suggesting adequate politico-moral alternatives is, at best, politically inadequate. At its worst it is blindingly dangerous.

Our political task today is to see that the U.S.S.R. (or any nation) is not tempted to catastrophic nuclear action in a belief that it is unconstrained by another power *and* to see that the arms race does not continue until it escapes rational control. Nuclear weapons are here to stay. For as long as humankind endures it will live with nuclear weapons. If all that presently exist were to be destroyed, we would still have the knowledge of how to construct them. Since that is true and there is no reason to believe conflict will soon be rooted out of international affairs, we must accept our present uncertain and threatening time as an opportunity to create international structures that will inhibit large-scale wars. Those who believe that nuclear war is necessarily evil must work to see that it is made as unlikely as human affairs will allow. This will not be accomplished by those who wish to treat nuclear weapons as simply another, but larger, weapon in the arsenal or those who, paralyzed by the thought of nuclear war, urge immediate unilateral nuclear disarmament. The unadmirable exemplar of such intellectual paralysis remains Bertrand Russell, who, when the U.S. alone possessed nuclear weapons, proposed unilateral assault upon Moscow's nuclear plants—and who, when the U.S.S.R. attained nuclear weapons, urged unilateral nuclear disarmament by the U.S. Both proposals cut the Gordian knot by unpolitical and immoral means. No nation is to be long trusted as the sole custodian of nuclear weapons. The burden and the temptation would be too great. It is this temptation we would present to the U.S.S.R. if the U.S. were unilaterally to rid itself of nuclear weapons. We must search, in concert, for other means. It is a long and arduous road that lies ahead. Pacifists and just-war advocates could join forces on that long trek.

Second: If we escape military conflict between superpowers, there remains the possibility of a major power's waging war upon or militarily intervening in the affairs of a relatively small state. Vietnam, though fresh in the memory, stirs too many discords to serve everyone as a good example of the inability of a major power readily to exercise its will upon a much smaller weaker country. (I say this although it is a good enough example for President Carter. At his press conference on January 17, 1979, he said: "Certainly we have no desire, nor ability, to intrude massive forces into Iran or any other country to determine the outcome of domestic political issues. This is something we have no intention of ever doing in another country. We tried this once in Vietnam. It didn't work well. . . .") Nicaragua today serves as a better example. Here the history of U.S.-Nicaraguan relations is illuminating. At the beginning of this century the United States found it easy to impose its desires upon countries in Latin America. Sometimes it simply called in the Marines, as it did in Nicaragua in 1912. No military opposition and no effectual criticism. In the mid-twenties the U.S. tried the same measures but met serious resistance from guerrilla forces under General Augustino Sandino. The prolonged fighting caused anti-Americanism to spread throughout Latin America and domestic criticism to build up within the U.S. By 1933 the Marines were withdrawn.

At the end of 1978 and the beginning of 1979 the U.S. was involved in rather ineffective mediation between Nicaragua's President Anastasio Somoza and the broad opposition front, including the Sandinist guerrillas, who were attempting to unseat him. It is a measure of the change in international affairs and of the inability of great powers to readily impose their wills that the U.S. was attempting to pressure Somoza into a legitimate plebiscite and that military pressure was out of the question.

The relation between the Nicaraguans and the U.S. has its counterparts in relations between other small countries and other great powers. Proxy wars—in which small countries are enlisted to do the fighting for other and greater countries—can still take place, e.g., Cambodia and Vietnam. Another example: Cuban troops in Africa can help fulfill Soviet intentions. Nevertheless, it has become true that for a major power the political cost of using its own military forces to impose its will has become increasingly prohibitive. The U.S. chose not to force a military option in Cuba, failed in Vietnam, abstained in Angola; the U.S.S.R. paid heavily to maintain its East European satellites when it crushed resistance in Hungary in 1956 and in Czechoslovakia in 1968. The People's Republic of China is not likely to attempt a military takeover of Taiwan. Admitting exceptions, the general rule is that it has become politically infeasible for a great power to impose its will on a weaker country directly and militarily.

Third: The likelihood of "liberation" uprisings within countries has increased dramatically. Such uprisings will present us during coming years with the most difficult political/moral problems. Early in 1979, Zbigniew Brzezinski spoke of the vast political awareness that has been gained by peoples around the world. I believe he was right and that many benefits will flow from that increased awareness. But there are dangers too. Pope Paul was acutely aware of both when, in 1967, he issued *Populorum Progressio,* speaking to the deep need for development in all its aspects and warning of the terrible consequences if that development did not take place:

> There are certainly situations whose injustice cries to heaven. When whole populations destitute of necessities live in a state of dependence barring them from all initiative and responsibility, and all opportunities to advance culturally and share in social and political life, recourse to violence, as a means to right these wrongs to human dignity, is a grave temptation.
>
> We know, however, that a revolutionary uprising—save where there is manifest, long-standing tyranny which would do great damage to fundamental personal rights and dangerous harm to the common good of the country—produces new injustices, throws more elements out of balance and brings on new disasters. A real evil should not be fought against at the cost of greater misery.[8]

It is the interpolated clause—"save where there is manifest, long-standing tyranny which would do great damage to fundamental personal rights and dangerous harm to the common good of the country"—that carries the greatest weight here, for whether such tyrannies exist is a question of judgment, but a judgment that many are ready to make when they look at many countries in the Southern tier. It is easy, at this date, to quote bishops, priests, and laypeople who see in violence the only alternative to continued tyranny in various countries of Latin America, Asia, and Africa; who now see recourse to violence as only a tactical question. Given the conditions in many of these countries, it is easy to sympathize with their positions. But to sympathize is not always to agree.

At the risk of losing the compassionate tone that Gordon Zahn brings to his analysis of this situation, I quote a single paragraph from one of his penetrating essays, "The Bondage of Liberation: A Pacifist Reflection" (*Worldview* 20 [March 1977]):

> One objection to "liberation theology" as popularly interpreted and applied is that it restores to respectability the "just war" morality that had become so thoroughly discredited by the excesses of World War II and, more recently, by Vietnam. Worse still, by effectively reducing the traditional criteria for such a "just war" to only two (just cause and right intention, both generously interpreted), it has opened the way to virtually uncritical support not only for wars of national liberation but for the full range of guerrilla tactics, not excluding indiscriminate acts of terrorism. Criteria such as proportionality, justice of the means, prospects of success, and others are either ignored or dismissed as secondary considerations.

I disagree with Zahn that just-war principles have been thoroughly discredited and would argue that it is exactly by those principles that one can condemn the excesses of World War II and describe the war in Vietnam as unjust. But Zahn and I agree that popular interpretations of liberation theology do not accord with either just-war principles or pacifism, the only alternatives now morally sanctioned within the Roman Catholic tradition.

Here I must modify significantly my earlier statements that modern war has a bad name and that it no longer provides heroic exemplars for us. Wars of "liberation" have enthusiastic supporters in religious communities. And Che Guevara, Camilo Torres, Nestor Paz, and even the former poet-pacifist Ernesto Cardenal are now being accorded the status of martyrs or heros. Many of the statements made by those who support the cause of revolution as it feeds and stokes "wars of liberation" bear the marks of a crusade mentality: absolute certainty in the justice of the cause; the division of contending forces into good and evil; the rejection of a neutral position; the willingness to take great risks and to "make the final sacrifice"; an unwillingness to make compromises. In brief, the transformation of political action into a religious cause, a holy war.

Behind many of the statements of those who speak most eloquently for revolution is the belief that in justice large, rich, stable countries owe to less developed, poor, economically unstable countries aid, assistance, and more equitable economic relations—and that the rich and powerful are not going to come across, that power and wealth must be wrested from them and their domestic lackeys, by force if necessary. This is accompanied sometimes by a belief or at least an uneasy suspicion that the Marxists have interpreted correctly the great swing and weight of history, that there is such a thing as the "wave of the future" and that those who do not ride it will be overwhelmed by it.

In brief compass one can do little more than note this phenomenon. It involves large issues—the largest actually; it has attracted compassionate and dedicated people; it has produced a library of theory and analysis; it has derived strength from and has cooperated in bloody fighting. It should be obvious, however, both to those who support and those who are critical of modern "wars of liberation," that they pose as great a challenge to traditional Catholic teachings on war as do the large nuclear arsenals of the superpowers.

Either traditional Catholic teaching on war—including just-war principles and pacifism—is bankrupt or it can today gain a purchase on the violence that threatens various communities. I think, I hope, I pray that the latter is the case.

I think that the latter is the case because traditional Catholic teaching situates war within an overarching theory of statecraft. One part of that theory stipulates a competent authority for the exercise of power in national and international affairs. The lack of a recognized competent international authority with executive power is one of the grave deficiencies of present political life. It is a necessary work to see that such an authority be established, the precise structure of which it is our present task to conceptualize—and then work for.

This is the point we come to when we acknowledge that the question of war and peace presents itself in new terms, when we attempt to evaluate it with an entirely new attitude. Major structures of international life must be changed—but not by violence. That change will not be made in a single leap no matter how hard we try. What we face is the arduous, patient work of seeing that the contending superpowers live together on the same planet, of assisting smaller and weaker countries to achieve the security and independence for which they struggle, of strengthening international structures that have exhibited the competence and authority needed to accomplish assigned tasks, of bringing needed institutions into being.

These large statements, necessarily general and abstract, should not blind us to the daily realities that alone give them meaning—the passions and suffering and longing of masses of men, women, and children, each of whom is of ultimate significance. The task we must engage in will demand the efforts of people of different political, national, racial, and religious allegiances. But those with a biblical view of humankind and our place in the universe can bring to this task a shared passion. It *is* a task in which pacifist and nonpacifist can cooperate. It is a part of Catholic teaching that there is a common good that transcends national boundaries. The obligation to seek that common good and alleviate as far as possible the underlying causes of war falls on pacifist and nonpacifist alike.

I hope and pray that traditional Catholic teaching on war is valid still and can guide us today, or the frail barriers that inhibit and limit violent conflict in our time are even frailer than one fears.

Notes

1. "Pastoral Constitution on the Church in the Modern World," n. 79, *The Documents of Vatican II*, ed. Walter M. Abbott, S.J. (New York: America Press, 1966), p. 292.
2. "Pastoral Constitution," n. 80, *The Documents of Vatican II*, p. 293.
3. Paul VI, Message to the special session of the United Nations on disarmament, delivered June 6, 1978, by Archbishop Agostino Casaroli, N.C. News Service, June 9, 1978.
4. *Letters of Rupert Brooke*, ed. Geoffrey Keynes (New York, 1968), p. 625. Quoted in Paul Fussell, *The Great War and Modern Memory* (New York: Oxford University Press, 1975), p. 25.
5. Ernest Hemingway, "Notes on the Next War," *Esquire* (September 1935).
6. John Courtney Murray, *Morality and Modern War* (New York: Religion and International Affairs, 1959), p. 14.
7. "Paul VI's Day of Peace," *New York Times*, December 16, 1967, p. 18.
8. Paul VI, *Populorum Progressio*, n. 30, in David J. O'Brien and Thomas A. Shannon, eds., *Renewing the Earth: Catholic Documents on Peace, Justice and Liberation* (New York: Doubleday, Image Books, 1977).

2

The Just-War Ethic and Catholic Theology: Dynamics of Change and Continuity

J. Bryan Hehir

Historical surveys of Christian teaching on war conventionally employ Roland H. Bainton's *Christian Attitudes toward War and Peace* as a convenient, if not definitive, classification of positions.[1] Bainton portrays a direct and continuing relationship between the just-war doctrine and the Catholic Church. The relationship is historical rather than doctrinal; the just-war ethic is not exclusively a Christian preserve, but it has been most extensively cultivated within the Roman Catholic moral tradition. In the face of this relationship Gordon Zahn has provided an alternative Catholic posture. In his personal witness and his professional research, Zahn has defined and exemplified the meaning of Catholic pacifism.

It is of some significance to record and examine the implications of the fact that in recent Catholic teaching Zahn's personal position has received substantial support. The purpose of this chapter is to revisit the just-war doctrine in light of the emergence of pacifist themes in contemporary Catholic teaching. The analysis will first review the historical linkage of the just-war ethic and the Church, then explore the content of contemporary Catholic teaching, and finally, probe the future directions in which Catholic theology and witness may move.

The Classical Case: Just-War Doctrine and Catholic Theology

LeRoy B. Walters concludes his illuminating study of five just-war authors with the observation that there exist several just-war theories within a single just-war tradition.[2] While acknowledging this doctrinal pluralism, the focus in this section is to specify the relationship between the just-war tradition and the Catholic tradition. This relationship can be illustrated with new clarity and precision today thanks to a series of excellent historical studies on just-war theories which have appeared in the last decade.[3] On the basis of these studies it is possible to distinguish four stages of development of just-war thought in the Catholic tradition. The four stages are associated with distinctive personalities: Augustine (d. 430), Aquinas (d. 1274), the Spanish Scholastics (Vitoria [d. 1546] and Suarez [d. 1617]), and twentieth-century papal teaching. In the context of this article it is possible only to identify the broad lines of development within the just-war tradition and to summarize the conceptual product of just-war norms as they exist today.

Augustine provided the basic rationale for other just-war theorists by utilizing a moral argument which legitimized the use of force as a means of implementing the gospel command of love in the political order.[4] Augustine's argument is political in the sense that his moral judgment on warfare emerged from an assessment of the possibilities and requirements of order in the political community. Augustine's theological anthropology is marked by an abiding consciousness of the effect of sin in human affairs. War is both the product of sin and a remedy for it; in a world marked by sin, the use of force by public authorities is a legitimate means of avenging evil. In the face of the New Testament ethic, most powerfully evident in the Sermon on the Mount, the use of force was problematical for Christians but not impossible to reconcile with the gospel. Augustine combined an ethic of intention with a powerful sense of the needs of public order in constructing a position which prohibited killing in self-defense, but acknowledged its possibility in social relations.[5]

Thomas Aquinas inherited the Augustinian position, accepted its basic rationale, and provided the just-war theory with a systematic set of criteria: just cause, legitimate authority, and right intention.[6] Following Augustine, Thomas located his analysis of just war within the framework of an ethic of charity and tied it directly to the needs of the common good. The taking of human life remained a major moral problem for those committed to the message and life of Jesus; it could be justified only by referring it to the defense of the common good. The purpose of the just-war ethic was not to rationalize violence, but to limit its scope and methods in a world where force was a tragic but necessary instrument of the political process.

The ambivalence of legitimizing even a limited use of force within an evangelical ethic appears in Thomas' discussion of the right of self-defense. Augustine had prohibited the killing of another in the name of self-defense. Aquinas accepted the measure, but only by using the principle of double effect: public authorities could directly will the taking of life, but private persons could *intend* only the deterring of aggression, not the death of the aggressor.[7] The principal role of Aquinas in the just-war tradition was that he systematized the limiting criteria which had developed since Augustine, and he added his immense authority in Catholic theological tradition to the just-war concept.

Aquinas did theology in the context of a unified Christian commonwealth with the Church established as the recognized moral authority. By the time Vitoria and Suarez addressed the problem of war two decisive changes had occurred. First, the emergence of the nation-state produced a qualitatively new center of secular political authority which challenged both the idea of a wider Christian commonwealth and the binding power of any universal moral authority higher than the state. Second, the impact of the Reformation eroded the spiritual and moral bonds of the Christian community which Augustine and Aquinas had taken for granted. Faced with a new political and religious context, the Spanish Scholastics labored to save the substance of the just-war ethic by revising its structure.[8] The emphasis of the normative teaching shifted from Aquinas' strong stress on just cause toward a concentration on questions of means used in warfare. The category of just-cause war was modified to allow for the possibility that both sides subjectively perceived themselves to have justifiable reasons for war. In the face of this principle, itself an accommodation to the secular nation-state, the moralists made a tactical retreat to the position of seeking to limit the scope of violence among states. In recasting the content of the just-cause category and in enhancing the status of judgments about the means of warfare, the Spanish Scholastics, and to an even greater degree the Protestant theologian Hugo Grotius (d. 1645), provided the foundation for the secular science of international law.[9]

Between the seventeenth and twentieth centuries the only innovative contribution to just-war thinking in the Catholic tradition was the work of Taparelli d'Azeglio (d. 1862) in the nineteenth century. His efforts to think about the international community as a subject of moral law provided the conceptual foundation for themes in twentieth-century papal teaching. For the purposes of this survey, it is more useful to examine the product of the papal teaching rather than its roots. The principal link in the relationship of the just-war tradition and papal teaching is Pius XII. In a detailed analysis of Pius XII's teaching on modern warfare, John Courtney Murray illustrates how Pius XII both affirmed the just-war ethic and modified its content.[10]

On the one hand, Pius XII's approach to war acknowledged the possibility that force could be used as an instrument of justice, although he consistently tried to place this question within the framework of the need for creating a more adequate political and legal structure for the international community.[11] On the other hand, Pius XII was sufficiently impressed, on both moral and political grounds, with the destructive capacity of modern warfare that he reduced the legitimate causes of war from three (defense, avenging evil, and restoring violated rights) to one: defense of one's nation or of others being unjustly attacked.[12] This marginal justification of the legitimacy of force in international relations foreshadowed the increasing discomfort which papal teaching would have reconciling modern weaponry with standards of reason and faith. At the same time Pius XII was vividly clear that pacifism as a moral posture was unacceptable.[13] As the Catholic Church entered the pontificate of John XXIII, the just-war doctrine was solidly in possession.

The Contemporary Development: Catholic Teaching 1958–1978

Thus far the description of the just-war ethic has been cast in historical terms, specifying the close and continuing relationship between it and the public position of the Catholic Church. Prior to examining the specific characteristics of contemporary Catholic teaching on war it is necessary to summarize the constitutive principles and categories of the just-war tradition as it stands today.

THE CONTENT OF THE JUST-WAR ETHIC

Two excellent essays by Ralph B. Potter and James F. Childress simplify the task of analysis and provide a means of summarizing the tradition.[14] Both Potter and Childress find in the just-war ethic an understanding of war as a rule-governed activity. Potter states the case synthetically:

> The logic generally applied by wise critics in thinking about right and wrong in the use of force is admirably simple in its basic structure. First, there is a strong presumption against the use of force. The burden of proof rests heavily upon anyone who would take arms against his neighbor. But secondly, it is conceded that certain exceptions must be made for the sake of the common good.[15]

As Childress observes, evaluating war as a rule-governed activity sets the just-war ethic apart from both the pacifist posture (all war is unlimited violence and unacceptable) and the realist position (war is too central to security to be restrained by moral categories). To explore the meaning of "rule-governed activity" takes us into the categories and questions which reason poses about the use of force and the taking of human life. Both Childress and Potter locate the origin of the just-war argument in "a strong moral and legal presumption against the use of force."[16] This presumption against war is reflected in the way Aquinas poses his *quaestio* regarding war: "Is fighting in war always a sin?"[17] In the pacifist tradition this "strong presumption" becomes in effect an absolute rule admitting no exceptions. The just-war ethic retains the presumption, but acknowledges exceptions to the rule.

Childress analyzes the structure of just-war moral reasoning by invoking W. D. Ross' distinction between a "*prima facie* duty" and an "actual duty." As Childress states the distinction:

> When two or more *prima facie* obligations appear to come into conflict, we have to assess the total situation including various possible courses of action with all their features of *prima facie* rightness and wrongness to determine what we actually ought to do. The phrase "*prima facie*" indicates that certain features of acts that have a tendency to make an act right or wrong claim our

> attention; insofar as an act has those features it is right or wrong. But our actual obligation depends on the act in its wholeness or entirety.[18]

In the moral problem of war, our *prima facie* obligation not to do harm to others is balanced against the fact that failure to use force will leave the innocent open to unjust attack or will leave centrally important societal values (justice, freedom of conscience, etc.) at the mercy of those who neither reverence nor honor them. The moral decision to use force in the just-war ethic arises, therefore, from a conflict of *prima facie* obligations. When the just-war ethic is legitimately invoked, the conclusion is that our actual moral duty is the need to use force as a last resort in defense of human life and the values which provide life with meaning and dignity. The just-war ethic, with its stringent tests and structured moral vocabulary, is designed not to legitimate war as an acceptable activity in society, but to limit war to those cases, and only those, where supremely important values are at stake. In such instances the obligation to defend such values overrides the presumption not to use force.

The content of the just-war ethic is comprised by the criteria and questions designed to assess when the *prima facie* obligation to do no harm or to abstain from using force can be overridden. In the development of the just-war tradition Aquinas' three basic categories of proper authority, just cause, and right intention have been expanded into a complex set of criteria usually classified in terms of *jus ad bellum* and *jus in bello*. The first set of tests involves: (1) legitimate authority; (2) just cause; (3) last resort; (4) need for a declaration of war; (5) reasonable hope of success; (6) proportionality (of the whole enterprise of the war in question); and (7) right intention. The second set of principles involves: (1) the immunity of noncombatants from direct attack; and (2) proportionality (of specific tactics).

Both Potter and Childress have examined the content of each of these criteria, and Childress has carried forward the essential inquiry of how the criteria should be weighed and related to each other. It is important to note that this articulated framework of moral analysis is the background in terms of which the just-war ethic has been invoked in Catholic teaching. Often the use of the principles, and even their meaning, was not clearly exposed, but the basic structure of moral reasoning was assumed. As a system of rational analysis open to explication and implementation it is open to use by all. Given the history of the ethic, however, its contemporary status in Catholic teaching is an issue of some significance. The rest of this chapter is devoted to specifying its status and speculating upon its future in Catholic theology.

PACIFISM WITHIN CATHOLICISM

In the twenty years since John XXIII took up the papal ministry, Catholic teaching on war has been in a state of movement. The principal development has been the legitimization of a pacifist perspective as a method for evaluating modern warfare. This has occurred as one piece of a larger pattern, so the pacifist orientation in contemporary teaching should not be seen as an isolated phenomenon. The task here is to assess both its meaning and its status in relationship to just-war thinking within Catholicism. The relevant texts which have produced the pacifist option are John XXIII's *Pacem in Terris* (1963), Vatican II's *Gaudium et Spes* (1965), and a series of statements by Paul VI during his pontificate (1963–1978).[19]

Both *Pacem in Terris* and *Gaudium et Spes* have contributed to the articulation of a pacifist position within Catholicism, but they have done so in different ways. The analysis of modern war in *Pacem in Terris* is notable for three reasons. First, the strong criticism of the arms race, and the balance of terror upon which it rests, is linked directly to positive proposals much like those of Pius XII, calling for structural reform of the international political and legal system. In Pope John's view the control of the arms race is one of several questions which exhibit the structural defect in international relations today. Second, *Pacem in Terris*, alone in the documents of contemporary papal teaching, provides no explicit endorsement of the right of self-defense for peoples and states. Third, the most explicit moral judgment asserted in the section on war seems to call into question the very rationale of just-war teaching. The rendition of the text has itself been the subject of extensive controversy. The most widely used version asserts:

> Therefore, in this age of ours, which prides itself on its atomic power, it is irrational to think that war is a proper way to obtain justice for violated rights.[20]

Some commentators, like James Douglass, have read this statement to mean that the conditions of modern war are such that no form of warfare can be justified.[21] The passage is, therefore, a pure pacifist assertion. Others, like Paul Ramsey, contend that such an interpretation cannot be sustained. Ramsey sees *Pacem in Terris* simply reaffirming the position of Pius XII: that defensive war is the only permissable recourse to force in the nuclear age.[22] This dispute over the "literal sense" of *Pacem in Terris* remains unresolved and may not be open to definitive resolution. In the face of contending views, the approach taken here is to place *Pacem in Terris* in the line of what preceded it and followed it in papal teaching. Since later documents consistently assert the right of legitimate defense for states, and yet make no attempt to reform, correct, or reinterpret *Pacem in Terris*, it seems reasonable to assume that the encyclical is not understood in Catholic teaching as proscribing the defensive use of force under very restricted conditions. Even if this reading of the text is accepted, it amounts to toleration of the use of force, not a moral endorsement. Both the tenor and the text of *Pacem in Terris* signaled a changing atmosphere in the Catholic evaluation of modern war.

In spite of his devastating critique of war, John XXIII provided no explicit endorsement of a pacifist position. This occurred for the first time in Catholic teaching in *Gaudium et Spes*. The tone of this conciliar reflection on war and peace is set by its expressed intention "to undertake an evaluation of war with an entirely new attitude." Two products of this new attitude are the endorsement of nonviolent philosophy and support for conscientious objection. The first occurs in the context of the conciliar reflection on the nature and meaning of peace: "We cannot fail to praise those who renounce the use of violence in the vindication of their rights, and who resort to methods of defense which are otherwise available to weaker parties too, provided that this can be done without injury to the rights and duties of others or of the community itself."[23] From the perspective of ethical analysis, an endorsement *in principle* of a nonviolent position would have been conceptually more clear. As the text stands in *Gaudium et Spes,* it is closer to being a pastoral commendation of those practicing nonviolence than it is a statement of moral principle. In spite of this ambiguity, it does not distort the text to find in this passage support for a pacifist position as a legitimate option for the Catholic conscience.

Such an interpretation is confirmed in the next paragraph by the discussion in *Gaudium et Spes* of the obligation of conscience in the face of policy directives. In language noticeably stronger than earlier authors had used, the council calls upon Christians to resist orders which violate the natural law. In this context *Gaudium et Spes* addresses conscientious objection:

> It seems right that laws make humane provisions for the case of those who for reasons of conscience refuse to bear arms, provided however, that they accept some other form of service to the human community.[24]

No distinction is made here between universal and selective conscientious objection. While this omission leaves some issues unresolved, the thrust of the statement as it stands makes clear that in supporting universal conscientious objection, the council has placed the Church in support of those who affirm a clear-cut pacifist position.

Both statements in *Gaudium et Spes* are strikingly different from a just-war position, and the statement on conscientious objection reversed the position taken by Pius XII a decade earlier. In the years after the council, Paul VI contributed to the direction taken in these statements by praising nonviolent methods of social change.[25] Taken together, a series of statements from *Pacem in Terris* through the speeches of Paul VI have established a new position from which Catholics can evaluate the moral problem of war. The question which inevitably arises in light of these statements is whether Catholic teaching has simply become pacifist. Such an impression can be garnered from some of the commentaries on recent Church teaching. James Douglass's position that *Pacem in Terris* is a pacifist document has already been cited.[26] John Yoder, in his work, *Nevertheless: The Varieties of Religious Pacifism,* classifies *Pacem in Terris* and Pope Paul's *Address to the United Nations* (1965) as examples of cosmopolitan pacifism.[27] In a statement submitted to the U.N. Special

Session on Disarmament (1978), Pax Christi, an International Catholic Movement for Peace, made the following judgment about the state of mind of Catholics:

> Concerned Catholics, in finding the traditional conditions for organizing violence inapplicable, are concentrating on the theology of peace, a theology based on the centrality of love and on seeing the imprint of the divine in every human creature.[28]

The difficulty with these statements is that they push the texts too far. The total content of recent Catholic teaching does not support a judgment that the Church has moved from a just-war ethic to a pacifist position. The reality is both more complex, less clear, and perhaps morally richer than such an absolute "conversion" would be. There has been a dimension of change in the normative doctrine on war; its significance can be evaluated from the texts examined above, and from others which support and complement these. But there has also been affirmed a significant line of continuity with the teaching of Pius XII, and with the moral tradition of the just-war ethic.

CATHOLIC TEACHING AND LEGITIMATE DEFENSE

The central theme which ties contemporary Catholic teaching to earlier just-war teaching is the repeated assertion of the right of states to legitimate defense. The relevant texts, in addition to Pius XII, are *Gaudium et Spes*, Pope Paul's U.N. Address (1965), and the Vatican statement, *The Holy See and Disarmament* (1976).[29] The substance of these assertions is basically the same: in a world of states, still devoid of an effective political-legal international authority, "governments cannot be denied the right to legitimate defense once every means of peaceful settlement has been exhausted."[30] Implied in this statement, and others like it, is a structure of moral argument which we have already examined.

The term "just war" does not appear in recent papal teaching, but if the right of legitimate defense is affirmed, then just below the surface of the affirmation lies what Ralph B. Potter has called the "moral logic" of just-war theory. This moral logic is the set of questions used to determine when recourse to arms is a "legitimate" act of defense and when it is not. To assert the right of states to defend themselves without providing a moral framework for the assertion is to leave the road open to indiscriminate uses of force. The assertion requires an ethical calculus defining both the legitimate ends and limited means which keep the use of force within the moral universe.

In fact *Gaudium et Spes* uses the traditional ethical calculus but does not identify it as such. The categories which legitimize some forms of force and prohibit others invoke terms like just defense, rely upon the principle of proportionality, and use the rule of noncombatant immunity as the key concept in the council's condemnation of weapons of mass destruction. The prominent use of the traditional categories illustrates that, even in the document which formulated a pacifist option, Catholic moral theology retained the conviction that war is possible, may be necessary in the name of justice, and, if necessary, must be a rule-governed activity pursued within a fabric of moral restraints.

The use of the traditional ethical calculus is also reflected in the way the arms race is treated in recent Catholic teaching. At one level the statements, from *Pacem in Terris* through *Gaudium et Spes* to *The Holy See and Disarmament*, are a relentless condemnation of the arms race. The passage from *Gaudium et Spes* is representative: "The arms race is an utterly treacherous trap for humanity, and one which injures the poor to an intolerable degree."[31] The judgment is reiterated with qualitatively new strength a decade after Vatican II. In an intervention at the United Nations, the Holy See urged that the arms race "be condemned unreservedly" because it is "a danger, an injustice, a theft from the poor and a folly."[32] Given the dimensions and danger of the nuclear arms race, the power of these statements establishes for the Holy See a position which is morally prophetic and politically important.

Equally significant, however, is the difference in tone and style in the papal discourse when it moves from condemnation of the arms race to constructive political change. The approach to arms control and disarmament is cautious and carefully drawn. It reflects awareness of the complexity of negotiating an agreement between sovereign states on an issue central to their security. The passage which typifies the recent teaching on disarmament is found in *Gaudium et Spes:*

> Hence everyone must labor to put an end at last to the arms race, and to make a true beginning of disarmament, not indeed a unilateral disarmament, but one proceeding at an equal pace according to agreement, and backed up by authentic and workable safeguards.[33]

The statements in Catholic teaching call for a fundamental change in the psychology and politics of interstate relations, from fear to mutual trust; understandably, they provide little guidance about which specific policy measures should be pursued to control the arms race. They do, however, offer a set of procedural criteria which reflect the approach just cited from *Gaudium et Spes*. The process of disarmament must be "gradual," "controlled," and "backed up by genuine and effective guarantees."[34] These operational guidelines are the product of a measured political realism in the face of a situation which urgently requires transformation, but which does not yield to simple solutions. The papal appeals for disarmament carefully try to incorporate both dimensions of the dilemma, prophetic vision and political wisdom.[35]

THE QUESTION OF COHERENCE

Sufficient exegesis of Catholic teaching on war since 1958 has been done here to illustrate the new state of the question. Whereas Bainton, and to some degree Pius XII, depicted an exclusive relationship between Catholic moral thought and the just-war ethic, the new situation is more complex. Today there are two moral responses offered to the Catholic conscience confronted by the moral dilemma of war. The first is the just-war ethic; the second is Christian pacifism. In a volume devoted to moral analysis it is not sufficient simply to describe the new factual situation. Moral positions must be submitted to the tests of consistency and coherence. The question for Catholic theology is whether the existing teaching forms a viable moral posture. In the new state of the question do we have moral complexity or simply contradiction in the two positions?

To assess the moral quality of contemporary teaching, it is necessary to begin with a recognition that pluralism is both a fact and a desired characteristic in Catholic moral theology today.[36] Yet, affirming pluralism as the context for moral teaching does not settle the questions of internal consistency and coherence. Pluralism cannot legitimize anarchy; for the concept to be analytically useful, there must be definite limits to pluralism. The limits define a framework of ethical perspective and discourse within which different methodologies and distinct moral judgements can be affirmed. The search for coherence begins with an assessment of whether the divergent conclusions of pacifism and the just-war ethic are rooted in some shared moral vision.

At the level of a general moral vision there are a number of perceptions and premises held in common by the pacifist and just-war positions. Both begin with a religious and moral conviction about the sacredness of life. This yields a positive responsibility to foster and preserve its sacred character, and a conviction that any taking of human life is a moral problem of the highest order. For both positions, therefore, war can never be explained as a purely technical or political problem. Nor will either position admit the "realist" view that once we pass from peace to war, we move from a world of moral restraint to a wasteland in which "anything goes."

As we have already seen in this chapter, the difference between the pacifist and just-war ethic surfaces when the presumption against using force is tested in a variety of conflict situations. The pacifist moral conviction about the inviolability of human life is so absolute, and the pacifist religious belief about the ministry and message of Jesus is so tied to a nonviolent meaning, that no conflict of values, even the defense of innocent life, can legitimize overriding the presumption. In the just-war ethic, as we have seen, the *prima facie* duty yields to an actual duty in which force is used in the name of justice. Briefly, the pacifist ethic has a single rule and it is absolute: force is never to be used; it is incompatible with the Christian vocation. The just-war ethic has a multiplicity of rules; it begins with the pacifist presumption, but it acknowledges the possibility of the presumption yielding to a rule-governed use of force, shaped by a multiplicity of criteria. Common premises yield diverse conclusions. The journey from premise to conclusion is shaped not only by different patterns of moral reasoning, but also by positions on theological anthropology and diverse readings of the empirical data of history.

An analagous relationship exists between the two forms of moral reasoning, however, and it is exemplified in the question of conscientious objection. The position of conscientious objection is a pacifist position; Gordon Zahn has described its moral significance in his writings, and has witnessed to its political significance in World War II. The position of selective conscientious objection is a product of just-war reasoning;[37] one arrives at the position by an application of the just-war criteria to a specific conflict. For the pacifist conscience, selective conscientious objection is not an option, since it implies that some uses of force would be legitimate. The new state of the question in Catholic moral thought is illustrated by the fact that during the Vietnam War the bishops of the United States placed the institutional Church in support of both conscientious objection and selective conscientious objection.[38] The two positions cannot logically be held by the same person; they are products of distinct patterns of moral reasoning. The initial question of coherence put to contemporary Catholic teaching is whether the positions can be held by different persons within the same faith community. It is not sufficient simply to say that both positions have been supported in Catholic teaching. The teaching must be tested by standards of theological discourse. The new state of the question requires systematic inquiry which will examine what the internal logic of each position is, how they are related, and whether they can be held in tandem.

The systematic inquiry will have to go beyond the initial question of personal conscience and test the coherence of the existing teaching at two levels of church life. John Courtney Murray has pointed out that the just-war teaching always had a dual purpose: to set the right terms for public debate on war, and to inform the Christian conscience.[39] The first level involves the Church as an institution in policy debate in society; the second level is a pastoral function directed at the conscience of each believer. The ethical coherence of the new state of the question must be tested in terms of the Church's institutional and pastoral functions. Hence, the question of coherence is not only whether there can be pacifist and just-war Christians in the same faith community. It is also the question of what the public position of the Church shall be. At this level, participating in the policy debate of society, the moral pluralism within the community becomes more problematical. The implications for public policy of a pacifist and a just-war position are significantly different. The distance which pacifist churches keep from the policy questions is testimony to this fact. Since the Catholic conception of Church teaching includes the policy dimension as an integral element, one level of the inquiry about coherence is how to project a policy position out of a pluralist setting within the Church. These are challenges which arise from the internal logic of the new state of the question; as theological inquiry responds to them, it will have to confront one other factor, a sign of the times, at both the policy and pastoral level: the moral dilemma of the nuclear age.

THE NUCLEAR ISSUES

The onset of nuclear weapons had a dual impact on the ethics of warfare: it created a new moral category and it posed a qualitatively new moral problem. The new category emerged as the professional and popular understanding of the destructive capacity of nuclear weapons increased. The empirical data pushed the debate on the morality of war beyond Bainton's distinction of pacifism and just-war ethics. Between these categories moralists posited a position of nuclear pacifism. The position is grounded in just-war premises (some uses of force are legitimate) but terminates in a pacifist conclusion (nuclear weapons cannot be used). Nuclear pacifists agree with the conclusion of Professor Michael Walzer in *Just and Unjust Wars*:

> Nuclear weapons explode the theory of just-war. They are the first of mankind's technological innovations that are simply not encompassable within the familiar moral world.[40]

While some commentators, like James Douglass, have used this conclusion to argue that the just-war ethic itself is no longer viable,[41] it can be argued with equal cogency that its viability is demonstrated precisely in the guidance it provides for affirming a position of nuclear pacifism. Catholic teaching has in fact used the just-war categories to assess the morality of nuclear weaponry, and the magisterial statements illustrate a development of moral perspective within the framework of the traditional criteria. Pius XII made the first official response to the question of the morality of nuclear weapons in 1954. John Courtney Murray correctly concluded that it is not possible to find in Pius XII's position an absolute proscription of nuclear weapons.[42] The logic of Pius XII's argument was to classify nuclear weapons as simply another use of force, then to employ the traditional criteria. His key category of judgment was the principle of proportionality:

> In any case, when the employment of this means entails such an extension of the evil that it entirely escapes the control of man, its use ought to be rejected as immoral.[43]

The document of Vatican II, twelve years later, has a different tone and a broader moral conclusion. While not identifying nuclear weapons by name, the strongest moral statement of the council declares:

> Any act of war aimed indiscriminately at the destruction of entire cities or of extensive areas along with their population is a crime against God and man himself. It merits unequivocal and unhesitating condemnation.[44]

This condemnation is preceded and followed by commentary on "modern scientific weapons." After making the judgment just cited, the conciliar text continues: "The unique hazard of modern warfare consists in this: it provides those who possess modern scientific weapons with a kind of occasion for perpetrating just such abominations."[45] The source of the moral judgment in the conciliar text is the principle of noncombatant immunity. It certainly is a prohibition of the use of *strategic* nuclear weapons. Whether it can be said to be a definitive position of nuclear pacifism, condemning *all* use of nuclear weapons, is less certain. It is undoubtedly closer, however, to that position, in tone and substance, than Pius XII's statement.

Paradoxically, the unique moral problem posed by nuclear weapons is not the *use* of them but the *threat* to use them in a policy of deterrence. Nuclear pacifists, clear on the question of use, are themselves divided on the morality of deterrence policy. Deterrence is the hard case for policy and the limit case for the ethics of policy. Pius XII did not have to face the problem, and Vatican II's response is less than precise. *Gaudium et Spes* reflects the inherent complexity of the problem in the contrast between its ringing condemnation of total war and indiscriminate *acts* of war, and its nuanced and cautious evaluation of deterrence: "Whatever be the case with this method of deterrence, men should be convinced that the arms race in which so many countries are engaged is not a safe way to preserve a steady peace."[46] In this passage at least, no clear moral judgment is made about deterrence *in se*; rather the emphasis is placed on the arms race *in toto*, and the moral imperative is directed at moving the world away from the balance of terror. On the basis of his personal knowledge of the positions held by key bishops in the conciliar debate, James Douglass has argued persuasively that they believed they were passing judgment on both the act of waging war and on the intent to wage it.[47] In this reading the words of *Gaudium et Spes* would reach beyond *acts* to the *preparation* for such acts of total war. Only a hesitancy to judge the actual *intentions* of statesmen prevented the council from condemning deterrence policy.

Since no other analyst has had access to the material used by Douglass, his interpretation must be accorded significant weight in evaluating the meaning of the conciliar statement. His reading does, however, go beyond the text of the statement.[48] It is not the purpose here to dispute his view, but simply to indicate that the hesitancy of the council to condemn deterrence pure and simple has an objective foundation. The caution in the conciliar text should not be attributed to a failure of moral courage. The complexity of the politico-moral problem of deterrence demands caution. The point is not that any moralist finds the paradox of deterrence acceptable; it is rather the paucity of alternatives which are both morally acceptable and politically viable.

The limit case of deterrence is shaped by a series of interlocking elements. First, the fundamental moral issue is the relationship between an intention to act and the execution of an action. Classical moral theology asserts that a formed intention to do evil carries the same degree of culpability as the doing of evil. The would-be assassin is morally guilty of murder even if his plan is frustrated. The policy of deterrence today is based upon a declared intention to do what just-war ethics could never legitimize.

A second issue involved in deterrence policy, however, requires that an ethic of intention be fused with an ethic of consequences. As *Gaudium et Spes* observed in its description of deterrence: "Many regard this state of affairs as the most effective way by which peace of a sort can be maintained between nations at the present time."[49] This sentence captures the complexity and the uniqueness of the problem of deterrence. It is precisely this judgment, that the *threat* of nuclear retaliation may in fact be preventing the *use* of nuclear weapons, which gives some moralists pause before simply condemning deterrence policy because of the evil intent involved. If the intention to retaliate and the actual use of nuclear weapons both violate the ethics of war, is there a lesser evil in a threat which remains unfulfilled?

A third question which makes the calculation of consequences intractably difficult is the way in which the intent to act, the perception of that intention by one's adversary, and the possibility of moving from intention to action are related in deterrence policy. Specifically, a perceived wavering of intention to act may tempt one's adversary to act; a threatening, overbearing intention may frighten one's adversary into action. A radical or unilateral move, taken with the best of motives, but having as a consequence a "destabilizing" effect on the strategic balance, may increase the chance that deterrence will fail and the *use* of nuclear weapons will become the moral problem.

These literally insoluble dilemmas have produced a variety of responses to the morality of deterrence policy. One position, the ideal-type of nuclear pacifism, moves from a prohibition of the use of nuclear weapons to condemnation of deterrence policy because of the intent to use.[50] A second position, refusing to classify nuclear weapons in a unique moral category, argues that some uses of nuclear weapons are conceivably legitimate; on that basis it legitimizes some forms of deterrence policy.[51] A third position prohibits any use of nuclear weapons, but tolerates the deterrent,[52] employing some variant of Michael Walzer's position:

> Supreme emergency has become a permanent condition. Deterrence is a way of coping with that condition, and though it is a bad way, there may well be no other that is practical in a world of sovereign and suspicious states. We threaten evil in order not to do it, and the doing of it would be so terrible that the threat seems in comparison to be morally defensible.[53]

The Catholic bishops of the United States implicitly adopted the first position in a statement made in 1976. Going significantly beyond *Gaudium et Spes*, they declared: "With respect to nuclear weapons, at least those with massive destructive capability, the first imperative is to prevent their use. As possessors of a vast nuclear arsenal, we must also be aware that not only is it wrong to attack civilian populations, but it is also wrong to threaten to attack them as part of a strategy of deterrence.''[54] This cryptic passage cries out for exposition.

To specify the contribution of the statement to the wider debate, it is helpful to situate it in the categories already employed in this chapter. The passage has some affinity with nuclear pacifism in placing primary importance on the non-use of nuclear weapons. At the same time it stops short of an absolute prohibition on nuclear weapons by the qualifying phrase ''those with massive destructive capability.'' Does this mean that tactical nuclear weapons are to be treated as indistinguishable from large-scale conventional weapons? If so, the statement is not one of nuclear pacifism.

Paradoxically, the caution in the judgment on the use of nuclear weapons is matched by a startling clarity of judgment about deterrence policy. The bishops' statement acknowledges none of the ambiguity inherent in the linkage between intention and use in deterrence theory. The statement simply applies the classical theory of intention to condemn deterrence policy. In summary, the surprising character of the bishops' declaration is that it has more of an absolute character concerning deterrence than it has about use.

Finally, the statement stops noticeably short of specifying the implications for policy and personal conscience of its condemnation of deterrence. Instead, it shifts its concern to the imperative to work for arms control and disarmament. In doing this the statement reflects a relationship with both Walzer's position and *Gaudium et Spes*.

This survey of magisterial texts from 1954 to 1976 shows Catholic moral theory struggling with the same ''rationality of irrationality'' which nuclear policy has posed for analysts in many disciplines. At one level it is possible to draw from the theory a strong tone of condemnation of the whole enterprise of nuclear strategy. At a second level there are sufficient qualifications in the statements, as well as concessions to the complexity of the nuclear issues, that a final judgment on Catholic teaching remains an open question.

Future Directions: Ethics and Ecclesiology

In this concluding section the focus of the chapter shifts from a retrospective inquiry of tracing recent developments in Catholic theology of war and peace to a prospective attempt to identify emerging issues in the debate. The purpose is not to predict the future, but to place the new state of the question in a broad theological context. As Walters, Russell, and others have shown, the analysis of war fits into the larger framework of Catholic moral theology. In addition to the moral context, as students of Roland Bainton and Ernst Troeltsch know,[55] the Christian moral response to war and peace has always been related to an ecclesiological analysis of the Church's role in society. The future direction of Catholic teaching and witness about war and peace will derive in part from developments in ethics and ecclesiology.

ETHICS: MORAL NORMS AND HUMAN LIFE

One area of inquiry, as yet not systematically examined, is the way in which some of the themes which have produced both pacifist witness and pacifist theology among Catholics have moved in a distinctly different direction from some key questions presently being examined by moral theologians in the Catholic tradition. Implicit in the pacifist position is the conviction that human life has an absolute value; it has such intrinsic worth that no conflict of values justifies taking human life.

It is important to observe two characteristics about this moral posture. First, it applies to other issues besides warfare, most notably opposition to abortion, capital punishment, and euthanasia. Second, the moral sensitivity of Catholics to the value of life has undoubtedly been catalyzed by increasing dangers to life in contemporary society, as evidenced by the threat of total war, widespread resort to abortion, and the often murky debate about "death with dignity." Gordon Zahn makes explicit the basis of his position on both war and abortion in the following response to those advocating liberal abortion policies:

> There is that matter of "absolutizing" the right to life, and to this I am ready to plead guilty. At a time when moral absolutes of any kind are suspect and the fashions in theological and ethical discourse seem to have moved from situationalism to relativism and now to something approaching indifferentism, it strikes me as not only proper but imperative that we proclaim the value of every human life as well as the obligation to respect that life wherever it exists.[56]

In support of this position, Zahn and others in the Catholic community seek to eliminate the exceptions which have legitimized the taking of human life (e.g., the just war or capital punishment). In the wider Catholic theological community there is substantial support for the attitude of enhancing the value and protection given human life. At the same time it is clear that Zahn and many theologians would divide over questions of method and, in virtue of this difference, over specific moral decisions. To illustrate the difference in method, it is useful to take the principle from the just-war ethic which serves as a point of contact with the pacifist perspective: the principle of noncombatant immunity.

In traditional just-war teaching the principle prohibits the direct taking of civilian (innocent) life. Within the just-war ethic the principle of noncombatant immunity functions in a deontological manner, admitting no exceptions. The application of the principle by just-war theorists, however, invoked the distinction between direct and indirect killing. This meant that while "absolute value" was given civilian life by noncombatant immunity, the just war also had a means to deal with conflict situations in which civilians would knowingly be killed in a legitimate military attack.[57]

Within the past decade, moral theologians have begun a systematic re-examination of the direct-indirect voluntary[58] (i.e., the double-effect) which has been the basis for the distinction between direct and indirect killing. The research has arisen in response to a sense of dissatisfaction with the method of resolving "conflict situations" across a range of moral questions (war, abortion, sexual and medical ethics). The tenor of the movement is revisionist, not revolutionary; Richard McCormick conveys the spirit of the enterprise while concluding a painstakingly careful review of the literature: "This study would very tentatively conclude, therefore, that the traditional distinction between direct and indirect is neither as exclusively decisive as we previously thought nor as widely dispensable as some recent studies suggest."[59]

The essence of the revisionist effort is to recast the moral calculus for decision making in conflict situations. The principle move is to devalue the role of direct vs. indirect intentionality and to place at the center of the calculus the concept of proportionate reason. Again, to use McCormick, who has both contributed original insights to the revisionist effort and has interpreted much of its early work for the American Catholic community:

> If one examines carefully all the instances where the occurrence of evil is judged acceptable in human action, a single decisive element is at the heart of the moral analysis: proportionate reason as here described.[60]

The arguments which lead to and support the revisionist case, as well as the various forms the argument assumes, are beyond the scope of this chapter, but its implications for the evaluation of war and peace are legitimate concerns. The revisionist position means a rejection of the notion of intrinsic evil in the sense of determining the morality of an action apart from its circumstances and consequences. In placing the notion of proportionate reason at the center of moral evaluation, the revisionist argument contextualizes moral decision-making and seeks to move Catholic moral thought more decisively in the direction of a sophisticated teleological approach.[61] All of the classical conflict-cases, including war, are influenced by the revisionist argument. It is not possible to trace the consequences here, but it is possible to indicate the difference in orientation between the revisionist method and the perspective of a Catholic pacifist like Gordon Zahn. The significant difference for the purpose of this essay lies in a style of moral reasoning which produces divergent answers to specific moral problems. The revisionist position introduces a dimension of flexibility into the decision-making process precisely because of its teleological character. The concept of proportionate reason pushes the ethical calculus in the direction of assessing all the factors of a problem, of not giving one aspect of an action a unique weight, and it explicitly acknowledges that "the basic analytic structure in conflict situations is the lesser-evil or morally avoidable-unavoidable evil.''[62] The revisionist position does entail the prospects of ''doing evil to achieve good.'' The distance of this position from Zahn's is indicated by a contrast which Zahn drew between the classical just-war ethic and the spirit of contemporary Catholic pacifism:

> All the old calculations aimed at determining ''proportionality,'' weighing ''good'' effects against ''bad,'' and making possible the choice of the ''lesser'' evil are rendered meaningless by the simple refusal to accept any degree of evil as an appropriate Christian objective.[63]

This critique of just-war reasoning was made prior to the debate about moral norms initiated by the revisionists. If anything the new questions would intensify Zahn's critique. The reason is that the style of the pacifist case is designed to foreclose the possibilities of exception to the rule of not taking human life. Flexibility, a broadly based moral calculus, and an ethic which tries to find its way through conflict situations by a process of negotiating the lesser evil are all inimical to the dike the pacifist would build against the threat to life posed by modern war. The style of the revisionist case involves a willingness to re-examine even those principles within the double-effect calculus which provide the kind of absolute judgments the pacifist sees as necessary when dealing with human life. The two positions, therefore, are grounded in basically different conceptions of moral reasoning. This does not mean they are devoid of common ground. Among the conflict situations which have come under the revisionist critique, none has been handled with such delicacy and caution as the question of civilian life in warfare. Richard McCormick has taken up the subject on three distinct occasions in order to demonstrate that one can use the revisionist approach and still preserve ''virtually exceptionless'' rules like noncombatant immunity.[64] The pacifist position would be satisfied by this conclusion but not by the process of reasoning which supports it.

The purpose of raising the complex and far-reaching debate on moral norms in an essay on war and peace is to illustrate how broader theological themes can influence the specific conclusions on the ethics of force. Seen in light of the work of McCormick and other revisionists, the new state of the question on war and peace is only one dimension of a larger debate between those who see an imperative to draw distinct lines with little or no qualification on issues of human life, and those who find the life issues precisely the kind of ''conflict-case'' which require a rethinking of key concepts in Catholic moral theology. Obviously the issue of ethical methodology is not exhausted by the war-peace debate, but it will undoubtedly affect the direction that debate will take.

ECCLESIOLOGY: THE MORAL POSTURE OF THE CHURCH IN SOCIETY

A second way in which the contending positions about the morality of war lead to a larger theological debate is the intersection between ethics and ecclesiology. The pacifist position has historically been related to a conception of the Church which Troeltsch and others have designated as sectarian. The term implies a counter-cultural posture for the Church, confirmed in the view that the ethics of discipleship and the obligations of citizenship are normally in tension and often in opposition. The sectarian position has been most clearly exemplified in the peace churches where the ethical imperative of pacifism has produced an ecclesiological position. Stanley Hauerwas has crystallized the ecclesiological premise of a pacifist commitment:

> It is the duty of the church to be a society which through the way its members deal with one another demonstrates to the world what love means in social relations. So understood the church fulfills its social responsibility by being an example, a witness, a creative minority formed by its obedience to nonresistant love.[65]

Hauerwas recognizes that in contrast to this conception of the Church in society, the just-war ethic has been tied, theologically and historically, to another understanding of the Church's role. This view, prominently present in papal social encyclicals, assumes that the Church has a positive responsibility to participate in the process of building a more just and peaceful human society. To use the formulation of Vatican Council II, although the Church has no specific political mission as it pursues its religious ministry, it contributes to the protection of human rights, the promotion of human dignity, and the unity of the human family.[66] A corollary to this conception that the church and state should collaborate in promoting human welfare has been the notion "that the Christian must be willing to employ force and violence to secure the good."[67] In Troeltsch's terms the just-war ethic presupposed a "church" model of presence in society, most vividly exemplified in medieval Catholicism, but open to other forms of implementation. Such a "church" position was based on premises about the relationship of nature and grace, faith and reason, and the proper form and purpose of Christian social ethics.

The relevance of these two conceptions of the role of the Church in society with their correlative forms of an ethic of war, is that it places in perspective the new state of the question in Catholic life. In Hauerwas' essay the classical case for pacifism and sectarian ecclesiology is reaffirmed. A pacifist conception of Christian witness assumes "that the church will be composed of a relatively small minority" of Christians who have accepted nonresistance as a way of life.[68] It is not clear that contemporary Catholic pacifists presume that "the nonresistant Church" has either a sectarian or minority character. Gordon Zahn speaks of the need for the Catholic peace movement to reach "that great majority of Catholics, lay and clergy, who are not yet alert to the pacifist implications of their religious tradition."[69] The statement reflects a consistent theme of Zahn's persistent witness to peace: his determination to build a pacifist constituency solidly within the institutional Church. The analytical question, raised earlier in this essay, is not whether such a constituency is compatible with a Catholic conception of faith—it clearly is—but whether the institutional Church should take this position. Zahn is clear about his view; he speaks of making "the Catholic Church" the principal focus of pacifist witness, of "converting it into the effective vehicle for peace it ought to be."[70]

In examining the future of the war-peace debate within Catholicism, questions will undoubtedly be raised, on both historical and analytical grounds, about this mix of pacifism and what has been a Catholic conception of social ethics and the place of the Church in society. To cite one example which points toward deeper theoretical questions, Zahn understandably is both supported and gratified by the continuing cry for peace of the Holy See in recent years. The premises of the Church's relationship to the state upon which many of these statements (e.g., *Pacem in Terris*; Paul VI at the U.N.; Paul VI to Special Session on Disarmament, 1978) rest, however, is not the conception which traditionally sustained the sectarian witness of pacifism. The acceptance of the state is theologically and politically more positive and the expectations of the capacity of the state are higher than in a sectarian position. Zahn speaks of a "redefinition of the proper relationship between church and state" which has occurred in Catholicism as the result of a new approach to questions of war and peace.[71] Such a redefinition occurred at Vatican II and is embodied in the documents *Dignitatis Humanae* and *Gaudium et Spes*,[72] but it would be difficult to show that the new formulation substantively resembles the view of church-state relations that has traditionally sustained a pacifist option for an *ecclesial community*.

Another form of the ecclesiological question is raised by Charles E. Curran in an article arguing for a greater recognition of theological pluralism in the Church. Central to his case is the need for consistency: pluralism needs to be acknowledged and legitimized in both personal and social ethics. Previously, Curran argues, such pluralism was recognized by the magisterium in social issues, but not in personal moral questions. Today there are two adversaries of pluralism: some still deny its legitimacy in the personal realm, while others expect the community to be of one mind on social questions. In cautioning against such a position Curran acknowledges:

> There is no doubt that the model of the church proposed here will not be as prophetic as some people in the church think it should be. For many reasons we all want the church to be prophetic, but we must understand this in terms of a broader ecclesiology. There will always be a tension between the prophetic aspect of the community and the freedom of the individual believer.[73]

The classical peace churches have not been shaped ecclesiologically on the basis of expecting a tension between prophetic witness and the individual believer. The expected tension is between the prophetic ecclesial community and the wider society. As Hauerwas puts the case: "The Christian is dependent for his knowing and doing the good on the forgiveness and regeneration of the gospel, but not all men share this knowledge and experience. Because of this the Christian cannot speak to society as if it were capable of acting in terms of the demands of the gospel."[74] The theological and ecclesiological premises of Hauerwas' statement are qualitatively different from those of John XXIII in the opening paragraphs of *Pacem in Terris*; he argues that the moral law governing all social relations, from the interpersonal to the international, is inscribed in the nature of the person and is accessible to reason.

Zahn's theology and social ethic seems to be designed to combine a pacifist ethic with a church-type ecclesiology. One of the open issues in the new state of the question is whether this mix is logically and theologically possible.

The question is implicit in a recent essay by Professor George Lindbeck, who argues that the future of the Christian church may lie in a model which is sociologically sectarian but theologically Catholic.[75] Lindbeck's focus is somewhat different from the church-sect relationship which has been examined here, but it offers categories which can be applied to this question. To some degree the mix Lindbeck proposes is analogous to the ecclesiological strategy Zahn has been proposing for Catholics in the peace movement. Lindbeck has not addressed, however, the question of whether a sociologically sectarian church could tolerate the kind of pluralism in social ethics advocated by Curran.

Neither the ethical nor the ecclesiological questions which have been raised in this concluding section can be settled in this essay. The state of the question on war is precisely the pluralist position Curran has advocated. Such a position has displaced the just-war ethic as the exclusive Catholic response to war and peace, but it has not divorced just-war ethics and Catholic teaching. The pluralism clearly legitimizes a pacifist option for Christians within the Catholic community, but it has not produced a pacifist position for the Catholic Church in society. Some commentators seem to feel that the present state of the question is or should be a transitory formulation on the way to a more clear-cut pacifist option for Catholicism. This essay raises questions about that possibility because its author is not of the view that this would be the optimal ecclesiological or ethical road for Catholicism to take. But clearly we are in the midst of extended debate on precisely this point. Gordon Zahn has helped bring us this far, and undoubtedly will continue to be one of the preeminent voices in the continuing conversation.

Notes

1. R. H. Bainton, *Christian Attitudes toward War and Peace* (New York: Abingdon Press, 1960).
2. LeRoy B. Walters, Jr., "Five Classic Just-War Theories: A Study in the

Thought of Thomas Aquinas, Vitoria, Suarez, Gentili, and Grotius," (Ph.D. diss., Yale University, 1971), pp. 419–20.

3. In addition to Walters, cf. F. H. Russell, *The Just War in the Middle Ages* (London: Cambridge University Press, 1977); J. Johnson, *Ideology, Reason, and the Limitation of War: Religious and Secular Concepts, 1200–1740* (Princeton, N.J.: Princeton University Press, 1975).

4. Russell, *Just War in the Middle Ages* (pp. 16–39) provides a synthetic statement of the theological and moral reasoning supporting Augustine's position.

5. Russell's argument is that Augustine provided theological grounding for Christian participation in war by "spiritualizing" the content of the Sermon on the Mount: it referred to the inner disposition or intention of the Christian, not principally to external actions, pp. 16–18. Walters makes a similar observation about Aquinas' use of the biblical data: "In answering the apparent biblical objections to war, Thomas' tactic was to limit severely the application of the biblical texts. Such limitations gave Thomas 'space' to develop his own thought in a way which did not contradict the Scriptures." Walters, "Five Just-War Theories," pp. 61–62.

6. Walters has taken the three criteria of Thomas and placed them within the larger framework of his ethical theory; none of the earlier commentators has provided such an extensive analysis of Aquinas' thought, pp. 60–199.

7. The treatment of self-defense by Thomas provided the first formulation of the rule of double-effect, which then became a permanent feature of Catholic moral thought: *Summa Theologiae*, II-III, q. 64, a. 7.

8. For the changing context in which Vitoria and Suarèz wrote see: J. T. Delos, "The Sociology of Modern War and the Theory of Just War," *Cross Currents* 8 (1958): 248–265. For internal changes wrought in the ethical argument, see Walters, "Five Just-War Theories," pp. 201–409 and Johnson, *Ideology,* pp. 150–203.

9. For Grotius' contribution to just-war and international law, see Walters, "Five Just-War Theories"; H. Lanterpacht, "The Grotian Tradition in International Law," *British Yearbook of International Law* 23 (1946).

10. J. C. Murray, "Remarks on the Moral Problem of War," *Theological Studies* 20 (1959): 40–61.

11. The theme of international order was a consistent dimension of Pius XII's teaching; see Christmas Address 1941, 1951, 1952, 1953 in V. Yzermans, ed., *Major Addresses of Pius XII,* vol. 2 (St. Paul: North Central Publishing Co., 1961).

12. Murray, "Remarks," pp. 45–46; esp. fn. 12.

13. Murray makes the point that Pius XII was speaking to a particular situation, but the statement on conscientious objection seemed to have the force of a general principle for Pius XII; the text is the *Christmas Message* 1956, cited in Murray, p. 53.

14. R. B. Potter, *The Moral Logic of War* (Philadelphia: United Presbyterian Church, n.d.); J. F. Childress, "Just-War Theories," *Theological Studies* 39 (1978): 427–445.

15. Potter, *The Moral Logic,* p. 9.

16. Ibid., p. 7.

17. Thomas Aquinas, *Summa Theologiae,* II-II, q. 40.

18. Childress, "Just-War Theories," p. 430.

19. The encyclicals of John XXIII, the conciliar text, and Pope Paul's Address to the United Nations are found in J. Gremillion, *The Gospel of Peace and Justice: Catholic Social Teaching Since Pope John* (Maryknoll, N.Y.: Orbis Books, 1976).

Pope Paul has also made a major statement each year on the occasion of the Day of Peace—an observance he initiated within the Church.

20. This version is the way the text is translated in A. Flannery, *Vatican II: The Conciliar and Post-Conciliar Documents* (Collegeville, Minn.: Liturgical Press, 1975). Flannery is translating the *Pacem in Terris* paragraph as it is used in *Gaudium et Spes*, fn. to n. 80.

21. James Douglass, *The Nonviolent Cross: A Theology of Revolution and Peace* (New York: Macmillan, 1966), p. 84.

22. Paul Ramsey, *The Just War: Force and Political Responsibility* (New York: Scribner's, 1968), p. 78.

23. *Gaudium et Spes*, n. 78., in D. J. O'Brien and T. A. Shannon, *Renewing the Earth: Catholic Documents on Peace, Justice and Liberation* (New York: Doubleday, Image Books, 1977), p. 260.

24. *Gaudium et Spes*, n. 79, ibid., p. 262.

25. Paul VI, *Message for Day of Peace*, 1976.

26. Douglass asserts the nonviolent content of *Pacem in Terris* several times in his chapter "The Nonviolent Power of *Pacem in Terris*," *Nonviolent Cross*, pp. 86, 94, 95.

27. J. Yoder, *Nevertheless: The Varieties of Religious Pacifism* (Scottsdale, Pa.: Herald Press, 1971).

28. Pax Christi, "Some Moral Aspects of Disarmament," statement submitted to the Special Session of the U.N. on Disarmament, May-June 1978, p. 3.

29. *The Holy See and Disarmament* (Vatican City: Tipografia Poliglotta Vaticana, 1976).

30. *Gaudium et Spes*, n. 79; O'Brien and Shannon, *Renewing the Earth*, p. 262.

31. *Gaudium et Spes*, n. 81; ibid., p. 264.

32. *The Holy See and Disarmament*, pp. 1, 2.

33. *Gaudium et Spes*, n. 82; O'Brien and Shannon, *Renewing the Earth*, p. 264.

34. *The Holy See and Disarmament*, p. 7; cf. *Pacem in Terris*, n. 112, Gremillion, *Gospel of Peace and Justice*, p. 225.

35. The message of Paul VI to the U.N. Special Session on Disarmament exemplifies this balance; speaking of disarmament it said: "It seems to be a problem situated at the level of a prophetic vision, open to the hopes of the future. And yet one cannot really face this problem without remaining solidly based upon the hard and concrete reality of the present" (May 24, 1978).

36. Among others, Charles E. Curran has addressed the dimensions and implications of pluralism in Catholic moral theology: "Today there exists a plurality of methodologies which are employed by Catholic moral theologians, so that it is much more accurate to admit the existence of Catholic moral theologies when speaking in a strict sense about the methodological approaches to questions of moral theology or Christian ethics"; in *Catholic Moral Theology in Dialogue* (Notre Dame, Ind.: University of Notre Dame Press, 1976), pp. 254–255. Curran specifically notes that pluralism extends beyond questions of method to particular moral issues.

37. For an analysis of selective conscientious objection, see R. Potter, "Conscientious Objection to Particular Wars," in D. Giannella, ed., *Religion and the Public Order* (Ithaca, N.Y.: Cornell University Press, 1968), pp. 44–99; P. Ramsey, *The Just War*, pp. 91–140; J. Finn, ed., *Conflict of Loyalties: The Case for Selective Conscientious Objection* (Indianapolis, Ind.: Pegasus, 1968).

38. U. S. Catholic Conference: *The Catholic Conscientious Objector*, October 15, 1969; *Declaration on Conscientious Objection and Selective Conscientious Objection*, October 21, 1971, (Washington: U.S. Catholic Conference).

39. Murray, "Remarks on the Moral Problem of War," pp. 56–57.

40. Michael Walzer, *Just and Unjust Wars: A Moral Argument with Historical Illustrations* (New York: Basic Books, 1977), p. 282.

41. Douglass opens his chapter on "The Anatomy of the Just War" with the judgment that "the state of just-war doctrine in contemporary Catholic thought is roughly equivalent to that of the prohibition against contraception: it has lost its cogency in terms of current theological thought and continues in use primarily as a point of reference for those who wish to go beyond it," *Nonviolent Cross*, p. 155.

42. Murray, "Remarks," p. 49.

43. Pius XII: *Allocution to the World Medical Congress*, 1954; cited in Murray, "Remarks," p. 51.

44. *Gaudium et Spes*, n. 80; O'Brien and Shannon, *Renewing the Earth*, p. 263.

45. Ibid.

46. *Gaudium et Spes*, n. 81; ibid.

47. Douglass, *Nonviolent Cross*, pp. 112–123, esp. p. 122.

48. Douglass acknowledges that *Gaudium et Spes* "is silent on the morality of deterrence," *Nonviolent Cross*, p. 119.

49. *Gaudium et Spes*, n. 81; O'Brien and Shannon, *Renewing the Earth*, p. 263.

50. W. Stein, ed., *Nuclear Weapons and the Christian Conscience* (London: Merlin Press, 1961).

51. Ramsey, *The Just War*, cf. chapters 13, 14, 15.

52. J. B. Hehir, "The New Nuclear Debate: Political and Ethical Considerations," in R. A. Gessert and J. B. Hehir, *The New Nuclear Debate* (New York: CRIA Special Studies, 1976), pp. 35–76. Cf. also P. S. Corden, "Moving Beyond the Just-War Tradition," in H. P. Ford and F. X. Winters, eds., *Ethics and Nuclear Strategy* (Maryknoll, N.Y.: Orbis Books, 1977), pp. 157–180.

53. Walzer, *Just and Unjust Wars*, p. 274.

54. National Conference of Catholic Bishops, *To Live in Christ Jesus: A Pastoral Reflection on the Moral Life* (Washington, D.C.: U.S. Catholic Conference, 1976), p. 34.

55. Ernst Troeltsch, *The Social Teaching of the Christian Churches*, 2 vols. (New York: Harper and Row, 1960).

56. Gordon Zahn, "A Religious Pacifist Looks at Abortion," *Commonweal* 94 (May 28, 1971): 282.

57. Charles E. Curran makes a similar point about Catholic moral teaching on abortion: "It is not exact to say that in the past Catholic theology condemned all abortion. Catholic theology realized the possibility of some conflict situations and tried to solve these conflict situations by the application of the principle of the direct and indirect effects." Curran, *Catholic Moral Theology in Dialogue*, p. 258.

58. The most comprehensive survey of the research is to be found in R. McCormick and P. Ramsey, *Doing Evil to Achieve Good* (Chicago: Loyola University Press, 1978). The first chapter is McCormick's Père Marquette Lecture (1973), "Ambiguity in Moral Choice," which presents, with relentless virtuosity, a thorough, fair, and incisive survey of the literature.

59. McCormick and Ramsey, *Doing Evil*, p. 50.

60. Ibid., p. 45.

61. Ibid., p. 261.

62. Ibid., p. 38.

63. G. Zahn, "The Great Catholic Upheaval," *Saturday Review* 54 (September 11, 1971): 54.

64. McCormick and Ramsey, *Doing Evil*, pp. 42–44, 264–65; cf. also "Notes on Moral Theology," *Theological Studies* 39 (1978): 113–116.

65. Stanley Hauerwas, *Vision and Virtue: Essays in Christian Ethical Reflection* (Notre Dame, Ind.: Fides Publishers, 1974), pp. 211–212.

66. *Gaudium et Spes*, n. 42; Gremillion, *Gospel of Peace and Justice*, pp. 276–277; cf. also J. C. Murray, "The Issue of Church and State at Vatican II," *Theological Studies* 27 (1966): 580–606.

67. Hauerwas, *Vision and Virtue*, p. 198.

68. Ibid., p. 212.

69. G. Zahn, "The Future of the Catholic Peace Movement," *Commonweal* 99 (December 28, 1973): 340.

70. G. Zahn, "Carrying Our Weight in The Catholic Peace Movement," *America* 133 (September 20, 1975): 145.

71. Zahn, "The Great Catholic Upheaval," p. 25.

72. Cf. Murray, "The Issue of Church and State at Vatican II."

73. C. E. Curran, "Ten Years Later: Reflections on *Humanae Vitae*," *Commonweal* 105 (July 7, 1978): 428.

74. Hauerwas, *Vision and Virtue*, p. 206.

75. George Lindbeck, "The Sectarian Future of the Church," in J. P. Whalen, S.J., ed., *The God Experience: Essays in Hope* (Westminster, Md.: Newman Press, 1971), pp. 226–243.

3

Just-War Criteria

James F. Childress

Introduction

Pacifists and proponents of just-war theories really need each other. This proposition is more serious than an aesthetic view that variety is needed or that the richness of Christianity requires these different perspectives. Just-war theorists need pacifists to remind them of their common starting point: the moral presumption against force and war. And pacifists need just-war theorists to provide a public framework for debates about particular wars and for the restraint of the practice of war. I propose to focus on the criteria of just wars, particularly their bases, interrelations, order, weights, and functions in order to indicate why pacifists have a stake in them. Among the pacifists who have contributed significantly to this debate with just-war theorists is Gordon Zahn, who was an active participant in a conference where I presented an earlier version of this essay.[1] Not every pacifist—probably not even Zahn himself—and not every proponent of just-war theories will find this analysis acceptable, but it is important to reconstruct just-war criteria in order to determine whether they can and should be significant in public debates about war and its conduct.

I shall begin with our "historical deposit" of just-war criteria, now accessible in a number of fine studies.[2] Then I shall offer a rational reconstruction of these criteria. Although we should begin with the deposit of criteria in our tradition, we cannot stop there if just-war criteria are to be defensible and usable for policy-makers, citizens, and church people. It is not sufficient to posit traditional criteria, without an indication of their presuppositions, grounds, interrelations, and functions. In a recent article entitled "Just War Theory: What's the Use?" James T. Johnson considers the implications of this "broadly defined collection of practical principles" called just-war theory.[3] He accepts "classic just-war theory" (which is actually more a tradition than a single theory) as normative. But he offers few arguments for taking particular "classic" formulations as normative and for viewing later developments as decline rather than progress. While my approach is different, I think it is complementary rather than contradictory. I shall try to show how these traditional criteria can be reconstructed, explicated, and defended in relation to the *prima facie* duty of nonmaleficence (the duty not to injure or kill others). Then I shall reconstruct their grounds and interrelations before considering their order, weights, and functions. Although the whole argument is designed to indicate why the pacifist has a stake in just-war criteria, I shall focus on this issue when I examine the functions of just-war criteria.

The Logic of **Prima Facie** *Duties*

The following criteria frequently appear in comprehensive just-war theories: legitimate or competent authority, just cause, right intention, announcement of intention, last resort, reasonable hope of success, proportionality, and just conduct. All these criteria taken together, with the exception of the last one, establish the *jus ad bellum,* the right to go to war, while the last criterion focuses on the *jus in bello,* right conduct within war, and includes both intention and proportionality, which are also part of the *jus ad bellum.*[4]

Many analogues to these criteria emerge when people reflect morally about several forms of conduct including the use of force and disobedience to the state.[5] For example, Pauline Maier shows that many American colonists in the eighteenth century justified and limited their resistance to England by appealing to criteria in the Whig tradition, which established several preconditions for justified violence: the ruler's violation of the ends of government, the failure of "all due means of redress," support by the people, right intentions and motives, reasonable chance of success, and proportionality. When the colonists acted, these criteria, as Maier notes, "proved to be as much a burden as a guide."[6] Similar criteria are sometimes operative even when a person's ethical methodology appears to exclude them. For example, Dietrich Bonhoeffer, a theologian who was put to death for his involvement in the July 20, 1944 plot to assassinate Hitler, justified tyrannicide by some of the criteria of traditional just-war and just-revolution theories although his theological-ethical methodology appeared to exclude rules and principles. His "operative guidelines," for which his theological-ethical methodology made no provision, included: clear evidence of serious misrule; respect for the scale of political responsibility and authority (those lower in or outside the political hierarchy should act only after others have failed); reasonable assurances of successful execution; tyrannicide as a last resort; minimal necessary force.[7] As in many justifications of revolution or tyrannicide, Bonhoeffer found a surrogate for the authority of the government in the political hierarchy; others have also appealed to the "lesser magistrates" and finally to the people.

Actually we formulate and use criteria that are analogous to those that determine whether a war is just and justified whenever we face conflicting obligations or duties, whenever it is impossible to fulfill all the claims upon us, to respect all the rights involved, or to avoid doing evil to everyone. Sometimes we confront two or more *prima facie* duties or obligations, one of which we cannot fulfill without sacrificing the other(s). In this sort of dilemma, we justify sacrificing one *prima facie* obligation to fulfill another only when we can answer certain questions: we need to know whether we have a just cause, proper intentions, a reasonable hope of achieving the end, a reasonable balance between probable good and evil, no other courses of action that would enable us to avoid sacrificing the obligation, etc. Thus, the criteria for assessing wars and several other actions are similar because war and these other actions sacrifice some *prima facie* obligation(s)—a sacrifice that must be justified along certain lines suggested by the criteria. While the fact that force is used is important, it is only one of numerous human actions that stand in need of justification because they sacrifice *prima facie* obligations. Just-war criteria can be illuminated by the language of *prima facie* obligations and the *content* of the particular obligations (not to injure or kill others) that the justification of war must override.

First, let us consider the notion of a *prima facie* obligation or duty (which I use interchangeably in this context). W. D. Ross introduced the distinction between *prima facie* and actual obligations to account for conflicts of obligations (which he thought to be "non-existent" when fully and carefully analyzed). When two or more *prima facie* obligations appear to come into conflict, we have to assess the total situation, including various possible courses of actions with all their features of *prima facie* rightness and wrongness, to determine what we actually ought to do. The phrase *prima facie* indicates that certain features of acts that have a *tendency* to make an act right or wrong claim our attention; insofar as an act has those features it is right or wrong. But our actual obligation depends on the act in its wholeness and entirety. For "while an act may well be *prima facie* obligatory in respect of one character and *prima facie* forbidden in virtue of another, it becomes obligatory or forbidden only in virtue of the totality of its ethically relevant characteristics."[8] Although some *prima facie* obligations are more stringent than others (e.g., nonmaleficence is more stringent than beneficence), it is not possible to provide a complete ranking or a scale of stringency of obligations.

To hold that an obligation or duty is *prima facie* is to claim that it always has a strong moral reason for its performance although this reason may not always be decisive or triumph over all other reasons. If an obligation is viewed as *absolute*, it cannot be overridden under any circumstances; it has priority over all other obligations with which it might come into conflict. If it is viewed as *relative*, the rule stating it is no more than a maxim or rule of thumb that illuminates but does not prescribe what we ought to do. If it is viewed as *prima facie*, it is intrinsically binding, but it does not necessarily determine one's actual obligation.

As individuals or members of institutions, we have a *prima facie* duty not to injure others. Injury may mean an unwarranted or unjustified harm or violation of rights, or it may mean inflicting actual harm (e.g., shooting someone) which may or may not be warranted or justified. In the first sense, it is, of course, always wrong by definition; an obligation not to injure others wrongfully would be absolute rather than *prima facie*. In the second sense, it is *prima facie*. Insofar as an act injures another, it is *prima facie* wrong and stands in need of justification. Although Joseph Fletcher and others imply that killing (which I am treating for the moment under injury) is morally neutral, William Frankena rightly insists that some kinds of action (including killing) are "intrinsically wrong." For they are

> always *prima facie* wrong, and they are always actually wrong when they are not justified on other moral grounds. They are not in themselves morally indifferent. They may conceivably be justified in certain situations, but they always need to be justified; and even when they are justified, there is still one moral point against them.[9]

If the fifth (or sixth) commandment means "Thou shalt not kill," it is *prima facie* rather than absolute, for the Hebrews admitted killing in self-defense, capital punishment, and war. If it means "Thou shalt not commit murder," it can then be taken as absolute, but it leaves open the question of which killings are to be counted as murder.[10]

It is not necessary to defend Ross's intuitionism in order to hold that injury and killing are intrinsically *prima facie* wrong. For Ross both fall under the obligation of nonmaleficence. For Rawls, there is a "natural duty" (i.e., owed to persons generally) not to injure or harm others and not to inflict unnecessary suffering; this natural duty can be derived from the original position.[11] Christian theologians might derive this obligation not to injure or kill others from the norm of *agape*. The claim that injury and killing are *prima facie* wrong is thus compatible with a number of philosophical and religious frameworks.

An overriden or outweighed *prima facie* obligation continues to function in the situation and the course of action one adopts. It leaves what Robert Nozick calls "moral traces." It has "residual effects" on the agent's attitudes and actions. As A. C. Ewing suggests,

> If I have a *prima facie* obligation which I cannot rightly fulfill because it is overruled by another, stronger *prima facie* obligation, it does not by any means follow that my conduct ought to be unaffected by the former obligation. Even if I am morally bound to do something inconsistent with it, it should in many cases modify in some respect the way in which the act is performed and in almost all it should affect some subsequent action.[12]

For example, if I think that a stronger obligation requires me to break a promise, I should at least explain the situation to the promisee, ask him not to hold me to the promise, apologize for breaking it, and even try to make it up to him later. At the very least, Ewing goes on to say, the *prima facie* obligation to keep the promise "should always affect our mental attitude toward the action" to the extent of evoking regret.[13]

One important difference between many Protestant and Catholic interpretations of just war appears at this point: the appropriate attitude toward a just war that overrides the *prima facie* duty not to injure or kill others. In accord with their belief in the universality of sin, many Protestant theologians such as Reinhold Niebuhr insist that the decision to wage war is always "the lesser of two evils," which they understand as "moral" as well as physical evils. Thus, remorse and repentance are proper responses. With St. Augustine they stress that wars should be both just and mournful.[14] Many Catholic theologians, joined by some Protestants, most notably Paul Ramsey, insist that "an act of self-defense or an act of vindictive justice, although imposed by circumstances which are regrettable, is morally good." For them, "war is not the lesser of two evils, but the lesser of two goods (one of which [i.e. peace] appears, at the moment of choice, unattainable)."[15] Regret may be appropriate, but not remorse.

Whether a war that justly and justifiably overrides the *prima facie* duty not to injure or kill others should evoke regret or remorse may be debatable, but it not only engenders certain attitudes but other obligations as well. The traces or residual effects of the overridden *prima facie* duty are extremely important as will be clear in my discussion of just-war criteria such as right intention, proportionality, and just conduct.

Before I develop those criteria, I want to summarize and amplify some implications of the *prima facie* duty not to injure or kill others; they are actually presuppositions of many just-war theories that include both *jus ad bellum* and *jus in bello*.

First, because it is *prima facie* wrong to injure or kill others, such acts demand justification. There is a presumption against their justification, and anyone who tries to justify them bears a heavy burden of proof.

Second, because not all duties can be fulfilled in every situation without some sacrifices (this inability may be understood as natural or as the result of sin), it is necessary and legitimate to override some *prima facie* duties. Some other duties may be more stringent and thus take priority over the duty not to injure others. For instance, the *prima facie* duty to uphold justice or to protect the innocent. War thus can be a moral undertaking in some circumstances.

Third, the overridden *prima facie* duties should affect the actors' attitudes and what they do in waging the war. Some ways of waging war are more compatible than others with the overridden *prima facie* duties not to injure or kill others. War can be more or less humane and civilized. War and politics, or peace, are not two totally separate realms or periods.[16] Both are subject to moral principles and rules, and, indeed, to many of the same principles and rules. War ought to fall within many of the boundaries that are also important in peace.

Theorists and practitioners are commonly tempted to make war merely an extension of politics so that it requires very little to justify waging war; or they are tempted to make politics and war so discontinuous that once one enters the state of war, previously important moral, political, and legal considerations become irrelevant. Two points need to be affirmed: On the one hand, war must be justified because it violates some of our *prima facie* obligations, not because it is totally immoral or amoral or utterly discontinuous with politics; on the other hand, it can be more or less humane insofar as it is conducted in accord with some standards that derive from the overridden *prima facie* obligations and other obligations that endure even in war. Furthermore, however much continuity there is between peace and war, peace remains the ultimate aim of a just war.

A model of war as a rule-governed activity stands in sharp contrast to a model of war as hell, which is accepted by most pacifists and by many "realists" who recognize no restraints other than proportionality. Both models are evident in the following passage from Rolf Hochhuth's play, *Soldiers*:

> Bishop Bell of Chichester: "We denigrate our men if we suggest that they require directives to tell them that the burning of defenseless persons is murder."
> P.M. (savagely, not looking at Bell): "War is murder. The murderer is the man who fires first. That man is Hitler."

According to one view, war is hell, murder, and there is thus only the crime of war, within which anything goes, for "all's fair. . . ." According to another view, war is a game-like (not in a frivolous sense) or a rule-governed conflict, within which one may legitimately injure, kill, and destroy, but not commit war crimes such as injuring or killing defenseless persons who are noncombatants or excombatants.[17] For the view that war is "total" and without limits, the only critical moral factor is the decision to wage war, and moral blameworthiness may attach to the side starting the war, sometimes even to the side firing the first shot. For the view that war is a rule-governed activity, the *jus in bello* becomes very important. Any adequate theory, however, should *not* concede that *jus ad bellum* is unimportant because some moral principles and rules persist in war. There is an important and irreducible difference between peace and war, and for that reason the *jus ad bellum* remains indispensable. That difference, however, is not equivalent to the difference between morality and amorality or immorality.[18]

Grounds of Just-War Criteria

Most of the criteria traditionally associated with just-war theories emerge because war involves a conflict between *prima facie* obligations (when it is just and justified) and because the overridden *prima facie* obligations forbid us to injure and kill others. Many of these criteria apply in other areas, as I have suggested, because of similar conflicts between *prima facie* obligations, not because the *prima facie* obligations not to injure or kill others are involved at every point. Nevertheless, the *content* of the *prima facie* obligations that are overruled in just wars certainly shape the criteria, particularly those having to do with *jus in bello*, since the conduct of the war should be as compatible as possible with the overridden *prima facie* obligations.

The first criterion of a just war is right or legitimate authority, which is really a presupposition for the rest of the criteria. In fact, it determines *who* is primarily responsible for judging whether the other criteria are met. As Quentin Quade indicates, "the principles of Just War become operative only *after* the classic political question is answered: who should do the judging?"[19] Answering the authority question is a precondition for answering the others; it thus cannot be dismissed as a "secondary criterion."[20] After the proper authority has determined that a war is just and justified and thus overrides the *prima facie* obligation not to injure and kill others, citizens, including subject-soldiers, face a different presumption. Whereas the proper authority has to confront and rebut the presumption against war, the subject-soldier now confronts the presumption that the war is just and justified because the legitimate authority has so decided in accord with established procedures.[21] In all political orders, the subject has a moral right/duty—although not a legal right—not to fight if the war is manifestly unjust. And in a democracy, the citizen is ruler as well as subject and thus has a greater responsibility to apply these criteria to war. As subject, however, the presumption ought to be that the authorities, if they are legitimate and have followed proper procedures, have decided correctly.

The requirement of a *just cause* is simply the requirement that the other competing *prima facie* duty or obligation be a serious and weighty one, e.g., to protect the innocent from unjust attack, to restore rights wrongfully denied, or to re-establish a just order. Because war involves overriding important *prima facie* obligations not to injure or kill others, it demands the most weighty and significant reasons.

These obligations cannot, however, be overridden if there are other ways of achieving the just aim short of war. War is the *ultima ratio, the last resort*. The requirement that war be the last resort does not mean that all possible measures have to be attempted and exhausted if there is no reasonable expectation that they will be successful. Nor does it necessarily mean that the side that first resorts to armed force should be condemned.[22]

Insofar as a formal *declaration* is sometimes required, it stems not only from the nature of political society, but also from the requirement that war be the last resort. Ultimata or formal declarations of war "are the last measures of persuasion short of force itself."[23] Although a formal declaration of war may not be appropriate for various reasons, the significance of this criterion, broadly understood, should not be underestimated. Conceding that the best publicists differed on the necessity of a declaration, Francis Lieber defended it because "decent regard for mankind" and "public good faith" require that a government explain and justify its departure from peace.[24] A failure to announce the intention of and the reasons for waging war is a failure to exercise the responsibility of explaining and justifying exceptional action to those involved, including the citizens of one's own country, the enemy, and third parties who have to decide how to respond. An announcement of intentions and explanation of reasons may be more appropriate than a formal declaration of war.

The requirements of *reasonable hope of success* and *proportionality* are closely related. If war has no reasonable chance of success, it is clearly imprudent. But more than a dictate of prudence is involved in the demand for a reasonable hope of success. If none of the just and serious ends, none of the other *prima facie* obligations, could be realized or fulfilled through the war, a nation should reconsider its policy which, after all, involves overriding stringent *prima facie* obligations. Nevertheless, numerous qualifications are in order. This criterion applies more clearly to offensive than to defensive wars. And in any war success may be broader than "victory." As Lieber wrote of John Brown's raid: it was irrational, but it will be historical! Success could include witnessing to values as well as achieving goals; for instance, a group might engage in resistance in order to retain self-respect even in its demise. Regarding the limited Jewish resistance in Nazi Germany, some Jewish thinkers have insisted that if the holocaust comes again, Jews must not "die like sheep." Although Ralph Potter has derived the criterion of reasonable hope of success from the moral prohibition of suicide and from the fact that statesmen are stewards of a nation,[25] heroic acts such as falling on a grenade to save one's comrades may be fitting for individuals and suicide itself may be justifiable in some cases, particularly if it can be noble witness to some higher values in the face of certain and imminent death. Even if a nation has good reason to think that it will be defeated anyway, its vigorous resistance may preserve significant values beyond number of lives and retention of territory or sovereignty. Furthermore, what is "reasonable" depends on the situations in which actors have to make responsible decisions; retrospective judgments by others should include only what the actors could and should have foreseen. Finally, this criterion appears only to exclude totally useless, pointless, or self-indulgent warfare which reasonable people cannot expect to achieve goals or to express values. Such warfare is excluded because it cannot override the *prima facie* duties not to injure or kill others, duties as binding on states as on individuals.

Regarding *proportionality*, Ramsey writes:

> It can never be right to resort to war, no matter how just the cause, unless a proportionality can be established between military/political objectives and their price, or unless one has reason to believe that in the end more good will be done than undone or a greater measure of evil prevented. But, of all the tests for judging whether to resort to or to participate in war, this one balancing an

> evil or good effect against another is open to the greatest uncertainty. This, therefore, establishes rather than removes the possibility of conscientious disagreement among prudent men.[26]

Here too defensive measures are less restricted than offensive ones, but this criterion includes the welfare of all countries and peoples and not merely one's own country. Certainly the weight of the cause and the probability of success enter the discussion of proportionality, but the probable negative consequences must also be considered—even beyond the negative feature of injuring or killing others.

The last major criterion of the *jus ad bellum* is right or just *intention* (which along with proportionality is very important in particular battles, engagements, and acts *within* war and not merely for the war as a whole). For the war as a whole, right intention is shaped by the pursuit of a just cause. But it also encompasses motives; for example, as St. Augustine and others have insisted, hatred is ruled out. Some would hold that the dominance, if not the mere presence, of hatred vitiates the right to wage war even if there is a just cause. For example, McKenna holds that a "war which is otherwise just becomes immoral if it is waged out of hatred."[27] Such a contention, however, is difficult to establish, for if all the conditions of a just/justified war are met, the presence of vicious motives would not obliterate the *jus ad bellum* although they would lead to negative judgments about the agents. Insofar as these vicious motives are expressed in disproportionate force, the infliction of unnecessary suffering, etc., one may condemn the belligerent for violating the *jus in bello*. Nevertheless, this criterion of right intention understood not merely as pursuit of a just cause but also as proper motives remains significant in part because war is conducted between public, not private, enemies. Furthermore, an attitude of regret, if not remorse, is appropriate when a *prima facie* obligation is overridden.

Another interpretation of right intention focuses on *peace* as the object or end of war. It too bridges the *jus ad bellum* and *jus in bello*, and I shall emphasize its impact on the conduct of war. St. Augustine and many others have affirmed that peace is the ultimate object, end, or intention of war. In short, war as injury, killing, and destruction is not an end in itself but a means to another end—a just or better peace. Even apart from the justice that is sought, peace retains its moral claim during war and thus constitutes an ultimate or final objective. There is a duty to restore the "normal" state of affairs as quickly and surely as possible.

It may be dangerous, however, to stress that it is urgent to restore peace, especially if peace is defined as the absence of conflict rather than a specific set of relationships which may include conflict. For such an emphasis may engender support for a quick, brutal, and total war, which may undermine the limits set by the *jus in bello*. Paul Ramsey holds that unless there is a morality that intrinsically limits the conduct of war, "then we must simply admit that war has no limits—since these can hardly be derived from 'peace' as the 'final cause' of just wars."[28] But if one does not misconstrue peace as the total absence of conflict, one can see how the *prima facie* obligation not to injure or kill others persists even in the midst of war by mandating the ultimate object of peace. And through the object of peace (but not only this way) it imposes other restraints on the conduct of war. Since the aim of war is "a just peace," John Rawls contends, "the means employed must not destroy the possibility of peace or encourage a contempt for human life that puts the safety of ourselves and of mankind in jeopardy."[29] General Orders No. 100 of 1863 held that "military necessity does not include any act of hostility which makes the return to peace unnecessarily difficult."[30]

If peace does not require mutual good will, it at least requires some trust and confidence. Thus, perfidy, bad faith, and treachery are ruled out in part because they are destructive of the ultimate object of peace. If they are prevalent in war, to restore and maintain peace becomes very difficult short of the total subjugation of the enemy. Acceptable ruses of war, according to one commentator on the laws of war, are "those acts which the enemy would have had reason to expect, or in any event had no reason not to expect."[31] Perfidy or treachery involves the betrayal of a belligerent's confidence that is based on moral and/or legal reasons (such as the expected protection of prisoners of war). This requirement of good faith derives not only from the ultimate end of peace but also from the respect for the humanity of the enemy that is expressed in a number of *prima facie* obligations.

The *prima facie* obligation not to injure or kill others should also more directly affect the choice of weapons and methods to fight wars than through the ultimate object of peace. Since this *prima facie* obligation is not cancelled even when it is overruled, its impact can be seen in various restrictions of the *jus in bello*.

First, the immediate object is not to kill or even to injure any particular person but to incapacitate or restrain him.[32] The enemy soldier is not reduced to his role as combatant, and when he surrenders or is wounded, he ceases to be a combatant because he ceases to be a threat. He is now an excombatant. As a prisoner of war, he is entitled to certain protections. As a wounded person, he is entitled to medical treatment equal to that of one's own wounded comrades.

Second, directly to attack noncombatants is not legitimate. This principle is sound even if the distinction between combatant and noncombatant is contextual and thus is partially determined by the society and the type of war. In the gray areas, noncombatants include those persons whose functions in factories and elsewhere serve the needs of the person *qua* person rather than his or her role as military personnel. Thus, while food is essential for the soldier to function, it is indispensable for him as a human being. And chaplains and medical personnel primarily serve the soldier as human being even when their ministrations indirectly aid the war effort.

Finally, indiscriminate methods of warfare are prohibited by this principle.

Third, the original *prima facie* obligation not to injure others also excludes inflicting *unnecessary suffering*. Thus, cruelty (inflicting suffering for the sake of suffering) and wanton destruction (destruction without a compelling reason) are wrong. Such acts are not essential to the war effort. Acts that appear to fall under these vague categories of "cruelty" and "wanton destruction" are not cruel or wanton if they are "necessary." The relation between military necessity and such categories is a serious problem area in the *jus in bello*.[33] At any rate, certain weapons (such as dum-dum bullets and explosive or inflammable projectiles weighing less than 400 grams) are prohibited because they are calculated to cause "unnecessary suffering" or "superfluous injury." The rationale is simple. An ordinary rifle bullet or a projectile weighing less than 400 grams is designed to incapacitate only one person. To make the bullet or projectile do more damage to that one person is to inflict suffering that is unnecessary or superfluous.[34] That suffering offers no military advantage. (Of course, not all suffering that offers military advantage is necessary and justified.)

Fourth, even the indirect, incidental, or obliquely intentional effects on civilians must be justified by the principle of proportion.

I have not tried to offer an exhaustive list of the requirements of the *jus in bello*, but rather to show that some restrictions emerge from the continued pressure of the *prima facie* duty not to injure or kill others even when it is overridden by the *jus ad bellum*. That duty persists and imposes restrictions indirectly through the ultimate object of peace and directly as in the protection of certain classes, avoidance of unnecessary suffering, and care for combatants who are *hors de combat*.

Order, Weight, and Function of Criteria

How can these criteria be used to assess particular wars? How can we determine when a war is just/justified or unjust/unjustified? Various applications of just-war criteria have been proposed and used: (1) Some just-war theorists contend that the inability to meet any single criterion, such as last resort, renders a war unjust. Each criterion is necessary and all are collectively sufficient.[35] (2) The criteria establish *prima facie* duties, which follow the logic of such duties: the criteria should be met unless they are overridden by more stringent duties.[36] (3) No single criterion must be met, but at least several criteria must be satisfied before a war can be justified. A war should approximate the criteria, even though it cannot fully satisfy them. (4) The criteria are "rules of thumb" or "maxims" that identify some morally relevant considerations; they illuminate but do not prescribe what we ought to do. (5) The criteria could be arranged in a serial or lexical order so that some must be met before others can even be considered. For example, if there is no "just cause," there is no reason to consider proportionality, for the war cannot be justified.

There are other possible ways to apply just-war criteria, and these five approaches can be combined in various ways. For example, some of the criteria could establish necessary conditions for justified war, or at least *prima facie* duties, while others could serve as rules of thumb. The fifth approach is especially promising, and one possible serial or lexical order is suggested in my arrangement of the criteria in the previous section. Whether this fifth approach, perhaps in combination with one or more of the others, could be developed is a subject for further reflection. It is unfortunate that philosophers and theologians have not devoted more attention to the order, mode of application, and weight of the various criteria.

Proposals on these matters will depend, in part, on a particular theory's *substantive* view of justice and other moral principles. But they are not reducible to substantive interpretations of justice, for my tentative order in the preceding section could be justified in terms of the logic of overriding *prima facie* duties. For the most part, the conception of just-war criteria in this essay is independent of substantive views of justice. It is not purely formal, however, for it hinges on material moral principles or *prima facie* duties (e.g., the duty not to injure or kill others). But it is intended to be accessible to many different theories of justice.

It is important to examine the possible *function* of just-war criteria in a society that has several competing theories of justice and the pacifist's stake, if any, in such a function. Many recent attempts to restate just-war criteria apparently treat them as questions that policy-makers and others ought to consider. These criteria constitute a formal framework and structure for moral debates about the use of force. They are important and even essential because of the *prima facie* duty not to injure or kill others. And they identify the kinds of questions that should be answered affirmatively before war—and other acts that override *prima facie* duties—can be justified. Perhaps because they are a *framework*, they can serve to organize and orchestrate disputes in the public arena; even pacifists could and did appeal to these criteria to condemn the war in Vietnam. In democratic theory and practice, formal procedures can accommodate conflicts about moral convictions and interests; they do not dictate the material outcome. Similarly, just-war criteria constitute a formal framework within which different substantive interpretations of justice and morality as applied to war can be debated. For example, the formal interpretation holds that it is morally mandatory to determine that one has a "just" cause, but exactly what constitutes a "just" cause will depend on substantive convictions about justice and morality. This formal function of the criteria is hardly what traditional just-war theorists expected, for they developed their criteria within substantive theories of justice and the common good.

Paul Ramsey prefers to translate *justum bellum* as "justified war" rather than "just war," in part because he does not think that a substantive theory of justice in relation to ends can be developed or that one side can legitimately claim justice while denying it to the other.[37] Such an approach fits with a formal understanding of these criteria. When a policy-maker raises these formal questions of the *jus ad bellum* and gets affirmative answers, resort to war is "justified" although we cannot say that it is "just." A procedural justification is possible even when we lack a substantive theory of justice. Ramsey is more willing to provide content for *jus in bello* at least in terms of a principle of discrimination that rules out direct attacks on noncombatants. Indeed, he says very little about *jus ad bellum,* concentrating instead on *jus in bello.*

Some critics of a formalist interpretation of just-war criteria contend that it cannot be accepted or supported because it does not serve, in fact, to restrain and limit war. Nevertheless, one of its manifest functions can be viewed as restraining and limiting war because it holds that only some wars, and only some acts within war, justifiably override the *prima facie* duty not to injure or kill others. It fulfills this function, however, in the context of the legitimation of war as an exceptional practice. Its function is both positive (legitimization) and negative (limitation). It justifies but also restrains.

Some critics are not satisfied with this explanation of the dual function of just-war theories.[38] They insist that this formalist interpretation fails to give clear and precise determinations regarding the justification of actual wars. In particular, they contend, it fails to give clear and precise *negative* answers. It fails to specify when particular wars or acts within wars are unjust/unjustified. In short, these critics wonder whether a formalist interpretation of just-war criteria can overcome the deficiencies of most formalist theories in ethics: they are empty and vacuous. Agreement is possible precisely because they do not involve material content.

What these critics expect of just-war criteria is available only within *substantive* theories. There is no single substantive theory of just war. But these critics ask that the just-war criteria serve the same function now that they served in a different era, when (presumably) there were strong shared convictions about justice and accepted arbiters of justice of and in war. This is impossible in a pluralistic society. But even in a pluralistic society, just-war criteria as defined in this essay have an important function: to serve as a framework for debates about *which wars,* if any, are justified.

Just-war criteria within a substantive theory should indicate when war is unjust and conducted unjustly. They should define not only "just" cause, but also "innocence," "discrimination," etc. I have not tried to develop a substantive theory of just war in this essay. My task has been more limited but not, I think, insignificant: I have tried to show that just-war criteria are important and even indispensable moral standards apart from any particular theory of justice. They are, I have argued, explicable by reference to the notion of *prima facie* duties and, specifically, to the *prima facie* duty not to injure or kill.

If we accept this *prima facie* duty of nonmaleficence, and if we accept the responsibility to think morally about the use of force in a sinful world, we should be committed to a framework and procedure of reasoning that is at least analogous to just-war criteria. Furthermore, it is important to secure support for this formal framework in order to avoid the amoral approaches to power that only appreciate "national interest" (as defined in nonmoral terms) or Machiavellian maneuvers. If pacifists admit that there will always be "wars and rumors of wars"—an admission that will depend on their theology and anthropology—then they too have an important stake in the moral assessment of wars and acts within wars. They too should be committed provisionally to something analogous to just-war criteria.

There may be some misunderstanding of the nature and function of just-war criteria: they are not designed to answer the question of the justification of war in general but the question of the justification of particular wars. That is, they do not determine *whether* war as an institution or practice can ever, or in principle, be justified; they rather indicate *when* particular wars can be justified. They presuppose an affirmative answer to the question whether war can ever be justified and then pinpoint the conditions required for the justification of any particular war. Just-war criteria thus are not involved in the debate between the pacifist and the just-war theorist over *whether* war can ever be justified. This debate hinges on general theological, anthropological, and moral convictions (e.g., sin, the place and function of the state, and political responsibility). It focuses on whether any moral principles and values, such as justice, can ever outweigh or override the *prima facie* duty of nonmaleficence.

But if just-war criteria presuppose an affirmative answer to the question whether war can ever be justified, how can the pacifist appeal to these criteria in discourse about a particular war? Sometimes in the moral assessment of particular wars, pacifists are ignored or excluded on the grounds that "we already know their conclusions." Because pacifists do not accept the premise of just-war theories that war can, in principle, be justified as an exceptional practice, so the argument goes, they cannot participate openly and impartially in the debate. But this argument is not cogent. Pacifists can apply the criteria of just war, as accepted by other groups, to a particular war. They can be sensitive to the implications of the criteria, whether they are satisfied by the factual circumstances, etc. They need not accept the premise of just-war theorists; their premise may be only that "of all possible wars, one that meets these criteria is less evil than one that does not."

In conclusion, pacifists and just-war theorists are actually closer to and more dependent on each other than they often suppose. They share a common starting point, which just-war theorists sometimes overlook: nonviolence has moral priority over violence, and violent acts always stand in need of justification because they violate the *prima facie* duty not to injure or kill others whereas only some nonviolent acts need justification (e.g., when they violate laws). While pacifists can remind just-war theorists of this presumption against violence, pacifists also need just-war theorists. In a world in which war appears to be a permanent institution, debates about particular wars require a framework and a structure, which can be provided by the criteria of the just-war tradition, properly reconstructed. In addition, there are degrees of justice and humanity within violence and warfare, and the just-war theorist can emphasize these moral constraints which the pacifist view of war as hell or murder (shared by some realists) tends to obscure. Even the pacifist has a stake in the integrity of just-war criteria as the coin of the political realm. The pacifist finally cannot be satisfied with that coin, just as the just-war theorist finally cannot be satisifed with the weight pacifism gives to the duty not to injure or kill that both recognize. What they share, however, can be neglected only at great peril to all of us.

Notes

1. Gordon Zahn was a participant in the International Law of War Symposium sponsored by the United States Catholic Conference. An earlier version of this essay was discussed at this symposium. In addition, this essay benefited from the criticisms and suggestions of several persons including Stanley Hauerwas, James Johnson, Ernest Lefever, James McCartney, Richard McCormick, Paul Ramsey, John Reeder, LeRoy Walters, and John Howard Yoder, and from general discussions of its basic ideas at the University of Chicago Divinity School, a symposium on "Concepts of Justice and Moral Obligation in Relation to War" at Princeton University, and Duodecim. All the third section and most of the second section of this essay appeared in this form in "Just-War Theories: The Bases, Interrelations, Priorities and Functions of their Criteria," *Theological Studies* 39 (September 1978): 427–445, and is used here with permission of the editor, Walter Burghardt, S.J.

2. See Frederick H. Russell, *The Just War in the Middle Ages* (New York: Cambridge University Press, 1975); James T. Johnson, *Ideology, Reason, and the Limitation of War* (Princeton, N.J.: Princeton University Press, 1975); LeRoy B. Walters, Jr., "Five Classic Just-War Theories: A Study in the Thought of Thomas Aquinas, Vitoria, Suarez, Gentili, and Grotius" (Ph.D. diss., Yale University Press, 1971).

3. James T. Johnson, "Just War Theory: What's the Use?" *Worldview* 19 (July–August 1976): 41–47.

4. Ralph B. Potter, Jr., *War and Moral Discourse* (Richmond, Va.: John Knox, 1969), p. 61. One of the best systematic examinations of just-war criteria is Potter's article, "The Moral Logic of War," *McCormick Quarterly* 23 (1970): 203–233.

5. James Luther Adams, "Civil Disobedience: Its Occasions and Limits," in *Political and Legal Obligation: Nomos XII,* ed. J. Roland Pennock and John W. Chapman (New York: Atherton, 1970), p. 303. Cf. James F. Childress, *Civil Disobedience and Political Obligation: A Study in Christian Social Ethics* (New Haven: Yale University Press, 1971), chap. 4. Paul Ramsey, *Christian Ethics and the Sit-in* (New York: Association, 1961), p. 104. Cf. Paul Ramsey, *War and the Christian Conscience* (Durham, N.C.: Duke University Press, 1961), and *The Just War: Force and Political Responsibility* (New York: Scribner's, 1968). For an attempt to apply just-war criteria to organ transplants on the grounds that both are

instances of "the controlled use of regrettable violence," see James B. Nelson, *Human Medicine* (Minneapolis: Augsburg, 1973), chap. 7.

6. Pauline Maier, *From Resistance to Revolution: Colonial Radicals and the Development of American Opposition to Britain, 1765–1776* (New York: Knopf, 1972), chap. 2, "An Ideology of Resistance and Restraint."

7. Larry L. Rasmussen, *Dietrich Bonhoeffer: Reality and Resistance* (New York: Abingdon, 1972), all of Part 2, but esp. pp. 145–46, 154–55.

8. W. D. Ross, *Foundations of Ethics* (Oxford: Clarendon, 1939), p. 86. Cf. Ross, *The Right and the Good* (Oxford: Clarendon, 1930), chap. 2. "*Prima facie*" does not mean "apparent" in contrast to "real," for *prima facie* duties are real although they are distinguished from "actual" duties.

9. William K. Frankena, *Ethics*, 2nd ed. (Englewood Cliffs, N.J.: Prentice-Hall, 1973), p. 55. Frankena holds that some kinds of acts are "intrinsically *prima facie* wrong" (55–56). In his article "The Moral Logic of War," Ralph Potter states the presumption against the use of force in two different ways. First, he states that our "common life is sustained by a strong moral and legal presumption against the use of force" (203). Second, he holds that the use of force "always involves an exception to the rule which forbids us to do harm to our neighbor *without due cause*" (206, my italics). The second statement is faulty; for if the rule forbids us to do harm without due cause, the just-war criteria are designed to establish when there is "due cause." Thus a just war is not an exception to the rule as stated; it is rather built into the rule.

10. For some of the issues, see J. J. Stamm with M. E. Andrew, *The Ten Commandments in Recent Research* (London: SCM, 1967), pp. 98–99, which views what is prohibited as "illegal killing inimical to the community." See also Solomon Goldman, *The Ten Commandments* (Chicago: University of Chicago Press, 1963).

11. John Rawls, *A Theory of Justice* (Cambridge, Mass.: Harvard University Press, 1971), pp. 113–114.

12. A. C. Ewing, *Second Thoughts in Moral Philosophy* (London: Routledge and Kegan Paul, 1959), p. 110.

13. Ibid. Ross says that "we do not for a moment cease to recognize a *prima facie* duty to keep our promise, and this leads us to feel, not indeed shame or repentance, but certainly compunction, for behaving as we do" (*The Right and the Good*, p. 28). For a criticism of the view that *prima facie* obligations retain their tendency to be binding and thus occasion some measure of moral regret, see Maurice Mandelbaum, *The Phenomenology of Moral Experience* (Baltimore: Johns Hopkins, 1969), pp. 79–81.

14. See Henry Paolucci, ed., *The Political Writings of St. Augustine* (Chicago: Regnery, 1962), pp. 162–183, and Roland H. Bainton, *Christian Attitudes Toward War and Peace* (Nashville, Tenn.: Abingdon, 1960), p. 98.

15. Joseph C. McKenna, S.J., "Ethics and War: A Catholic View," *American Political Science Review* 54 (1960): 658, cf. 650. For Ramsey's theoretical statement, see *Deeds and Rules in Christian Ethics* (New York: Scribner's, 1967), pp. 187–188. It may be useful to mention some trends in recent Catholic moral theology that are similar to the language of *prima facie* duties proposed in this essay. Without going into some differences that are also important, Richard McCormick notes that some of the "proportionalists" in recent Catholic theology who have been suspicious of the language of "intrinsic evil" have adopted arguments that resemble Ross's use of *prima facie* right and wrong. Such proportionalists do not hold that

actions have no meaning in themselves but "only that no final assessment of rightness or wrongness can be made until more has been said of the action than that it is [for example] 'breaking a promise' " (Richard McCormick, S.J., "Notes on Moral Theology 1977: The Church in Dispute," *Theological Studies* 38 [1978]: 103). They also hold that nonmoral evils (e.g., killings) are to be avoided as far as possible, but admit that such evils may be justified in conflicts of values and disvalues. Such conflicts may give rise to regret but not to moral remorse. The proportionalists are suspicious of the language of intrinsic evil because of the way it has been used in some recent theological and magisterial literature (e.g., to hold that direct sterilization is wrong regardless of the circumstances), because it seems more at home in a deontological than a teleological setting, and because it is confusing. As I understand the debate, my argument is not as close to the position taken by the proportionalists (such as McCormick, Schüller, Janssens, and Fuchs) as to the position developed by Albert R. DiIanni, S.M. in "The Direct/Indirect Distinction in Morals," *The Thomist* 41 (1977): 350–380. DiIanni distinguishes nonmoral evil (e.g., death) from the free causation of that evil (e.g., homicide). The latter has "at least minimal *moral* meaning in itself prior to consideration of intention and circumstances." Thus, DiIanni construes concepts such as homicide as "bearers of a negative *moral* meaning (as intrinsically evil in a weak sense) and not merely as bearers of negative ontic or pre-moral meaning." This weak sense of "intrinsically evil" (which he also calls the *prima facie* moral meaning of negative acts in the tradition of Ross) implies that the negative moral ought is always relevant but it is not always decisive. Even when an action that is *prima facie* or intrinsically evil is justified in particular circumstances, it should engender "creative regret" but not guilt.

16. Paul Ramsey, *The Just War,* pp. 55, 142, 143, 475, and passim.

17. The formulation of the ideas in this paragraph is indebted to some lectures on war by Professor Michael Walzer at Harvard University, Fall 1972. Walzer's *Just and Unjust Wars: A Moral Argument with Historical Illustrations* (New York: Basic Books, 1977) appeared after this essay was written. It is one of the most important books on just-war theory in this century. See my review in *The Bulletin of the Atomic Scientists* 38 (October 1978): 44–48.

18. In Paul Ramsey's thought, e.g., the emphasis is on the continuity between politics and war. Thus he concentrates on the *jus in bello,* holding that the "*laws* of war are only an extension, where war is the only available means, of the rules governing any use of political power." See *The Just War,* p. 144, cf. 475. Unfortunately, this emphasis on the continuity between politics and war may be excessive, since Ramsey does not pay enough attention to the *moral* issues in crossing the line between ordinary politics and war—the *jus ad bellum.* One of Ramsey's former students, James T. Johnson, is trying to reconstruct the *jus ad bellum.* See "Toward Reconstructing the *jus ad bellum,*" *Monist* 57 (1973): 461–488.

19. Quentin L. Quade, "Civil Disobedience and the State," *Worldview* 10 (November 1967): 4–9.

20. James T. Johnson, "Just War Theory," p. 42. He appears to think that legitimate authority was a "secondary criterion" for St. Augustine as well, but Augustine's writings indicate that the authority of the prince or state or God's direct authorization is indispensable for just war. See Paolucci, *Political Writings of St. Augustine,* pp. 163–166 and passim. In his attempt to reconstruct the *jus ad bellum,* Johnson does not address this criterion except in passing, in part because of

limitations of space but also because he thinks that the current de facto definition of right authority (wherever there is sovereignty, there is right authority) is politically workable, although it has some moral difficulties. See "Toward Reconstructing the *jus ad bellum,*" p. 487, n. 46. Any adequate just-war theory must seriously address this question: "Who decides?" Even in the use of these criteria for justifying and limiting revolution, surrogates for the established authority are often found in the revolutionary elite or the "people." See also Richard Neuhaus's suggestions in Peter L. Berger and Richard J. Neuhaus, *Movement and Revolution: Conversation on American Radicalism* (Garden City, N.Y.: Doubleday, 1970), pp. 164–178.

21. See John A. Rohr, *Prophets without Honor: Public Policy and the Selective Conscientious Objector* (Nashville, Tenn.: Abingdon, 1971), p. 98, and Ramsey, *The Just War,* pp. 98, 274–275, 360, and passim.

22. James T. Johnson does not emphasize the criterion of "last resort," in part because he thinks that it tends to be understood as condemning the first use of force. See "Just War Theory: What's the Use?" p. 44, and "Toward Reconstructing the *jus ad bellum*," p. 487 (where this criterion is not included in the reconstruction).

23. McKenna, "Ethics and War," p. 650.

24. See James F. Childress, "Francis Lieber's Interpretation of the Laws of War: General Orders No. 100 in the Context of His Life and Thought," *American Journal of Jurisprudence* 21 (1976): 34–70. This quotation comes from Lieber's "Laws and Usages of War," a lecture given at Columbia Law School, Dec. 3, 1861.

25. Potter, "The Moral Logic of War." p. 219.

26. Ramsey, *The Just War,* p. 195.

27. McKenna, "Ethics and War," p. 652.

28. Ramsey, *The Just War,* p. 152. On the dangers of an excessive emphasis on the end of peace, see Johnson, "Just War Theory," pp. 43–44.

29. Rawls, *A Theory of Justice,* p. 379.

30. See Childress, "Francis Lieber's Interpretation of the Laws of War," pp. 49 and 63–65.

31. Frits Kalshoven, *The Law of Warfare: A Summary of Its Recent History and Trends in Development* (Leiden: Sijthoff, 1973), p. 102.

32. Cf. Ramsey, *The Just War,* pp. 397, 502, and passim.

33. See Childress, "Reinhold Niebuhr's Critique of Pacifism," *Review of Politics* 36 (1974): 477–481, and "Francis Lieber's Interpretation of the Laws of War," pp. 63–65.

34. *Weapons That May Cause Unnecessary Suffering or Have Indiscriminate Effects.* Report on the Work of Experts (Geneva: International Committee of the Red Cross, 1973), pp. 12–13. The quoted passage is from the St. Petersburg Declaration of 1868. See also Morris Greenspan, *Soldier's Guide to the Laws of War* (Washington, D.C.: Public Affairs, 1969).

35. See Johnson, "Just War Theory: What's the Use?" pp. 42, 46.

36. In "A Reappraisal of the Just-War Tradition," *Ethics* 84 (1974): 167–173, D. Thomas O'Connor uses Ross's language of *prima facie* duty to apply to the criteria of *jus ad bellum* and *jus in bello*: "The rules of just warfare are *prima-facie* duties because they define abstract moral obligations. Thus, a nation ought not to violate a principle of just warfare unless a more important principle takes precedence." O'Connor does not, however, try to show how the principles of just warfare are themselves derivative from certain *prima facie* duties.

37. Ramsey, *War and the Christian Conscience,* pp. 15, 28, 31–32. It is important

to emphasize, as Joel Feinberg has pointed out, that one and the same act need not be both just and justified. It may be *just and unjustified* (e.g., although it renders various parties their due, it violates some other moral principles or has terrible consequences), or it may be *unjust and justified* (e.g., an unfair act is required to prevent a disaster). See Feinberg, "On Being 'Morally Speaking a Murderer,' " in *Ethics*, ed. Judith J. Thompson and Gerald Dworkin (New York: Harper and Row, 1968), pp. 295–297.

38. Similar criticisms were suggested by John Howard Yoder in an exchange in an Evening Dialogue on "Can Contemporary Armed Conflicts Be Just?" at the Woodrow Wilson Center of the Smithsonian Institution, Washington, D.C., October 5, 1978. Yoder, James J. Johnson, and I presented papers, to which Bryan Hehir and Seymour Siegel responded. Since at that time and subsequently John Howard Yoder's similar criticisms emerged in the context of an oral debate, I do not wish to suggest that he holds them, at least in the form they take in this essay.

4
Pax Christi

Joseph Fahey

Pax Christi International

Albert Camus in *The Plague* states that we live in an age in which if a teacher says "two and two is four" they send him to the gallows. These words well apply to the founder of Pax Christi, Bishop Pierre-Marie Théas of Lourdes, France. Bishop Théas was a champion of peace during World War II and his life was distinguished by his commitment to preach the gospel of peace despite its consequences.

Bishop Théas's pastoral letters strongly condemned the persecution of Jews in occupied France, the deportation of young workers to Germany, and the destruction of the village of Montpezat. The price that he paid for his saying that "two and two is four" to the Nazis was his own arrest in 1944 and incarceration in the State Prison at Compiègne. The Nazis had planned to deport him to a concentration camp in Germany, but the train that was to take him was blown up by the Resistance.

While he was in the State Prison at Compiègne some fellow prisoners—members of the Resistance—asked him to conduct a day of meditation for them. Bishop Théas shocked them by choosing the theme "Love Your Enemy." A fellow prisoner argued that this theme was "impossible" and the Bishop responded: "I cannot preach anything else to you but what he has said: 'Love your enemies. Not more—not less.' "[1] The next day the Bishop received permission to celebrate the Eucharist for the first time in prison. He offered the liturgy for Germany. That very same day the French prisoners of Compiègne were sent to Buchenwald.

This ministry of reconciliation led Bishop Théas to inspire the formation of Pax Christi shortly before the end of the war. Bishop Théas stated that "To make peace, one must learn to forgive, for to forgive is to make peace."[2]

While Bishop Théas is generally credited with the founding of Pax Christi, he himself credits a group of French Catholic laymen. In an article which appeared in *The American Ecclesiastical Review* in 1949 Bishop Théas explains the origins of Pax Christi:

> During the first weeks of 1945, a few Catholic French laymen, former victims of the Nazi regime, got the idea of organizing in France a crusade of prayer for Germany. Accordingly they came to seek approbation from the author of this article, who was at that time Bishop of Montauban.
>
> The war was not yet over; the Germans were still fighting in the Eastern part of France. Innumerable French prisoners and political refugees were dying in German Camps. In the hearts of many Frenchmen there was, naturally, a growing and violent animosity against the Germans.
>
> Despite all this, it seemed that the movement inaugurated by these pious laymen deserved approval. And so we granted it. The movement was inspired by the spirit of the Gospel which commands us to love our enemies, to pardon injuries, and to pray for those who persecute us. Thus it happened that during the first months of 1945, Christians in France, encouraged by several French Bishops, were praying for the Germans and, in particular, for the downfall of Nazism. This was the first activity of the *Pax Christi* movement.[3]

While Bishop Théas credits a group of French laymen for the inspiration for Pax Christi, it was he who formally founded it by giving it episcopal sanction. There is no doubt also that Bishop Théas' actions, which were mentioned earlier, were the founding premise from which Pax Christi later developed.

Thus it can be seen that the first months of Pax Christi were concerned with reconciliation between the French and Germans. In May 1945, after the surrender of Germany, the movement took on international dimensions when the directors of Pax Christi urged their members not only to pray for Germany, but for peace between all nations. In the words of Bishop Théas, "Quickly the movement, encouraged by the Hierarchy, grew to great proportions. From Germany we received the most fervent and enthusiastic support."[4]

Pax Christi twice received the blessing and commendation of Pope Pius XII. The approval of the Holy Father, which was given on June 3, 1947, and May 26, 1948, was received through Monsignor Montini (later Pope Paul VI):

> The Holy Father is pleased to know that at a time when men are working so energetically for peace—and so often in vain—the Crusade of *Pax Christi* is spreading everywhere the Christian concept of peace and creating, by the prayers of its members and the circulation of its literature, an atmosphere of universal understanding which will be the basis for a true and lasting reconciliation between men and nations.[5]

The early work of Pax Christi was to encourage a Church Crusade of Prayer for the Family of Nations. Allied to this work was the publication of a quarterly report (in French and German), international meetings between the French and the Germans, and an international pilgrimage of Pax Christi to Lourdes in 1948.[6] The movement also met in Oropa, Italy, in April of that year.

Following these early developments, the movement quickly spread to other European countries. Today there are sections in France, Germany, Spain, Italy, Switzerland, England, Austria, Belgium (Flemish and French), Ireland, Luxembourg, and the Netherlands. The two countries in which Pax Christi exists outside Europe are the United States and Australia. In addition, the movement is presently making plans for the dramatic spread of Pax Christi to Third World nations.

Pax Christi is presently known as the International Catholic Movement for Peace and its headquarters are in Antwerp, Belgium (Kerkstraat 150, B-2000, Antwerp, Belgium). Bernard Cardinal Alfrink is the honorary international president and Bishop Luigi Bettazzi is currently the Pax Christi international president. The vice-presidents are Bishop Thomas Gumbleton (U.S.A.) and Dr. Maria Lucker (Germany). The international secretary is Mr. E. De Jonghe of Belgium.

Each national section of Pax Christi is required by the international constitution to have a bishop president and the movement maintains a very close working relationship with the Catholic Church in each country, although Pax Christi is not an official organ of the Catholic Church. This gives Pax Christi considerable freedom of priorities and affords it the opportunity of taking positions which may be considered in "advance" of contemporary Church teaching on justice and peace.

While the activities of Pax Christi sections vary according to local needs, there is a common concern for such issues as disarmament, the primacy of conscience, peace education, contacts with the Church in Eastern European countries, and the arms trade. Present activities of Pax Christi International involve the publication of an international newsletter, the hosting of conferences on such issues as disarmament, peace education, nonviolence, and the formation of a global world order. Pax Christi International meets once a year and hosts an annual pilgrimage for European young people. A common concern of all Pax Christi sections is to encourage their membership to study and act on the Church's teachings on peace. Many sections are also very much committed to ecumenical activity and most allow non-Catholic membership in the movement.

Pax Christi U.S.A.

Pax Christi was founded in the United States in 1973 and developed from the organization known as Pax which existed from 1962 to 1972. Eileen Egan had a great deal to do with the founding of Pax Christi U.S.A. and the original committee included Bishops Carroll Dozier and Thomas Gumbleton, Edward Guinan, Eileen Egan, Clare Danielsson, Gordon Zahn, and Joseph Fahey. In 1974, internal disagreements over the role and function of Pax Christi caused a temporary period of suspension of activities. The movement was reorganized in May 1975 at a meeting called by Bishops Carroll Dozier and Thomas Gumbleton. The meeting, which was held at Manhattan College, included some forty Catholic peace leaders from around the country.

Strong endorsement was given to Pax Christi and there was common concern that Pax Christi should be a broadly based movement which appealed not only to pacifists but to those who believed that some use of violence was at times unavoidable. Many felt that the time was right for a collaborative peace organization which would work with the Church to make peacemaking an important priority in American society. At the same time it was recognized that Pax Christi had the freedom to take unpopular positions regarding peace issues and thus could be an added voice of conscience within the American Church and society.

A major result of the meeting was the approval of a Statement of Purpose which reads as follows:

> Pax Christi U.S.A. intends to contribute to the building of peace and justice by exploring and articulating the ideal of Christian nonviolence and by striving to apply it to personal life and to the structures of society. Pax Christi U.S.A. invites concerned Catholics to respond to the Church's call to evaluate war with an entirely new attitude and to take an active role in making secure a peace based on justice and love.
>
> As a section of Pax Christi International, Pax Christi U.S.A. seeks with the help of its episcopal members to establish peacemaking as a priority for the American Catholic Church. To accomplish this, Pax Christi U.S.A. will work with various Catholic communities and agencies, and will also collaborate with other groups committed to nonviolent peacemaking.
>
> Pax Christi U.S.A. will find its strength in the efforts of committed individuals to follow the Gospel imperative of peacemaking—an imperative repeated throughout the Christian tradition, most recently by Pope Paul VI: "If peace is truly desired, then it is possible, and if it is possible, then it is a duty."

Following approval of this statement a twelve-person Executive Council was established to supervise Pax Christi activities.[7] It was further decided that membership in Pax Christi is free following written support of the Statement of Purpose. Five dollars would entitle one to receive Pax Christi publications.

Pax Christi has since held national assemblies in Dayton, Ohio; Detroit, Mich.; Memphis, Tenn., and New York City. Pax Christi has also hosted three National Days of Peace in honor of the Holy Father's annual Day of Peace message and each meeting was well attended, especially by members of the hierarchy. Pax Christi was very active in the Call to Action process and has published a number of newsletters and publications which deal principally with the arms race. Pax Christi also actively worked with the Religious Committee of the Mobilization for Survival in planning activities for the Special Session on Disarmament held at the United Nations in 1978. In addition, many Pax Christi chapters (Pax Christi is organized on a state-wide basis) have hosted conferences and prayer and reflection days, and have supported movements which address themselves to individual moral issues.

At its meeting in March 1978, the Executive Council (consisting of twelve elected persons including three bishops) approved the following revised priorities for Pax Christi U.S.A.:

PAX CHRISTI PRIORITIES

Disarmament

Pax Christi U.S.A. seeks to foster both nuclear and general disarmament. It believes that the construction and possession of nuclear weapons represents a profound immorality in the contemporary world. Pax Christi U.S.A. seeks to reorient the priorities of our national government away from heavy arms spending and trading to policies which have as their chief concern the truly human survival of all people. Far from weakening the United States, disarmament will strengthen it and help it become a more constructive leader among nations.

A Just World Order

Pax Christi U.S.A. seeks to explore alternatives to the present international system of competition and mistrust. Only through the establishment of a global authority can human needs be met justly and nonviolently. Pax Christi strongly endorses the United Nations as a path to a more human and just world order. It is officially represented at the United Nations as a non-governmental organization.

The Primacy of Conscience

Pax Christi U.S.A. supports all who, for reasons of conscience, refuse to bear arms. It also upholds selective conscientious objection: the responsibility of every person to evaluate the morality of every war and to refuse to bear arms if a particular conflict does not meet Just War principles. Pax Christi endorses the establishment of the World Peace Tax Fund, which will allow individuals to follow the dictates of their conscience and donate their tax funds to peace groups, peace education and human needs.

Education for Peace

Pax Christi U.S.A. seeks to examine militarism in education, and to replace military and ROTC programs in our nation's schools and universities with programs in justice and peace education. Catholic schools, especially, should become centers for justice and peace education. Pax

Christi members are urged to approach Catholic military schools or schools with ROTC programs in their area to suggest creative alternatives.

Alternatives to Violence

Pax Christi U.S.A. is convinced that if we as individuals and as a nation and globe are to survive, we must pursue the Gospel mandate of nonviolent living. We must develop programs in nonviolent spirituality, nonviolent resistance and reconciliation, and nonviolent civilian and social defense.

In regard to these priorities, members of Pax Christi U.S.A. will carefully evaluate government budgets as well as existing and proposed legislation. They will support those policies and laws which promote peace and justice at home and abroad. They will oppose those which do not, and will formulate alternatives where they are needed.

Pax Christi U.S.A. members also commit themselves to a life guided by the Christian principles of nonviolence and justice for all people. Accordingly, members of Pax Christi U.S.A. will examine their own personal wealth and career objectives in the light of those ideals.

It can be seen from the above priorities that Pax Christi has a positive thrust and is committed not only to reforming certain aspects of American life (particularly in relation to the arms race) but also to creating a new American culture which is based on the gospel spirit of nonviolence and reconciliation. At present, the national coordinator of Pax Christi U.S.A., Sister Mary Evelyn Jegen, S.N.D. is organizing specific programs for the implementation of Pax Christi's priorities and some are in operation. The national address of Pax Christi U.S.A. is 3000 N. Mango Ave., Chicago, Illinois 60634.

Pax Christi and the Just War

Historically, Pax Christi was not founded as a pacifist organization but as a movement which was committed to making the Roman Catholic Church's teachings on peace more widely known in the world. At the time of the founding of Pax Christi in Europe the Catholic Church's moral theologians and teachings were firmly rooted in "just-war" thinking. After World War II, Pax Christi found itself in a situation in which the just-war principles were still operative, and, to some extent still relevant. Two important changes, however, have caused the Pax Christi movement to question the relevancy of the just-war principles in contemporary times.

The first is the vast increase in the development of indiscriminate weaponry. The United States and the Soviet Union can destroy the world and themselves many times over. Since World War II, the United States has spent some two trillion dollars on arms and the Soviet Union has surely spent near that amount, though exact figures are not available. The bomb dropped on Hiroshima (which in nine seconds killed 78,000 people and doomed 100,000 more) is now obsolete. The smallest bomb in our current arsenal is two-and-one-half times as powerful as the Hiroshima bomb. The development of MIRVed missiles (which place many independently targetible warheads on one missile) as a result of SALT I vastly increased our over-kill ratio and there is no sign that things are slowing down. Today all countries spend over 400 billion dollars on weaponry and one quarter of the world's scientists and technologists are engaged in weapons research and development. In addition, the SALT agreements between the United States and the Soviet Union have strengthened and institutionalized the arms race rather than limiting it or pointing to disarmament.[8]

The second change which has caused Pax Christi to question the relevance of the just-war principles is an increasingly positive theology of peace as enunciated by Popes Pius XII, John XXIII, Paul VI, and John Paul II, and Vatican Council II. In addition, moral theologians, as well as local Bishops' Conferences, have issued teachings which severely question the relevance of the just war to nuclear weaponry. The Fathers of Vatican II stated:

> The horror and perversity of war are immensely magnified by the multiplication of scientific weapons. For acts of war involving these weapons can inflict massive and indiscriminate destruction far exceeding the bounds of legitimate defense. Indeed, if the kind of instruments which can now be found in the armories of the great nations were to be employed to their fullest, an almost total and altogether reciprocal slaughter of each side by the other would follow, not to mention the widespread devastation which would take place in the world and the deadly aftereffects which would be spawned by the use of such weapons.
>
> All these considerations compel us to undertake an evaluation of war with an entirely new attitude (*Gaudium et Spes,* n. 80).

What is this "new" attitude? The Council Fathers tell us:

> With these truths in mind, this most holy Synod makes its own the condemnations of recent Popes, and issues the following declaration:
>
> Any act of war aimed indiscriminately at the destruction of entire cities or of extensive areas along with their population is a crime against God and man himself. It merits unequivocal and unhesitating condemnation (*Gaudium et Spes*, n. 80).

Without stating it explicitly, the Council Fathers held that there is no such thing as a "just" nuclear war. Also, the condemnation of indiscriminate weapons was one of the two condemnations issued at Vatican II. The importance of this condemnation cannot be emphasized too much. It is quite clear that the world's bishops viewed the use of indiscriminate weapons as the single overriding moral issue that our world faces today.

But the Fathers of the Council were not merely content to discuss the use of these weapons; they also addressed themselves to the larger issue of the global arms race. After stating that deterrence "was not a safe way to preserve a steady peace" they pronounced:

> Therefore, it must be said again: the arms race is an utterly treacherous trap for humanity, and one which injures the poor to an intolerable degree. It is much to be feared that if this race persists, it will eventually spawn all the lethal ruin whose path it is now making ready (*Gaudium et Spes*, n. 81).

The Council then proceeded to seek the "total banning of war" by international accord and to argue that the only way out of the arms race is the establishment of an international authority which can settle disputes through nonviolent means.

Pope Paul VI, in his Day of Peace messages, has called the arms race a "scandal" and has consistently called for positive measures of justice which alone can end war. In fact, an impartial reader of Pope Paul's statements on war may well conclude that since the Holy Father hardly mentions or refers to just-war thinking (and always speaks of a positive definition of peace) he has embraced the philosophy of nonviolent pacifism which characterized the early Christians. In his last address to the 1978 Special Session on Disarmament at the United Nations (delivered by Archbishop Casaroli) Pope Paul stated that he refused to believe that humankind

> is not capable of exorcising the demon of war which threatens to destroy him, even if this demands of him immense efforts and a reasonable *renunciation of old-fashioned concepts that continue to set peoples and nations at odds* [italics added].[9]

A strong case can be made here that the Holy Father is primarily referring to the Cold War with its consequent philosophy of deterrence (or MAD—mutually assured destruction) when he speaks of a "renunciation of old-fashioned concepts." But it may also be inferred that the Pope is referring to the excesses of nationalism since he immediately calls for a "new international order capable of eliminating wars and the causes of wars and thus making arms superfluous." By further implication (and this must be placed in the full context of other papal and conciliar statements) it is clear that the very concept of a "just war" in this latter half of the twentieth century is not only questioned but challenged. Is the Catholic Church moving away from its centuries-old tradition of the "just war" and toward a positive philosophy of international relations that would outlaw war itself? The answer is patently "yes." But this does not, of course, mean that many Catholics are ready to embrace the position of their leadership. That is why Pax Christi's mission of education for peace is so vitally important in our time.

Furthermore, the Vatican not only denounced the use of indiscriminate weapons but it questioned the very possession of armaments in general. In

1976 the Holy See was asked to present testimony to the United Nations on disarmament. In an excellent summary of Church teachings on the matter the Holy See declared, "The Arms Race: It is to be condemned unreservedly." The document then went on to say:

> The obvious contradiction between the waste involved in the overproduction of military devices and the extent of unsatisfied vital needs . . . *is in itself an act of aggression* against those who are the victims of it. It is an act of aggression which amounts to a crime, for *even when they are not used*, by their cost alone *armaments kill the poor by causing them to starve* [italics in original].[10]

The document then went on to condemn the philosophy of deterrence by stating *"the present situation of would-be security is to be condemned"* (italics in original). In his 1977 Day of Peace message Pope Paul called for the elimination of "this senseless cold war" which "must one day be resolved in the ruination of Peace and of countless human lives."

Because of these developments, Pax Christi finds itself in a much different situation than it did after World War II. When Pax Christi was founded it was understandable that it would give primary allegiance to "just-war" thinking. Later developments of the arms race together with the far more positive Church teachings on peace have caused Pax Christi itself to stop talking of the "just war" and to call for a new international order based on nonviolence and justice.

It should be obvious to the reader that Pax Christi is not a purely pacifist movement but rather a mainstream peace organization which attempts to live up to the teaching of the Church on the matter of global peace. Some have referred to Pax Christi as a "conservative" movement since its basic position is to live up to the Church's teachings on peace and justice.

I have attended three International Council meetings of Pax Christi and served on the International Executive Committee from 1975 to 1978 and thus attended other international meetings in this capacity. I also (with Bishop Gumbleton) attended a 1977 conference sponsored by Pax Christi at the Catholic University in Louvain, Belgium, on the theme "European Security in an International Context," as well as a disarmament meeting in Belgium in February 1979. These meetings over the past four years have led me to the following impressions:

1. The concept of the "just war" in this nuclear age is hardly discussed by either the international movement or by Pax Christi U.S.A.

2. Since Pax Christi is broadly based with respect to positions on war and peace, there are some within the movement who still believe in possession of nuclear weapons, but they are not the majority. In fact, as more young people come into the movement, the thrust seems to be clearly away from the "just war" thinking.

3. Pax Christi clearly challenges the arms race and arms trade.

4. Pax Christi is seeking more and more religious contacts with Eastern European nations to break down the barriers of the Cold War.

5. Pax Christi is centrally concerned with the concept of nonviolent civilian and social defense and much less with the concept of violent defense.

6. Pax Christi is active in almost every country, promoting education for peace as an alternative not only to military education but also to the kind of education which promotes nationalism and the glorification and toleration of violence.

7. Pax Christi is an active promoter of the United Nations (and especially of its disarmament work) as the alternative to a system of international anarchy.

Clearly the movement under the leadership of Cardinal Alfrink (and now under Bishop Bettazzi) has changed substantially since its origins and is becoming a far more positive force in promoting the Church's developing teachings on international peace.

Pax Christi U.S.A. and the "Just War"

Pax Christi in the United States is active in, and shares all of the concerns of the international movement. The United States section has never explicitly issued statements on the viability of the "just war" in its six years of existence in this country. As with the international movement, Pax Christi seeks to be broadly based and thus has within its membership some who subscribe to the concept of a just war.

It should be obvious, however, that the five priorities of Pax Christi U.S.A.—disarmament, a just world order, the primacy of conscience, education for peace, and alternatives to violence—are not based on the philosophy of the "just war." Instead, they are based on a far more positive program which seeks an international order based on justice and nonviolence. Pax Christi U.S.A. implicitly recognizes that the "just war" is not an adequate philosophy to confront a nuclear age. Instead it calls for nuclear and general disarmament (as does the Church) and views the possession of nuclear weapons as a "profound immorality in the contemporary world."

Pax Christi U.S.A. also seeks the creation of a just world order as an alternative to the "present international system of competition and mistrust." On an individual basis, Pax Christi believes in personal disarmament through conscientious objection or selective conscientious objection for those who believe in the "just-war" theory. It is on this issue that Pax Christi makes a specific reference to the "just-war" principles and speaks of "the responsibility of every person to evaluate the morality of every war and to refuse to bear arms if a particular conflict does not meet just-war principles." Thus Pax Christi U.S.A. does hold that the just-war principles are relevant on an individual basis but appears to be skeptical of their relevance as an instrument of national policy. (Indeed, the foreign policy regarding the use of military violence is not based on just-war thinking; the policy is based on deterrence and mutually assured destruction, which are hardly relevant to the notion of discriminate warfare.)

As part of its concern about the primacy of conscience Pax Christi believes that "Catholic schools, especially, should become centers for justice and peace education." In this context Pax Christi opposes military and ROTC programs in Catholic schools because of the clear implications these programs have for educating Catholic young people to accept or participate in a foreign policy which is demonstrably alien to Catholic principles on war and the arms race.

The fifth priority of Pax Christi—seeking alternatives to violence—is based on the assumption that we need something positive to replace the violence in our culture. Thus it calls for programs in "nonviolent spirituality, nonviolent resistance and reconciliation, and nonviolent civilian and social defense." Pax Christi is presently forming strategic programs and groups to seek to implement these priorities. Throughout all of this, Pax Christi U.S.A. seeks to "work with various Catholic communities and agencies, and will also collaborate with other groups committed to nonviolent peacemaking."

In summary, then, it is fair to say that Pax Christi does not believe that the just-war principles are relevant in a nuclear age and thus it proposes a positive path of disarmament, development, and justice. However, Pax Christi does not hold the just-war principles to be totally irrelevant since it permits them to be followed in the case of an individual conscience.

Deterrence and SALT II

Many in Pax Christi U.S.A. are coming to question the philosophy of deterrence, especially as it relates to SALT II. In many ways, deterrence has become the just-war theory of modern times. While many in the just-war tradition believe that we can never have a "just" nuclear war (and are thus "nuclear pacifists"), they nevertheless argue that it is morally tolerable to support the doctrine of deterrence. Much of this support is done on practical grounds, since its proponents argue that at least thus far we have *de facto* avoided a nuclear war and the arms race has in part contributed to that. In addition the proponents of deterrence do not strongly support this doctrine but rather see it as the lesser of the two evils which confront us. The argument for deterrence has, in short, taken on many of the dimensions of the just-war thinking.

But while the doctrine of deterrence may cause one to support it from a practical viewpoint, it must certainly be challenged from a moral viewpoint. The following are some arguments against deterrence:

1. Deterrence assumes that the only ultimate way nations can solve differences is through violence or the threat of violence.

2. Deterrence assumes that there will be constant hostility between two parties without any possibility of future trust or reconciliation.

3. Deterrence is based on the assumption that the only way to resist injustice is through threatening the total destruction of one's opponent rather than through the diplomatic, political, and economic conversion of that foe.

4. Deterrence is based on the fallacious assumption that "might makes

right" and that armed strength will guarantee security.

5. The use of deterrence is a violation of the ethical principles that "two wrongs do not make a right" and that "the end does not justify the means." If we want a world without war, enormous arms preparation will hardly guarantee that. As we sow, so shall we reap.

6. The most dangerous aspect of deterrence is the naive assumption that such weapons will never be used. Of the thousands of arms races in history only a *few* have not ended in war. The odds are clearly against us. Nuclear war—by accident, intention, or terrorism—is far more likely than we realize and every new weapon (the U.S. builds three nuclear weapons a day) only adds to our global insecurity.

7. Deterrence continues the Cold War rather than ends it. Pope Paul has called the Cold War "senseless" and has argued that it could cost "countless human lives."

8. The United States Catholic bishops have stated:

> As possessors of a vast nuclear arsenal, we must also be aware that not only is it wrong to attack civilian populations but it *is also wrong to threaten to attack them as part of a strategy of deterrence* [italics added].

Deterrence is, in short, a morally bankrupt philosophy whose continued development will not prevent war but in fact will cause it.

Is there a way out? Is there another strategy? The Catholic Church has long argued for an international authority to control and end the arms race. Surely we should give much more vigorous support to that concept than we do to deterrence.

In this context, the Executive Council of Pax Christi U.S.A. has taken the position of non-support of the ratification of the SALT II treaty. The SALT II treaty not only further institutionalizes the arms race but also endorses the doctrine of deterrence and mutually assured destruction as the formal basis of United States foreign policy. In light of the entire corpus of Catholic teaching on this matter it is extremely difficult to understand how Catholics can support deterrence, mutually assured destruction, the Cold War, or the arms race that is institutionalized by SALT II. If the just-war criteria present problems even when applied to conventional wars it is almost impossible to understand how one coming from a just-war tradition could support the doctrine of deterrence (even as a lesser evil) without violating the very basis of just-war thinking.

In this article we have spoken of the origins of Pax Christi International, and various international activities as they relate to the just-war philosophy. We have also discussed the implications for the just-war philosophy that result from an examination of the priorities of Pax Christi U.S.A. Kenneth Boulding has said that "if the human race is to survive we will have to change our thinking more in the next 25 years than we have in the past 25,000." Clearly, an examination of the just-war philosophy must be a part of our "change" in thinking. We not only cannot have a "just" war in this nuclear age, we must not have one. We must develop nonviolent alternatives to war which at the same time promote the formation of a human world order. Both Pax Christi International and Pax Christi U.S.A. are engaged in the search for these alternatives and let us pray that we discover them in time.

Notes

1. "Pax Christi Chapter Guidelines," Pax Christi, U.S.A., p. 1.
2. Ibid.
3. Pierre-Marie Théas, "Pax Christi: A Crusade of Prayer for All Nations," *The American Ecclesiastical Review* 121 (July 1949): 7.
4. Ibid., p. 8.
5. Ibid.
6. By this time Bishop Théas had been named bishop of Lourdes.
7. The members of the Executive Council in 1979 were Thomas Cornell, Vincent DiLalla, Bishop Carroll Dozier, Eileen Egan, Joseph Fahey, Bishop Thomas Gumbleton (President, Pax Christi U.S.A.), Mary Evelyn Jegen, S.N.D., Marjorie Keenan, R.S.H.M., Angela O'Gorman, Bishop Walter Sullivan, Gerard Vanderhaar, Gordon Zahn.
8. Cf. Marek Thee, "Arms Control: The Retreat from Disarmament, The Record to Date and the Search for Alternatives," *Journal of Peace Research* 14 (1977): 111.
9. Pope Paul VI, "Toward a Balance of Trust," Message of Pope Paul VI to the General Assembly of the United Nations Organization for its Session on Disarmament, in "Pope Paul VI: Two U.N. Addresses," The World Conference on Religion and Peace, 1977, p. 13 (pamphlet).
10. Testimony of the Holy See to the United Nations on disarmament entitled "Strengthening of the Role of the United Nations in the Field of Disarmament," May 7, 1976, found in "The Church and the Arms Race," Pax Christi U.S.A., 1977, p. 23 (pamphlet).

PART II
PACIFISM

5
Protestant Social Ethics and Pacifism

*Paul Deats**

Insofar as the main tradition in Protestantism is one of dissent and criticism, a Protestant social ethic is a difficult and precarious achievement. Further, the nineteenth-century environment in the United States provided a setting in which many Protestants deepened their inclinations to be individualists in religion as well as in economics and politics. Still further, Protestants have typically thought of themselves as a minority; and, even when there has been a Protestant dominance in numbers and/or ethos, the impact upon public policy has been more that of an implicit cultural pattern than of a self-consciously articulated ethic.

On the other side of the equation in the title of this essay, many pacifists have, by temperament or persuasion, revealed a strain of anarchism, a distrust of government, and an inclination to accept an ethic of duty or obedience binding only upon individuals or sects in an evil world.[1]

Thus, whether by selective affinity or some other factor, many Protestants who have been pacifists have focused more upon the duty to refrain from preparation for or participation in war, upon the protection of the right to conscientious objection to military service, and upon binding up the wounds of war, rather than upon challenging the phenomenon of war itself. In other words, we who see ourselves as pacifists have not always been reluctant to occupy the "sectarian" posture recommended by some critics. In the course of this essay I suggest first that there are significant and instructive exceptions to this set of reinforcing expectations, and then that the "sectarian" model ought not to be accepted without question.

The principle institutional force in the United States for a Protestant social ethic was the Social Gospel Movement of the last third of the last century and the first third of this. This is not the place for a full discussion of its achievements and limits, but it is instructive to note three aspects of this movement which are relevant to the issues of pacifism and war. First, by and large the leaders of the Social Gospel were preoccupied with economic

*With the research assistance of Glenda Yoder, which is gratefully acknowledged.

rather than political problems. Second, they were concerned more with U.S. domestic problems than with international ones. Third, they did not give explicit attention to the role and responsibility of the Church.

The attack upon the Social Gospel came from within and was led by Reinhold Niebuhr. In a persistent criticism of the liberalism, idealism, and individualism[2] of Protestantism, he argued that the Social Gospel was unduly optimistic in its view of human nature and insufficiently attentive to the necessary role of coercion in human society. His early break with pacifism was of a piece with this criticism, for he affirmed that coercion was needed to achieve economic justice, especially in the class struggle. Later he would respond to the crisis of Western civilization posed by the Nazi threat and attack the complacency and irresponsibility of American neutralism, including *political* pacifism. Articulating a perspective of "Christian realism," Niebuhr both affirmed the relevance of sacrificial love in personal relations and rejected it in favor of justice as the operative norm in the affairs of groups (and in favor of balance of power as the operative norm in relations between states). Thus he set, for the decades since *Moral Man and Immoral Society* (1932), the almost insuperable difficulties of moving from an individual ethic *directly* to a social ethic, especially as this involved pacifism. Much of the pacifist/nonpacifist debate during and after World War II has been against this Niebuhrian backdrop.

But the stage for the debate was really set by Max Weber in 1918 in his famous essay "Politics as a Vocation."[3] Here he asserts that "all ethically oriented conduct may be guided by one of two fundamentally differing and irreconcilably opposed maxims": an "ethic of ultimate ends"—which is not identical with irresponsibility; and an "ethic of responsibility"—which is not identical with unbridled opportunism. No ethic can escape the *fact* that achieving "good" ends often requires the price of morally dubious or dangerous means. Even Weber does not distinguish clearly between *force, power,* and *violence* as he asserts that, although force is not the normal or only means in politics, "the decisive means . . . is violence." It is not only that the ethics of ultimate ends must go to pieces on the problem of the justification of means by ends, but that the salvation of one's soul should not be sought in the violent realm of politics. Still, Weber confesses that he is moved when a person of maturity, whether young or old, feels a responsibility for his conduct "with heart and soul." "Insofar as this is true," he suggests, the two ethics are "not absolute contrasts but rather supplements"; thus the vocation of politics requires them in tension, not isolation.

If Max Weber is thus led to consider these two ethics as supplementary rather than absolute contrasts, I suspect that the categories of pacifist and nonpacifist are themselves usually seen as too hard, too mutually exclusive, and even too comfortably isolated. As absolute contrasts they may frustrate an essential dialogue concerning peace. John Yoder suggested this in the introduction to his *Karl Barth and the Problem of War*.[4] "The chief result of past debate between pacifism and its critics has been to make clear that none of the traditional positions in the field of discussion has demonstrated a solution to the problems caused by war and especially by modern war.'' Yoder also notes in the ''Preface'' to his brief book on the varieties of religious pacifism:

> One of the constants of serious discussion about the Christian's participation in war is the nagging feeling the observer gets that the parties are talking past each other.[5]

What is true for the ''observer'' may be even more frustratingly true for the participants, each convinced that the other is not hearing. Yoder suggests that one reason for this is the fact that there is no single pacifist position; but it is also because the arguments on each side reflect a variety of ethical systems. Elsewhere, Yoder writes that Reinhold Niebuhr uses the pacifist issue ''as the clearest case of the essential problem of all Christian ethics, namely, how to bring down to earth the 'impracticable' teachings of Jesus.''[6] Still, he warns us and himself that discussion of war and peace may easily be transmuted into a comparison of ethical systems.

> The critical reader will have noticed as we moved through the inventory above that in most cases the kinds of models of ethical thought with which we were dealing represented attitudes not simply to war but to the whole problem of ethics. . . . The post-Niebuhrian non-pacifist will see all pacifism, as he rejects it, as utopian purism or as withdrawal. . . . The ''situation ethics'' advocate will reject pacifism for its inflexible principles rather than take seriously those pacifisms which calculate carefully in the situation or which preserve the integrity of the loving disposition of free decision in every context. *One is then not discussing war but talking past one another out of logically incompatible prior assumptions.* Each kind of pacifist position has its rootage in a wider context and should be evaluated only there.[7]

I hope, within the limits imposed in this essay, to suggest a few ways in which we can talk *with* rather than *past* one another. To this end, I propose to explore: (1) the adequacy of our definitions of pacifism; (2) the presuppositions concerning the nature of the state and politics underlying the discussion; and (3) a still further underlying conceptual confusion about violence and power. In the light of this discussion, I intend to ask whether pacifists, however chastened, can (4) bring together in their ethical discourse the ethics of absolute ends and of responsibility, and (5) engage in a theory of statecraft.[8] In this discussion I will refer to the contributions of such Protestant social ethicists as Reinhold Niebuhr, John C. Bennett, Paul Ramsey, Walter G. Muelder, and John H. Yoder.

A Critique of Definitions of Pacifism and the Possibility of Dialogue

The ''classic'' or ''traditional'' definition of pacifism is that identified with the witness of the historic peace churches, especially with the Mennonites. Its focus is on nonresistance to evil, maintenance of a steadfast witness of obedience to the gospel ethic of love (and even of purity), with no claim to effectiveness, since the results are in the hands of God. This is usually a "sectarian" position and is often eschatological or even apocalyptic in its expectation. It is the recommended posture of vocational pacifism, considered "valuable" by nonpacifists as a reminder both of the evil of war and of the demands of love. Its grounding is altogether religious and not at all pragmatic or prudential.

Several problems for dialogue and action flow from this position. Some who begin with this posture find it too inflexible and unresponsive and seek to modify it in the direction of nonviolent resistance, looking again at biblical sources as well as at current responsibilities. Others, often without systematic reworking of the position, move to "apply" the presumed gospel ethic to political decisions.

This kind of confusion feeds into a number of criticisms of pacifism. It is seen as *legalistic*—supplying answers before questions are put; *simplistic*—assuming the state can turn directly from violence, with love seen as too easy a possibility in history; *isolationist* and *neutralist* in facing international problems of order and justice—and thus *irresponsible*. Other criticisms extend to self-righteousness and an "easy conscience." But, the critics usually note, this is pacifism which makes some claim to political relevance, which moves toward nonviolence rather than toward nonresistance.

John C. Bennett, who stands within both the Social Gospel and the Christian realist traditions, and who refuses to acknowledge a "double standard" for personal and social ethics, contends that "pacifism is not a self-sufficient social strategy."[9] He cites four reasons. First, Christians have an obligation *both* to avoid violence and to restrain evil. Second, one should not expect nation-states to be pacifist. Third, a nonviolent strategy is not always available, and we must assume responsibility for short-run consequences. Finally, the policy of nonviolence contributes to suffering which pacifists cannot take upon themselves. Therefore, the way of pacifism is for individuals and minorities. Despite his refusal, Bennett's position finally closely resembles that of Niebuhr: "The Christian love ideal is individual rather than social. . . . Its primary concern is not the establishment of justice in society, but purity in the individual."[10]

I am quite prepared to admit that some, perhaps many, pacifists have been legalistic, even isolationist, and certainly often preoccupied with individual claims to conscientious objection to war. But I know relatively few who assume, in the "post-Niebuhrian" world, that love is a "simple possibility" or that we can move *directly* from a personal to a public ethic for the state. Further, as some evidence of the *un*easy conscience of many pacifists, I sense several emerging issues or shifts, on none of which there is unanimity, but there is at least a willingness to consider them as open questions: (1) Many are aware of the need to exercise public and political responsibility rather than to withdraw; they are uneasy with a "vocational'' designation even though they realize they constitute a minority. (2) Many struggle with the concept of ''police power''—at least a limited coercion exerted on behalf of a relatively just and legitimate public order, such as a U.N. peace-keeping force. (3) Many are surprisingly able to identify in spirit and goal with those who are oppressed in the struggle for liberation, even while they reserve the right to argue about appropriate means. One close observer wrote of the churches' responses to the World Council of Churches' Special Fund to Combat Racism, including humanitarian aid to guerrilla movements:

> One remarkable aspect . . . was that many pacifists felt able to give full support . . . while the most vociferous objections were raised from within traditionally non-pacifist churches.[11]

On the other hand, I sense that among many conscientious nonpacifists there are also open questions, mainly in the light of the new developments in warfare: (1) Many are less certain that mutual deterrence is fundamentally stable. In an unpublished paper in 1960 John C. Bennett acknowledged regarding the ''nuclear dilemma'' that he no longer had his earlier confidence that the deterrent would prevent war. (2) There is a growing suspicion that, in a conflict, neither side can—or will—limit its means, with the resulting escalation violating just-war criteria of proportionality and discrimination or noncombatant immunity. (3) Many are aware that, under the nuclear umbrella, there continue to surface conflicts which may become at the very least ''brush-fire wars.''

This brief review suggests both that there are ''varieties'' of pacifism and that clarification of such issues as nonresistance/nonviolent resistance might facilitate dialogue.

The Nature of the State

I have already noted that Max Weber held that violence is the ''decisive means'' in politics, although he qualified this by adding that it is not the normal or only means. It is certainly not true that all pacifists line up behind a consensus theory of politics, nor that nonpacifists agree on a coercive theory of the state, but it may be a good place for dialogue to begin. The fact that there is too little discrimination between coercion and violence will be treated in the next section.

Reinhold Niebuhr tended to emphasize coercion both within and especially between states, insisting that consent is never enough in itself to hold people together in political groups. John Bennett acknowledges that there is an interweaving of coercion and consent, and a healthier state needs to rely less on coercive means. But both Niebuhr and Bennett accept a negative role for the state in the restraint of evil; and this is especially true in affairs between states in the absence of strong international institutions, and in view of aggressive threats from totalitarian states. Bennett stresses the interdependence of preserving freedom and public welfare with the maintenance of order and security, but I suspect the priority has been on the last two.[12]

There is a strong pacifist position which accepts this negative view of the state, but draws the opposite conclusion about coercion. Mulford Sibley, concluding his survey of *The Political Theories of Modern Pacifism,* finds general assent to "the view that the modern state is essentially an engine of violence and tends to infuse its *ethos* throughout all life."[13] John H. Yoder, as a pacifist, seems to employ this view of the state. He contrasts the ethics of discipleship with the ethics of responsibility, choosing the former in obedience to God's operation in the realm of redemption, and sees the Church *coexisting with the violent state,* which lies in the order of conservation.[14] In a later article, Yoder distinguishes Jesus from the Zealots in his lower view of the state and higher view of the enemy.[15] "Revolutionary subordination" means to accept the *fact* of existing government but to discriminate in what is due to the state (e.g., taxes, but not fear and honor; judges and police, but not the death penalty and war).[16] For Yoder the Christian testimony does not provide any philosophic or practical foundations for government, but rather seeks to correct excesses of violence in the state.[17] It is worth noting that Yoder at least opens the door both to a partially positive view of the state and to a Christian witness to the state, but the overall evaluation seems consistently negative.

However, also as a pacifist, Walter G. Muelder stresses both the crucial importance of consent in the state and a positive evaluation of the state, as society organized for political ends, including justice. These two points are closely linked in his thought. He writes: "The political community is not basically an order of force, but of effective justice."[18]

Muelder quotes with approval the way in which C. H. McIlwain traces this conception to Augustine's *City of God*: "Justice and justice alone is the only possible bond which can unite men as a true *populus* in a real *res publica*."[19] Muelder warns against the over-emphasis on power and coercion as having "serious consequences for both theory and practice." It both inhibits constructive theory and "gives hostages to a situation which it wishes to transcend."

> By underestimating the real nature of the social bond and by ignoring the non-violent power of the moral cement of political institutions, the power theory of the state contributes to the appeal to power. Excessive concentration on the role of power reflects a view of man in which the non-rational, egocentric, and lustful deviations . . . are given major consideration.[20]

In Muelder's more positive conception, the normative expectation for the state must always be its grounding in participatory consent and its concern for social justice and welfare, despite historical deviations in actual states. Further, an important part of this conception hinges upon reliance on intermediate forms of cooperation and community within states and among states, such enterprises to both promote individual responsibility and serve as restraints upon the state.

I suspect that this different view of the state has powerful implications for relations between states and the achievement of international institutions which can both promote justice and restrain evil. Reinhold Niebuhr never fully relied upon evolving international institutions which he saw as lacking sufficient coercive sanctions to restrain aggressor states. But it is almost impossible for institutions beyond the nation state to emerge and to become effective without some relaxation of sovereignty by existing states. Paul Ramsey seems to put this process of change in almost the exact reverse order, as did Niebuhr, and thus frustrate the transnational development: "the moral right to use force cannot go down faster than the public authority and enforcement of a world community is organized."[21]

It should also be noted that both Niebuhr and Ramsey still focus on coercive sanctions. There is a serious neglect of the role and importance of the evolving ethos of a world community in which international consensus finds form and then juridicial expression with appropriate sanctions. It is also relevant that the strategy of those preoccupied with coercion is upon the limiting of war-making by balances of power—or of terror—rather than upon the achievement of forms of international institutions which would by their existence as well as by their sanctions enable limits on war.

As will be noted later, Yoder seems at times to qualify his understanding of the state as necessarily violent, but this is not consistently worked through. His position probably reflects different theological understandings of creation and redemption, as well as of the relation of the Church to the larger community, from those of Muelder. However, Muelder can be understood as deepening and transforming Yoder's "discrimination in what is due the state," thus moving from "revolutionary subordination" to "critical participation." Muelder is more at home in political philosophy and opens the way for fruitful dialogue between pacifists and nonpacifists on the nature of the state, the balancing of consensus, justice, and coercion, and the creation of centers of loyalty beyond the nation-state.

Coercion and Violence

Related to these divergent views on the basis of the state is the remarkable lack of conceptual clarity about violence by both pacifists and nonpacifists. Clarity in this regard might contribute to dialogue. All too often writers use as synonyms and without discrimination "violence," "coercion," and "power." I have already noted that for Reinhold Niebuhr such lack of clarity may be intentional, as when he criticizes the "too rigorous moral distinctions between forms of violent and non-violent coercion."[22] In this view the crucial distinction is coercion/noncoercion, and the pacifist protest against violence tends to be defined out of the argument. Most pacifists, even those careless in the use of these terms, assume that the distinctions are necessary, and some attempt to refine the terms. In the

World Council of Churches' discussions on "Violence, Nonviolence and the Struggle for Social Justice," the Cardiff Consultation turned to Gene Sharp for definitions.[23] *Power,* as the most inclusive term, is defined as "the totality of all influences, pressures, forces, and sanctions which may be applied in order to achieve an objective." *Coercion,* somewhat less inclusive, is said to mean "the taking away from a person, group or government of the capacity for continued action to achieve or maintain their objectives." In this model, *violence* refers to the means—"the infliction of physical harm or injury, or of death to persons, or the threat to do so." So also *nonviolence* refers to means—ranging from noncooperation through social and/or economic pressures to massive disobedience, but without the use or threat of physical harm or injury directly, with a focus on the killing of opponents. This much more restrictive use of violence reflects Paul Ricoeur's distinction which refers more directly to war:

> Thus, on the one hand, war does not summarize the whole of violence, in the measure in which the battle between states only imperfectly reflects the profound tensions of society; on the other, the states introduce a new dimension into collective violence by raising it to the level of war.[24]

It is precisely this violence "raised to the level of war" by the state to which the pacifist raises the strongest objection. Such violence is obviously the most massive and the easiest to escape control. It is also beyond the reach of most understandings of legitimization and consensus within a political community. And it is the violence which most readily goes beyond any set limits.

It is essential to Paul Ramsey's argument regarding the Christian and war that one aim at the "limited use of limited force." For him the ends for which wars are fought are not so important as the means, or just conduct.[25] This is probably because Ramsey accepts the inevitability of violent conflict between states, assuming that disarmament and international controls are not realistic possibilities. But LeRoy Walters' careful study of five just-war theorists lends credence to the inherent possibility that, once justified, a war cannot be effectively limited. He summarizes the argument of the theorists in general terms:

> . . . if one side has a just cause for war, then justice will only be promoted if that side is successful in winning the war; if the unrighteous side wins, justice will be frustrated. Thus the strictly moral concern for promoting justice was considered to be contingent upon the utilitarian question of military success. In view of this fundamentally teleological orientation, it is not surprising that the four later theorists answered in unison: "Yes, in war fought for a just cause, the end . . . does justify the use of all necessary military means."[26]

I find it instructive here to refer to Ramsey in his treatment of the decisive difference in argument before and after the *use* of armed force occurs:

> Once the decision is taken, however, and the foreign policy of a nation has undertaken a particular political use of armed force the presumption shifts in favor of the justice of the war that these processes have authorized.[27]

I am perfectly aware that the context here for Ramsey is the decision to *go* to war; but the same mindset, I suspect, works to justify whatever means are required to prosecute a war once begun.

The pacifist has serious questions concerning the crucial factor of limits once war has begun. Is modern war essentially unlimited, except in terms of mutual restraint regarding methods the other side is capable of using in retaliation? Does the process of escalation depend more on how the conflict goes and the available technological resources than on any moral doctrine of limits?

It may be useful to explore the notion of limits both moral and technological in terms of pacifist discussion on war as "police action." Mulford Sibley writes of this:

> The critic of pacifism will sometimes assert that if both war and violent revolution are repudiated, the pacifist must also renounce police activity; for, the argument will continue, police work is simply a kind of war. But the pacifist rejects this analogy. He admits, to be sure, that alleged policing in a repressive and class-ridden society may become violent. . . . But true police work . . . is basically preventive and non-violent; and in the marginal instances where physical force can be used constructively, the force is carefully controlled, employed discriminatingly as between and among individuals, and strictly subordinated to law.[28]

Walter Muelder agrees that the pacifist does not repudiate all coercion under all circumstances. But he insists that coercion must be under the restraint of law. Further, since militarism and national sovereignty reinforce each other, war is different *in principle* from police action within a state. If there is a trend in pacifist thought generally, it is to accept police action insofar as it uses limited coercion within a framework of law, but to recognize that this becomes war when the action moves beyond the community framework and into realms where limits are more difficult. The idea of a peace-keeping force on behalf of the United Nations moves in this direction, but at least one problem involves the reliance upon contingents from the armies of nation states, even though these are typically "lesser powers."

Pacifism and Responsibility

In his reply to his brother's early 1930's essay, "The Grace of Doing Nothing," Reinhold Niebuhr set forth the germ of his understanding of responsibility—that it is necessary to "try to use ethically directed *coercion* in order that *violence* may be avoided."[29] Throughout his career he continued to assume that responsibility meant to resist tyranny, to correct injury, to protect the weak from aggression both domestically and internationally. But he also came to understand, as he stated with clarity in *Christianity and Crisis* in February 21, 1966:

> The moral life of man is continually in the embarrassment of realizing that the absolutes of biblical and rational norms—which enjoin responsibility for the neighbor's welfare—can never be perfectly fulfilled, *either by the use of or abstention from* any of the instruments of community or conflict.[30]

John Howard Yoder is not always clear on the concept of responsibility. As I have suggested, he accepts in the main Niebuhr's negative understanding of the state, and he usually sees the *means* of violence as intrinsic to the understanding of responsibility. But perhaps as important in his rejection of the Christian's responsibility for the state is this notion of the Constantinian Church allied with the state. He sees the "fall" of the Church as her willingness to "make her membership identical with that of society and to serve as social cement, as guarantor of morale and cohesion for the social order of the day."[31] The Constantinian idea of responsibility is thus interpreted as one of *managing*, of *taking charge*:

> As used by Niebuhr this means not our obligation to concern ourselves with all needs around us in terms of the love ethic; it means rather an inherent duty to take charge of the social order in the interest of its survival or its amelioration by the use of means dictated, not by love, but by social order itself.[32]

What can a pacifist understand responsibility to mean; what is one responsible *for*? In reflective moments, pacifists and nonpacifists would agree that we are not to be responsible for maintaining the status quo of a given order, but to preserve *some* framework of order within which we can seek peace and justice. The pacifist is concerned with the *means* of preservation, with the processes of consent and the substance of justice, as well as with the instruments of order. But one of the pacifist's concerns with war as an instrument of achieving justice and preserving order is that the ethos of war-making is conducive to cheapening the value of life in every area and to extending the range and severity of coercive measures.[33]

But Yoder points not only to the means but also to the concept of managing and taking control, in response to which he argues for *withdrawal*, thus leaving the responsibility to be exercised by God. Here I turn to another Mennonite theologian/ethicist, Gordon Kaufman, who defines responsibility in terms of participation rather than managing and taking charge.[34] He notes that some pacifists find participation embarrassing because they thus accept coercive means. But Kaufman finds withdrawal as theologically embarrassing as attempts at participation, "for it leads to the negation of the very love in the name of which the withdrawal is made" (p. 7). Responsibility is claimed both for the neighbor and for society, deriving from our responsibility *to* God (p. 10). There are three aspects of this responsibility. The first is witnessing to the truth as we see it, but without attempting to make the other over into our image. The second facet of responsibility is acceptance of the neighbor, with whom we disagree about war, as a person, honoring the other's insights by listening to his or her understanding of responsibility, concerned more for the other's integrity before God than for *our* purity of interpretation. Thus there is no attempt to dominate, or to control or manage—to tell others what God's will is for them.[35] Some of us may take longer to think our way through one specific application of this, in which Kaufman argues that we ought to be prepared, "along with our negative witness, to *support* the military bill most in accord with the highest ideals and best insights of the total American society" (p. 16). This is involved in our helping our nation "come to a deeper understanding of her own faith, her own convictions, her own moral insights" (p. 17). Third, we are neither to forsake our near neighbor in a decision we take to be wrong nor to break off fellowship, but are even to help in its implementation. Kaufman is well aware that we will experience conflict among these three aspects and this opens the way for a Christian to support even a given conscription bill as "most adequate" but still to refuse personally to register under the bill. That the tensions and the risks of such an understanding are not beyond consideration by John Howard Yoder seems to be suggested in a 1977 essay, "The Christian Case for Democracy:"[36]

> I am not advocating systematic withdrawal from modern society as the "Christ against Culture" caricature . . . would indicate. The interlocking of society is far more than civil government. What we call government today is by no means only the sword. I am rather pointing to a great variety of styles of involvement, of which "the sword" is not the dominant paradigm.

Against this background of a chastened pacifist understanding of responsibility and a more tension-oriented conception of involvement, I turn to consider whether such a pacifist can articulate what Paul Ramsey calls a "theory of statecraft."

Pacifists and a Theory of Statecraft

Insofar as the mode of argument required in a theory of statecraft by Ramsey implies acceptance of some version of a just-war doctrine, most pacifists have in the past opted out, although Gordon Zahn and I have participated in continuing consultations on revisions of just-war arguments. LeRoy Walters notes that just-war doctrine was developed, at least by the four later theorists, as an alternative to the "dangerous" response of pacifism.[37] There is another reason, which may arise from this originating impulse. Most pacifists suspect that use of the just-war argument almost invariably turns out to *justify* a war, almost never to declare a war by one's own land as unjust. The pacifist suspects that the doctrine—or the commitments of those who use it—loads the consideration in favor of justification.

In "Can a Pacifist Tell a Just War?" Ramsey criticizes one pacifist, James Douglass, a Roman Catholic, of distorting the argument because of his personal commitment.[38] Ramsey rejects Douglass's "way of the cross" as a "political alternative." His criticism of Douglass hinges in part on fundamental *premises* regarding the use of nuclear weapons and in part on *judgments of fact* about the foreseeable consequences of threats of use as opposed to nonuse or nonthreats. Ramsey acknowledges that judgments of fact, and their implications for decision, are arguable in good faith, at least in principle. But he charges Douglass with "prescinding in advance" from drawing the proper conclusions from the facts.

It may be that there is no answer to this charge except to accept what Ramsey considers "proper conclusions"; but the facts are not that clear to some of us, even those of us pacifists whose conclusions regarding policy differ from those of both Douglass and Ramsey. This is especially true in the acceptance of a policy of nuclear deterrence to preserve a fragile peace—*if* such a policy can be kept stable, in fact. But this argument can proceed only if *both sides* are presumed to enter the debate in good faith.

The other answer may be seen to be an *argumentum ad hominem,* but I suspect that if it is such, it cuts both ways for Ramsey and his opponent. Let me explain. In *A Christian Method of Moral Judgment,* J. Philip Wogaman, not himself a pacifist, spells out "The Concept of Methodological Presumption" in ethics:

> I believe that we all actually tend to do our thinking on the basis of methodological presumptions, though we often do it quite unconsciously and therefore unclearly. We have instinctive points of . . . reference that constitute our initial presumptions . . . we place a conscious or unconscious burden of proof against apparent deviations from what seems to be right.
>
> The real question is not whether we have them but whether we are able to clarify and modify our initial presumptions on the basis of our ultimate value commitments.[39]

In illustration of the alleged lack of a relationship between presumptions and their "supposed theological foundations," Wogaman takes the case of Ramsey, "whose published judgments on foreign policy issues have rather consistently supported American military commitments and interests despite considerable change in his ethical methodology over the past thirty years." In the footnote explaining this illustration, Wogaman concludes:

> One may therefore question the extent to which his basic methodological position has been the determinative factor in his judgment on military and foreign policy issues—which is to say that his operative methodology has perhaps not been revealed fully in his methodological writings.[40]

Douglass is at least self-conscious and public about his commitments. I join Wogaman in wondering whether Ramsey is capable of making a negative judgment against a U.S. military policy of strength. For him to engage a pacifist in discussing a theory of statecraft, *both* would have to be self-conscious and open about their methodological presumptions and personal commitments.

There is at least room for argument whether the pacifist commitment as such precludes attempting a theory of statecraft. But there may be other obstacles. One is the idea that the pacifist moves *directly* from an individual gospel ethic to a social policy decision. Here it is helpful to refer again to John Yoder. Yoder distinguishes between "pacifism as a political policy for states and pacifism as an ethical principle for Christians" and goes on to insist that the judgments on the two levels "are not of the same order."[41] Certainly this reflects the posture of many pacifists who undertake ethical theory, if not all pacifists. A second obstacle, concerning responsibility, would seem to be overcome if we follow Kaufman's suggestion of participating, listening, witnessing, deciding, even while holding open, as all persons must, the possibility of personal refusal to any specific implementation of policy. I assume that nonpacifists share with pacifists the same kind of dilemma as they face the possibility that a community might decide against their own judgment, for example, a vote *not* to prepare for war. A third possible obstacle concerns risks, i.e., can the pacifist justify asking a community to incur the consequences of failure to go to war. Here it is well to recall Niebuhr's assertion that no policy can be perfectly fulfilled, whether one uses or abstains from the use of violence. Niebuhr obviously thought the risks of refusing war outweighed those of going to war and was willing to ask combatants and noncombatants in this country—and in others—to bear those risks. John Bennett once argued that a policy of nonviolence would contribute to—or risk—suffering which its proponents cannot take upon themselves.[42] But a policy of violence contributes to—and risks—suffering also, and not just on the part of its proponents.

In 1944 a commission appointed by the then Federal Council of Churches reported on "The Relation of the Church to the War in the Light of the Christian Faith." Among its findings was this sobering note: "It is almost never possible to will good in war-time without seeing the good that one wills bring evil in its train. *Neither* fighting in defense of the weak, nor refusing to fight while abuse of them goes on, can provide a way that is unambiguously good."[43] In the aftermath of war, one finds that one has risked victims who were unanticipated as well as side effects one could not foresee, to say nothing of the risks of losing the conflict. These risks are all too often taken for granted, while the critic of war is demanded to justify other risks. In these days it becomes necessary also to consider the risks of *preparation* for nuclear war itself, whether these mean the erosion of trust and democracy, the costs in terms of human welfare, or the more obvious risks of accidental war.

The argument of this section has been that the pacifist commitment as such does not preclude engagement in either the theory or practice of public debate and decision on policy, or in statecraft. This is, in fact, a part of the exercise of responsibility. Pacifist and nonpacifist alike have commitments which must be made public; both are obligated to consider the same facts and to foresee consequences; neither can advocate a policy free of risk.

Implications for the Role and Responsibility of the Church

The self-understanding of the Church in relation to war has been a problem at least since New Testament times, when Christians asked whether it was permissible to serve in the army of the Roman Empire—or whether a soldier in that army could become a Christian. This dilemma was not so much solved as stated in the just-war theory, in which the classical formulations presupposed the "proper authority" to be a Christian ruler in a Christian state. Twentieth-century ecumenical conferences have condemned war as such, but they have not been able to prescribe or sanction one position regarding participation as normative, whether the righteous warrior, the mournful warrior, or the absolute objector. The typical admonition is that the Church should hold persons in all three postures within its fellowship.

The historic peace churches have found their self-understanding of a vocation to peace-witness and peace-making challenged as they re-examine the import of responsibility in society. Those involved in the "New Call to Peacemaking" explore the expansion of responsibility for domestic and international justice as well as for peace, on the part of disciplined fellowship committed to nonviolence or nonresistance.[44]

I can only suggest the directions in which dialogue might continue as the churches wrestle with the tensions between participation in public policy decisions and Christian faithfulness or obedience. The Church is not a state, and Christians' basic loyalties are not to any state. The Church is a transnational fellowship both in intention and in fact. As such any one church helps its members who are also citizens to reflect on their participation in political choices, but it cannot identify any one state or economic or political order—or even civilization—as the necessary or final embodiment of its message. The Church stands loose to all institutions. This does not mean neutrality or indifference, but recognition of a higher loyalty. We can probably not expect all the fellowship of Christians to be committed pacifists, but we can expect that the Church will not bless a war or decide for the faithful that a war is justified. The Church must maintain the burden of proof against the war system. John Yoder interprets Karl Barth in this regard:

> The church's task is not to justify the use of force but to keep her distance from it. If the church as a matter of habit tolerates the use of force and planning for war on the part of the state, then she will not even know when the exceptional time has come when it would be justified for her to say a Christian "yes."[45]

It may be more appropriate for a church to find it necessary to call publicly into question a war as unjust, as, for example, when a government is prepared to go to war on behalf of a racist regime against groups seeking equal justice.

The Church has other responsibilities. It needs to keep open channels of communication between "enemies" even during the conflict, to serve as a reminder and embodiment of reconciliation before, during, and after a war. It also has a continuing pastoral task—to seek to build an ethos of world community and to build moral restraints into the character of Christians, which restraints will function in the lives of citizens, soldiers, policy makers, and resisters.

How God Acts

Walter Muelder finds the ultimate sanction for his pacifist faith in the character of God as intelligent and redemptive love. This is not the place to do more than to suggest three implications of this faith. First, war is not inevitable; God does not condemn us to have no way out of our march toward conflict. Second, war involves in some sense judgment as the tragic consequence of persistently evil human choices in a moral universe created by God; but we are not called to make ourselves the instruments of this judgment. Third, God will use our best efforts to prevent war and build peace, but God will not violate our freedom and save us from our wrong choices if we persist in them.

Conclusion

This essay began by suggesting that there has been a mutually reinforcing quality in much pacifism and much Protestant ethics. Many Protestants found that their pacifist inclinations were all too congenial to an individualistic and sectarian ethic and to withdrawal from public responsibility. These tendencies lent credence to the perception by other Protestants committed to another notion of responsibility that the pacifist witness, while in some ultimate sense important, was in a more immediate sense irrelevant. The argument in these pages has been an attempt to explore the possibilities of dialogue beyond stereotypes and into a more constructive dealing with the pressing issues of war and peace. If there are hints for reformulation of a Protestant social ethic, this will be a welcome but unanticipated dividend.

More directly the argument has tried to explore why and how pacifists who happen to be Protestants can recognize and deal with issues fundamental to their own self-understanding, both among themselves and in dialogue with others. One productive option might well be to work with those who may see themselves as "contingent pacifists" rather than as nonpacifists. Jonathan Glover borrows the term from John Rawls and clarifies its meaning in a philosophical treatment of *Causing Death and Saving Lives*. Despite resemblances to traditional just-war argument, Glover insists that "there is a very strong presumption against a war being justified." He argues the case against absolute pacifism and then concludes:

> To say all this is to lean over backwards to recognize the possibility of complex moral justifications for acts which would normally outrage the sensibilities of most decent people. The trouble with allowing the *possibility* of such acts being justified is that this view can be corrupted by enthusiastic "realists" into a defense of whatever war or atrocity is thought to serve their national or ideological interests.[46]

He adds: "One change must be to stop regarding killing in war as almost by magic immune from moral criticism."

There may be those among us who will decry this expanded dialogue and acknowledgment of "contingent pacifists" as "diluting" or "weakening" our witness. This is a risk I think worth taking, for the sake of the world and of our own self-understanding. My hope is that we will become more honest, more responsible, and more truly faithful in our response to the God who calls us to include justice in our vocation of peacemaking.

Notes

1. I have even heard Gordon Zahn confess that he did not easily become a member of any association in which his own behavior might seem to be bound by a majority decision.

2. The Social Gospel was a major attempt to counter this individualism, and with this attempt Niebuhr was identified.

3. *From Max Weber: Essays in Sociology*, trans. H. H. Gerth and C. Wright Mills (New York: Oxford University Press, 1946), pp. 77–129, especially pp. 78, 120–122, 127.

4. John H. Yoder, *Karl Barth and the Problem of War* (Nashville: Abingdon Press, 1970), p. 14.

5. John H. Yoder, *Nevertheless* (Scottdale, Pa.: Herald Press, 1971), p. 4.

6. John H. Yoder, "Reinhold Niebuhr and Christian Pacifism," in the *Mennonite Quarterly Review*, April 1955; Vol. 29, p. 101.

7. Yoder, *Nevertheless*, pp. 128–129, emphasis added.

8. "Statecraft" is the term Paul Ramsey uses to refer to carrying on the business of the nation-state. He assumes that this necessarily requires willingness to employ violent means. The issue he poses is whether the personal commitment of pacifism disqualifies one from any participation in political decisions, or statecraft.

9. John C. Bennett, *Christian Realism* (New York: Scribner's, 1947), p. 98.

10. Reinhold Niebuhr, "Christian Politics and Communist Religion," in John Lewis et al., *Christianity and the Social Revolution* (New York: Scribner's, 1936), pp. 442–443.

11. *Study-Encounter* 7 (1971): 4.

12. See the Preface to John C. Bennett, *The Radical Imperative* (Philadelphia: Westminster Press, 1975), pp. 7–10. Paul Ramsey affirms a positive view of the state, especially in the reliance on rulers and lesser magistrates, but he focuses on the seemingly prior requirement of order if justice is to be achieved and peace observed. Thus there is a premium on coercion.

13. Mulford Sibley, *The Political Theories of Modern Pacifism* (Philadelphia: The Pacifist Research Bureau, 1944 [rev. 1970]), p. 54.

14. John H. Yoder, "The Anabaptist Dissent," *Concern*, no. 1 (1954): 45–46.

15. John H. Yoder, "Jesus and Power," *The Ecumenical Review* 25 (October 1973): 449.

16. John H. Yoder, *The Politics of Jesus* (Grand Rapids: Eerdmans, 1973), p. 212.

17. John H. Yoder, *The Christian Witness to the State* (Newton, Kans.: Faith and Life Press, 1964), pp. 39–41.

18. Walter G. Muelder, "Concerning Power in the State," *The Philosophical Forum 5* (Spring 1947): 6.

19. C. H. McIlwain, *The Growth of Political Thought in the West* (New York: Macmillan, 1932), p. 158. Muelder also relies on the political theory of R. M. MacIver.

20. Muelder, "Concerning Power in the State," pp. 4–5.

21. Paul Ramsey, *The Just War* (New York: Scribner's, 1968), p. 199.

22. Niebuhr, "Christian Politics and Communist Religion," p. 457.

23. Appendix, "Some Definitions Related to the Struggle for Social Justice by Nonviolent Action," pp. 30–31 of the Report of the Consultation at Cardiff, Wales, mimeographed, World Council of Churches, Department of Church and Society, November 20, 1972.

24. Paul Ricoeur, "Non-violent Man and His Presence to History," in *History and Truth*, trans. Charles A. Kelbley (Evanston, Ill.: Northwestern University Press, 1965), p. 227. It is worth noting that in this early essay Ricoeur writes of unmasking "the violence of law and order," foreshadowing the discussions of systemic violence of the 1970s, but also clearly distinguishing these two types of violence—systemic and war.

25. Paul Ramsey, *War and the Christian Conscience* (Durham, N.C.: Duke University Press, 1961), pp. 128, 135.

26. LeRoy Walters, Jr., "Five Classic Just-War Theories," (Ph.D. diss., Yale University, 1971), University microfilms, p. 364. Walters includes a most interesting quotation from Grotius on whether a war might be unjust on both sides: "We are more likely to find both belligerent parties in the wrong than we are to find right on both sides," p. 329. Other theorists are Aquinas, Vitoria, Suarez, and Gentili.

27. Ramsey, *The Just War*, p. 275.

28. Sibley, *Political Theories*, pp. 66–67.

29. Reinhold Niebuhr, "Must We Do Nothing?" *The Christian Century* 49 (March 30, 1932). Emphasis added to stress the unusual distinction drawn by Niebuhr at this time.

30. Reinhold Niebuhr, "A Christian Journal Confronts Mankind's Continuing Crisis," *Christianity and Crisis* 26 (February 21, 1966), p. 13. Emphasis added.

31. John H. Yoder, "The Anabaptist Dissent," *Concern,* No. 1 (1954):47.

32. Yoder, "Reinhold Niebuhr and Christian Pacifism," p. 15.

33. See the reasons for protecting life in Sissela Bok, "Ethical Problems of Abortion," in *Hastings Center Studies* (January 1974).

34. Gordon D. Kaufman, "Nonresistance and Responsibility," *Concern*, no. 6 (November 1958): 5–29. It seems clear that Kaufman does not limit his conception of responsibility to the proponents of nonresistance.

35. Note the similar counsel in the World Council of Churches' report on "Violence, Nonviolence and the Struggle for Social Justice," p. 17: "Chris-

tians . . . must avoid the trap of seeming to dictate strategies and tactics to people living in distant and different situations.'' The context indicates that this applies to nonpacifists as well as to pacifists.

36. John H. Yoder, ''The Christian Case for Democracy,'' *Journal of Religious Ethics* 5 (Fall 1977): 222.

37. Walters, ''Five Just-War Theories,'' pp. 280–281.

38. Ramsey, *The Just War*, pp. 259–278.

39. J. Philip Wogaman, *A Christian Method of Moral Judgment* (London: SCM, 1976), pp. 43, 45.

40. Ibid., p. 246.

41. Yoder, ''Reinhold Niebuhr and Christian Pacifism,'' p. 6. I take it that Yoder would not argue that the two levels do not inform each other.

42. Bennett, *Christian Realism*, pp. 108 ff.

43. *Social Action* 10, no. 10 (December 15, 1944): 52. The commission was composed of theologians and church leaders.

44. ''The New Call to Peacemaking,'' Task Force on the Biblical and Theological Basis of Peacemaking, July 1977 Working Document. A crucial issue has been facing the implications of ''proclaiming one ethic for the church community and another for the world.''

45. Yoder, *Karl Barth and the Problem of War*, p. 39.

46. Jonathan Glover, *Causing Death and Saving Lives* (New York: Penguin Books, 1977), pp. 261, 284–285. Cf. Yoder, *Karl Barth and the Problem of War*, pp. 37–42.

6
Roman Catholic Social Ethics and Pacifism

Stephen E. Lammers

Anyone familiar with the history of Roman Catholic social ethics might find the title of this paper slightly odd. After all, many Roman Catholic social ethicists have been severe critics of pacifists and pacifist movements. Indeed, one could argue that Roman Catholic social ethics and pacifism stood in a negative relationship at most periods in Western European history.

At the same time, one would have to recognize that Roman Catholic moral life does not take all its sustenance from Roman Catholic ethicists. For example, one can find remembrances of pacifists in martyrologies. Usually these collections included one or two stories of saints killed because they themselves would not kill. Even Roman Catholic social ethics itself is not monolithic on this question. As early as 1919, the traditional formulation of the justifiable war was being used to justify a pacifist stance.[1] However, exceptions such as these are not the mainstream of either Roman Catholic moral life or Roman Catholic social ethics. In social ethics that mainstream is summarized in the following quotation:

> It is clear from what has been said that absolute pacifism is irreconcilable with traditional Catholic doctrine. Catholic exegetes likewise commonly reject the pacifist interpretation of Christ's teaching. His pronouncement on nonresistance to evil is taken as a *counsel* rather than as a *precept*, and for *private individuals* rather than *public authorities* since these would fail in an essential duty were they to offer no forceful resistance to violent aggressions from within or without. His warning to those who "take the sword" is commonly understood . . . to refer to those *who usurp the function* of rulers. . . . Nor is there any intrinsic contradiction between a just war and Christ's command that we *love our enemies. A just war expresses hatred of the evil deed rather than of the evildoer.*[2]

But that quotation does not represent the pluralism that exists within Roman Catholic social ethics today. At this particular point in their history, Roman Catholic ethicists find themselves discussing a number of alternatives, ranging from controlling nuclear deterrence to a complete withdrawal from politics on the grounds that all forms of modern war are immoral. It would be hard to point to an earlier period within Roman Catholic social ethics when such a variety of viewpoints existed. What is different about our time is that pacifism of one form or another is a live alternative for so many Christians.

In this paper I would like to discuss some of the reasons why Roman Catholic ethicists are considering pacifism once again. In order to do this I will review briefly some of the reasons for the past rejection of pacifism by Roman Catholic social ethicists. Then I will indicate some of the significant changes in the modern period, both within our understanding of pacifism and within Roman Catholic social ethics. In conclusion, I will indicate what I think are some of the unresolved issues if some form of pacifism is thought to be the best way to work a social ethic for Roman Catholic Christians.

Traditional Roman Catholic Social Ethics and Pacifism

Given the enormous literature that has been generated by the discussion of the term "pacifism," it would be best if we begin by having a tentative definition of the term. Initially I will be using the term to refer to opposition to participation in war. The grounds for the opposition to participation have been different at different periods in the history of the Roman Catholic Church. In the early period of the Christian Church, it appears that being a member of the Roman army involved participation in religious rituals, rituals which were forbidden to Christians. At the time of the Reformation, Christian pacifists claimed that pacifism was a charge given to the Christian community so that that community could live a certain kind of life, a life apart from the sword.[3]

For purposes of this essay, I would like to concentrate on the rejection of pacifism which has marked most of post-Reformation Roman Catholic social ethics. No doubt, opposition to the peace churches of the Reformation played a role in this rejection. However, this is certainly not all that was at stake.

In the first place, there was the discussion of Scripture which took place, and the role the Hebrew Bible played in that discussion. Given the theologian's assumption that the two testaments were understood to be united, pacifist claims which were based upon the New Testament threatened that assumed unity because war clearly was permitted in the Old Testament. Indeed, war had been blessed and commanded by God in the Hebrew Bible and thus war could not always be evil. The conclusion to be drawn from this was clear. The pacifists must have misunderstood the passages in the New Testament.[4]

Secondly, there was the predominant methodology of Roman Catholic ethics. This methodology of the natural law limited ethicists so that they could claim to know only that which could be known by all persons of good will; there was no special revelation in Christ determining what was right and wrong for society, no special knowledge in morals which was given to

Christians alone or for them as examples for, or teachers of, humankind. Once one accepted that basic methodological constraint, one sought points of contact between Roman Catholic ethics and the best of secular thought. In the discussion of war and peace, this meant taking from the tradition of Graeco-Roman thought the idea of the just war and developing it. This tradition discussed the conditions under which war could be done, how war should be done, and what should be done after war was completed.[5] Christian thinkers started with these questions and added to them. Theologians were also influenced by the early theorists in international law, theorists who were consciously not relying upon religious justifications.[6]

But there was more than methodology involved. There was the nature of war itself. I do not wish to romanticize war at earlier periods of human history, nor make it something which was so limited in its effects that ordinary people were not touched by it. However, relative to the extent of and the power of war in the modern world, war was a limited phenomenon. Also, until the nineteenth century, it was fought mainly by professional soldiers. The advent of large conscript armies had to await the French Revolution.

In addition, there was the social setting within which the Roman Catholic social ethicist worked. The Church was interested in the maintenance of certain regimes, regimes which ostensibly were friendly to the Church. This situation of privilege could hardly be maintained if social ethicists were arguing that the Roman Catholic faithful could not participate in war.

Finally, Roman Catholic social ethicists frequently misunderstood the grounds of the pacifist's opposition to war, and thus misread the pacifist to be saying that the individual's conscience was supreme, not only in faith and morals but in politics as well. In brief, it appeared that the pacifist was arguing that an individual could preempt the decision of duly constituted authority in a particular community, without necessarily paying any attention to what that authority had decided. This placing of conscience outside of the political hierarchy was rejected by Roman Catholic social ethicists. One could, and in some cases should, disagree with political authorities. What one could not do was ignore them in advance.

The theoretical structure which grew out of this is well known to most and thus I will give only a bare summary here. What Roman Catholic social ethicists did was accept the possibility that war could be done justly, defined those purposes which qualified as just purposes for waging war, put some constraints upon behavior in war, and finally, made it an obligation for the soldier to participate in wars. The soldier was not charged to consider the justice or injustice of the war in most cases. That decision was left to the political leader. There is no place in this structure for a consideration of pacifism, except as an aberration.

Changed Factors in the Consideration of Pacifism

Yet so much of the above has changed that pacifism is an option which is being considered seriously by Roman Catholic social ethicists. In what follows, I will try to indicate what I think are the important reasons for this change, with special attention given to Roman Catholic social ethics in America.

Perhaps the most important change which has occurred in Roman Catholic social ethics has come from its re-evaluation of the reality of war in this century. War is no longer imagined to be a conflict which is fought upon battlefields isolated from large population centers. The bombing in World War II made it clear to all that major war in this century involves the large-scale destruction of civilian lives and urban centers. The organization of war since that conflict has done nothing to change that perception of the facts. Indeed, the deterrence policies of the superpowers have led many persons to claim that the willingness to destroy civilian life is a necessary concomitant of modern war. The basic difficulty with these deterrence policies is that they make enemy population centers targets of attack, should war come, and they have led to the situation where one's own population centers are not defended against attack. With deterrence understood as at least a commitment to attack enemy population centers should that prove necessary, the problem of modern war is exposed.[7]

Given the nature of war in this century, the popes have been increasingly hesitant to justify war as a method of achieving justice. The papal statements of this century have stressed the horrors of war, and beginning with the letters of Pius XII, the popes have restricted the right of war to defense against attack. No longer is it just, according to papal teaching, to make war in order to punish injustice.[8] In this area, papal teaching has led the way, rather than followed a consensus of ethicists.[9]

The documents of Vatican Council II demonstrate how these developments in papal thought were taken up by the leaders of the Roman Catholic Church. In *Gaudium et Spes,* the discussion of war is put within the context of social justice, especially economic justice. Peace is understood as "an enterprise of justice" (Isa. 32:7), and the result of human and divine love. The conciliar document, in a reversal of the normal procedure for the discussion of war, focuses first upon specific violations of the *jus in bello,* condemning both genocide and the indiscriminate destruction of large areas. The Council Fathers also ask respect for international conventions which govern conduct in war. In their discussion of the *jus ad bellum* the Council Fathers claim that legitimate defense is the only just cause for war and all of the restrictions which formerly applied to offensive wars are now applied to wars of defense. When they turn their attention to deterrence, the Council Fathers claim that deterrence is a structure which has maintained a kind of peace, not to be despised in itself but not the kind of peace which the Christian should be seeking as the goal of humankind. The arms race in particular comes in for critical comment, because the buildup of arms is a violation of social justice when it prevents nations from helping the poor.[10]

These severe comments about modern war found in both papal and conciliar documents and the negative attitude toward war as an instrument of justice are now reflected in American Roman Catholic social ethics. Typical of this new attitude is the following statement:

> . . . war must be limited to defense, by the *ultima ratio*, by proportionality in the use of force. The difficulty of verifying these controls in the nuclear age and translating them into meaningful political and strategic concepts has made warfare increasingly a moral (as well as rational and Christian) impossibility.[11]

But there have been other factors which have prepared the way for change. The social situation in which the ethicists do their work has changed dramatically in many countries. The Church is not formally dependent upon the state, nor does the state depend upon the Church for ideological support. This situation has left the Church in a more ambiguous situation but it has freed the Church to make critical comments about the behavior of the state. However, the relation between church and state remains ambiguous, as Gordon Zahn demonstrated in his study of the Catholic Church in Nazi Germany.

Zahn showed how the Catholic Church in Nazi Germany operated as a social control for the Nazi regime's war policy during World War II. The German Catholic bishops did not choose to help implement that war policy but, as a matter of fact, their action and inaction had the result that the Roman Catholic Church became an agent of the state in the state's pursuit of its particular goals. This occurred because the Roman Catholic Church would not take a stand against Hitler's wars, and individuals within Germany who questioned the justice of those wars were left without institutional supports. Because churchmen did not try to moderate the ferocity of the war nor serve as a focal point of opposition to the war, they found themselves acting as agents of the state, even if this was against their intent.[12]

For Roman Catholics in the United States, the situation was quite different. Indeed, World War II serves as the paradigm case of the just war, despite pacifist criticism of that war.[13] Even when certain policies of the Allies were condemned, Roman Catholic social ethicists did not condemn the war as a whole. Thus John Ford could argue during the war that the Allied bombing policy toward enemy cities was an unjustifiable policy; he did not, however, question the basic intent and purposes of the Allies, nor did he call the war itself unjustifiable.[14]

What has proved to be decisive for churchpersons in the United States was the war in Vietnam. First, it became clear to many that it was no longer possible to assume that the norms which Christians think are appropriate to govern behavior in war have anything at all to do with the norms used by the persons directing the war. For example, the norms of justifiable war, minimal as they might seem to many, did not seem to shape the policy decisions of American political and military leaders during the Vietnam conflict. If this framework of analysis was not accepted, then new frameworks had to be found.[15] Thus a review of the literature published by Roman Catholic ethicists during this period makes it clear that on the one hand many ethicists were using the criteria of the justifiable war in order to analyze the war in Vietnam while others were searching for a new way of understanding war. What Vietnam forced commentators to face was the possibility that not only were actions done in the war unjustifiable, such as the deliberate killing of civilians, but also they had to face the possibility that the war was being waged for an unjust cause. But the radical question, really not asked before, was the question concerning war itself as an instrument for preserving a minimum of order and justice in the world.[16]

It is out of this questioning of modern war as an instrument of justice that there has been a re-thinking of the relationship of the individual to the modern state.

But this re-examination of modern war has led not only to a questioning of the relationship of the individual to the state. It has also led to a discussion of distributive justice. Preparation for war demands enormous amounts of resources, resources which might be put to better use, especially within poorer societies. The problem of war today is not only that war is different in its potential ferocity, but that the preparation for war misdirects societies away from basic needs. In addition, there is the special problem of deterrence, in that one appears to be planning to do that which it would be immoral to do. The best that can be said for deterrence is that it does bring "peace of a sort."[17] However, it appears to be a peace which works against distributive justice because of the large amount of resources devoted to the deterrence structures.

Roman Catholic social ethicists are not simply looking at modern war as a different phenomenon from war in the past. They are looking at modern war with different eyes than in the past. Today, there is a pluralism of methodologies in Roman Catholic social ethics. No longer is the methodology of the natural law the only one possible. One can search for and insist upon the distinctively Christian elements in the Christian message. Thinkers who adopt this methodological stance have argued that if we seek out these distinctive elements, we will discover that we have no choice but to be pacifists. For example, James Douglass has argued that at the heart of the Christian message is the call for a transformative suffering for and with others. For Douglass, this call does not separate Christians from others, but unites them in a search for peace.[18]

But even if one does not wish to emphasize the distinctively Christian elements in Christian ethics, or if one wishes to deny that there are such elements, one finds that when one turns to the secular world there is a body of thought which finds that war is no longer a viable way to resolve conflicts. Thus, pacifism is no longer being recommended solely out of some religious vision, but because many are convinced that human society can no longer afford war if society itself is to continue.[19] However, this does not mean that these secular pacifists are no longer interested in the problem of justice. Often, they are committed to seeking justice through means other than war. In this sense, twentieth-century pacifism is different from pacifisms of the past. It is as a political option as well as an opportunity for religious witness that pacifism now has to be considered. Not only has the meaning of war changed in our time, but the meaning of pacifism as well. This is a new situation for Roman Catholic social ethics.

Continuing Issues in the Discussion of Pacifism

Paul Ramsey has argued that the move from pacifism to some kind of justifiable war discussion in the early Church should not be understood as some kind of "fall of the Church," but is better understood as an attempt by Christians to understand what love meant in the situation in which they found themselves at that particular period in the history of the Roman Empire.[20] The type of pacifism to which Ramsey refers is a pacifism of witness, a pacifism which did not take political responsibility for the larger world but only for the life of the Church. What I am going to do here is to take that comment of Ramsey's as a clue to what is happening in our own time, namely, that the move from justifiable war discussion to a discussion of pacifism is an attempt to discover what love means in our own historical circumstances. However, the pacifism under consideration here is not a pacifism of witness, but a pacifism of resistance. I agree with Charles Curran when he judges that the way of witness pacifism is not the way which the majority of the Roman Church will take.[21] Although this type of pacifism was recognized at Vatican Council II, it does not seem to be under consideration as a serious option by the majority of Roman Catholic social ethicists in America.[22]

What I will do in this section of the paper is point to those areas of discussion which need development and clarification if a pacifism of resistance is to be developed within Roman Catholic social ethics.[23] Although there is nothing in what follows that is addressed solely to Roman Catholic social ethicists, I hope that what follows is especially pertinent to them because of the role that the just-war tradition still plays within Roman Catholic social ethics.

The first point that should be made is that a pacifism of resistance calls for a new understanding of the act of refusing to participate in war, at least new in the American context and legally unrecognized until now. What has been recognized until the present is a pacifism of witness, the refusal to serve in any war because of reasons based upon religious beliefs or their equivalents. What has not been legally recognized is a refusal to serve in war because of a judgment that that particular war was unjust. I do not want to try to make the case here that a refusal to serve in war based upon the judgment that a particular war was unjust should be given legal recognition. Nor do I wish to argue that legal recognition should be extended to persons who refuse to serve based upon a pacifism of resistance. In the latter case, I would indicate that before such a case could be made, it would be necessary to develop a theory of the relationship of the individual to political society that would make it possible to give political significance to the act of refusal. That difficult work in political theory remains to be done.

A second difficulty that has to be faced by the ethicist is that the term "peace" lacks conceptual clarity in modern discussions. In many ways, discussions within religious ethics only reflect some of the conceptual difficulties in the discussion of peace in secular circles. Here we can learn from work which has already been done.

L. Gunnar Johnson has pointed out how contemporary peace studies are at a conceptual impasse. There is a basic disagreement over the meaning of the term "peace" itself. Certain authors see peace as the absence of war; others wish to talk about world justice in any discussion of peace; and still others are more interested in world order and the disorder in the current international system.[24]

As Johnson describes the *world without war* view, its adherents are united in the belief that the major obstacle to peace is war and in a search for what one must do to eliminate war.[25] One of the options available to a person holding this point of view is to argue for nonviolent solutions of conflicts. One of the difficulties of this view is that there is a perennial temptation to overlook or minimize the injustices which are being done to persons, especially if these injustices are not the result of killing force but rather the results of structural conditions. These situations of structural injustice are not easily addressed by the means of nonviolence. Indeed, it is at this point of the debate that the second conception of peace enters.

The second conception of peace, *peace as world justice*, really begins as a critique of the first conception. Peace in this second view must be something positive, not only the absence of war. The prevention of war is only part of peace; peace must also include the promotion of just conditions of life.[26] Thinkers in this second group thus focus on questions of social justice and the maldistribution of the goods of creation. One of the difficulties with this school is that often it does not pay attention to the institutions which are the doers of justice and injustice in the world. Thus begins the world order discussion of peace.

The *peace as world order* school notes that the international order is defective in a number of fundamental ways. First, there is the defect in the international system which permits nation-states to declare war for their own reasons. There is no international authority to judge disputes between nations. Second, there are numerous other problems which cannot be handled by nation-states. Global pollution of the air and the oceans is one example. What is suggested is that we must create international agencies adequate to the tasks which now must be done.[27]

I think that this ambiguity in the meaning of peace is mirrored in most discussions today. What we lack is a theory which links the institutions that will provide order, an idea of justice that would include justice between nations as well as within nations, and a new form of "conflict resolution."

What is especially urgent is a theory of the state and its powers which is appropriate for a world where it is possible to end humankind through the exercise of certain kinds of power. Even if we concluded that the nation-state should be replaced, we still must serve justice and peace while moving toward a new international system.

What we seem to have forgotten is that the discussion of justifiable war grew out of an understanding of the potentialities and the limitations of human political power. There were certain ends for which war was not appropriate as a means. Later, this discussion of war became part of a larger theory about the purposes of political action in a world with other national actors. The institutions of order and justice were linked with the means of order and justice.

What is needed today is an understanding of international life which does not ignore the realities of our current system while pointing the way to a more just system. In brief, for those persons who are pacifists because of their understanding of the nature of modern war and its inadequacy as a means to peace and justice, most of the problems of politics still remain. For that reason, one has to be wary of identifying too closely with any single understanding of peace as mentioned above. All of them have their limitations. If peace is to be a peace with any kind of justice, it will have to mean more than the absence of war. The absence of war may be quite important but the presence of economic injustice is also quite important, as is the fact that nation-states still reserve to themselves the right to declare war. The problem is not that these problems aren't recognized. The difficulty for a pacifism of resistance is that these situations of injustice and disorder have to be changed without resorting to war.

It is at this point that it becomes appropriate to ask questions about what skills we will need for this kind of pacifism to flourish. At this point, I can only recommend the encouragement of two different attitudes, both of which are important in traditional politics as well. These are creativity and a tragic vision.

The need for creativity should be clear by now. If one takes upon oneself the limitation that one will not make war, one will have to be especially creative in dealing with those situations where war is threatened or was used in order to secure either peace, order, or justice. At the same time, one will have to recognize that in some cases one will not be able to resolve all of the difficulties and that we will have to accept some injustice and some disorder because it will not be possible to use force in order to make a particular situation a more just one. In an age which does not want to recognize that there exist limitations upon the human will to good and thus does not want to recognize the existence of tragedy, insisting upon both creativity and tragedy will be difficult indeed.[28]

What I have said here should be understood as hopeful. Rarely have the signs of the times been more propitious for the reception of a totally new vision of society, one that is inspired by premises that are quite different from those which inspired the past of this country. At the same time, one has the impression that one of the things that need to be done is to encourage those persons who are disenchanted with modern society to continue to think hard about what society needs and how societies may resolve their conflicts. Here the answers of the past do not seem to be much help to us. Thus there is an opportunity here which should not be ignored by pacifists.

Even if I am wrong that a pacifism of resistance will become a major consideration within Roman Catholic social ethics, I think that it is no longer doubtful that pacifism, if not the option chosen by the Roman Catholic social ethicist, will be rejected only after long and careful deliberation. That step of rejection, carried out so casually in the past by Roman Catholic social ethicists, is for the first time a real choice that must be thought through for a world which holds both great promise and terrible possibilities. Unfortunately, one of the possibilities is that we will make it a world of no choice at all, because we will have made this world a place of death rather than a celebration of life.[29]

Notes

1. Alfred Vanderpol, *La Doctrine Scolastique du Droit de Guerre* (Paris: A. Pedone, 1919).

2. "Pacifism," *New Catholic Encyclopedia*, Volume 10, p. 856 (Italics in original).

3. Angel M. Mergal, *Spiritual and Anabaptist Writers* (Philadelphia: Westminster, 1957).

4. Cf. Michael Walzer, "Exodus 32 and the Theory of the Holy War: The History of a Citation," *Harvard Theological Review* 61 (1968): 1–14.

5. Cf. Roland Bainton, *Christian Attitudes toward War and Peace* (Nashville, Tenn.: Abingdon, 1960), pp. 17–43.

6. James T. Johnson, *Ideology, Reason and the Limitation of War* (Princeton, N.J.: Princeton University Press, 1975), pp. 64–75.

7. J. Bryan Hehir, "The Catholic Church and the Arms Race," *Worldview* 21 (July/August 1978): 13–18.

8. John Courtney Murray has written about this in *We Hold These Truths* (New York: Sheed and Ward, 1960), pp. 238–261.

9. Compare the encyclicals and speeches of Pius XII with the writings of moral theologians in the 1940s and 1950s. The pope is far more hesitant about the possibility of a justifiable war.

10. *Gaudium et Spes*, nn. 77–82.

11. "War," *New Catholic Encyclopedia*, Volume 14, p. 806.

12. Gordon Zahn, *German Catholics and Hitler's Wars: A Study in Social Control* (New York: Sheed and Ward, 1962).

13. The *Catholic Worker* is one place where this pacifist opposition is recorded. For an account of this criticism, see Patricia F. McNeal, *The American Catholic Peace Movement, 1928–72* (New York: Arno, 1978).

14. John C. Ford, "The Morality of Obliteration Bombing," *Theological Studies* 5 (1944): 261–309.

15. For one account of how just-war thinking had no impact upon frameworks used by the courts, see Peter Monkres, "Just-War Theology: Rejected by the Court," *The Christian Century* 92 (May 28, 1975): pp. 547–549.

16. Hehir, "The Catholic Church and the Arms Race."

17. *Gaudium et Spes,* n. 81.

18. James W. Douglass, *The Non-Violent Cross* (New York: Macmillan, 1968).

19. Cf. Peter Brock, *Twentieth-Century Pacifism* (New York: Van Nostrand Reinhold, 1970), pp. 213–264.

20. Paul Ramsey, *War and the Christian Conscience* (Durham, N.C.: Duke University Press, 1961), pp. 15–33.

21. Charles Curran, *Ongoing Revision in Moral Theology* (Notre Dame, Ind.: Fides/Claretian Press, 1975), p. 169.

22. *Gaudium et Spes*, n. 79.

23. By a pacifism of resistance, I mean a position which refuses to participate in war but which at the same time will *resist* injustice without using lethal force.

24. L. Gunnar Johnson, *Conflicting Concepts in Contemporary Peace Studies* (London: Sage Publications, 1976).

25. Ibid., pp. 9–13. For a Roman Catholic example of this, see Gordon Zahn, *An Alternative to War* (New York: Council on Religion and International Affairs, 1963).

26. Johnson, *Conflicting Concepts*, pp. 17–21. Cf. Thomas Merton, *Seeds of Destruction* (New York: Farrar, Straus and Giroux, 1964).

27. Johnson, *Conflicting Concepts*, pp. 25–31. Cf. Gerald and Patricia Mische, *Toward a Human World Order* (New York: Paulist Press, 1977).

28. See Stanley Hauerwas, *Truthfulness and Tragedy* (Notre Dame, Ind.: University of Notre Dame Press, 1977), for reflections on these matters in the context of medical ethics.

29. I would like to take the opportunity to thank Kimberly Lambert, my research assistant, who located much of the material used in preparation of this essay.

7
Sources of the Nonviolent Tradition in American Literature

Michael True

Violence is so much a part of American society in the late twentieth century that one is likely to think of it as the dominant characteristic of our culture. H. Rap Brown's observation, made in the late 1960s, that "violence is as American as apple pie" is supported by the actual violence of racism and sexism and the potential violence of our $130 billion annual military budget, which makes us the number one supplier of armaments to the world. Yet there is considerable evidence that violence is abhorrent to American culture. Numerous poems, essays, sermons, and novels, from the Colonial period to the present, suggest, in fact, that nonviolence is also "as American as apple pie." Or so historians are beginning to believe, as a result of important recoveries of our buried past.

Reclaiming a Lost Tradition

Although only occasionally recognized in standard histories of American culture, the literary record of nonviolence is extensive, dramatizing the search for nonviolent alternatives over a three-hundred-year period. These lines, from John Beecher's poem "Engagement at the Salt Fork," for example, describing the San Francisco to Moscow Peace Walk, as it crossed the Oklahoma prairie in the late winter of 1961, describe, also, the gentle, persistent strength of the American tradition of nonviolence:

> Like tumbleweeds before the wind we moved across the continent's huge heedless face. . . . Blasts, born on Yukon tundras, knifed us through and buffeted our sign: *Man Will End War or War Will End Man.*[1]

A knowledge of and appreciation for this tradition, available in imaginative as well as expository writings—poems and essays as well as songs and sermons—are obviously helpful to an understanding of where we come from, as well as where we might be going; they suggest the paths taken by people at critical times in our history, paths acknowledged, but often rejected by those pursuing the course of manifest destiny or economic domination and military conquest.

Reclaiming its place in the history of American culture is a recent victory for the nonviolent tradition, over formidable academic opposition. Military history and the glorification of heroes of violence still dominate most philosophies of history, but the great heroes of nonviolence are gradually making their way into books and courses of study. It is no coincidence that the black revolution, which made black history and literature available to us, has brought the history and literature of nonviolence—oral as well as written—along with it. That "ghetto" known as "the great Western and Christian tradition" has begun to recognize roots, long-hidden, of a radical, nonviolent past.

My purpose in this essay is to indicate what a history of that literary tradition might look like, referring not only to the extensive writings by political radicals arguing for nonviolent social change, but also to selected writings by conservatives attentive to the psychological implications of a violent culture. In some instances the writers are complete pacifists, people for whom nonviolence is a way of life; in other instances, they are non-pacifists, people committed to nonviolence as a tactic or interested in it as a subject for a particular story or poem.

Violence and Nonviolence

But before turning directly to a discussion of the literature, it may be useful to make every effort, in the midst of considerable confusion, to define the words *violence* or *nonviolence*. I. A. Richards says that developments in any area are often frustrated when we stick to formed definitions that do not really express the meaning and purpose of a concept. This is particularly true in relation to *violence*, a concept that has experienced considerable change in denotation and connotation since 1800, and *nonviolence*, a term that is less than one hundred years old.

In his valuable study, *Revolutionaries: Contemporary Essays* (1975), E. J. Hobsbawm said that "of all the vague words of the late 1960s, violence is very nearly the trendiest and the most meaningless," calling attention to a basic problem in discussions of this kind.[2] Hobsbawm and the late Hannah Arendt noted that the word *violence* did not even appear in the *International Encyclopedia of Social Science* (1968),[3] and implied that, in the apocalyptic rush of contemporary events, we may destroy ourselves as a civilization before we have any clear understanding, any word, to describe what has happened to us. Meanwhile, in the midst of what Hobsbawm calls "a general atmosphere of disorientation and hysteria"—represented over the past decade by a multiplicity of books and films extolling violence—old confusions perpetuate themselves. When the same word, *violence*, for example, is used to describe both the destruction of property, in the Boston Tea Party, and the possible destruction of millions of people in a nuclear war, we know that it does not accurately describe the two experiences.

The root meaning of *violence* comes from the Latin *violentia,* meaning vehemence, a passionate and uncontrolled force, the opposite of a calculated exercise of power. Traditionally, the word meant "to pervert some object, natural or human, from its 'natural' course of development" and "to exceed some limit or norm." Political theorists of the eighteenth century—Locke, Rousseau, Montesquieu—agreed that violence could not regenerate people or society, and, unlike later political philosophers, set limits to the justifiable province of violence.[4] Since Marx, however, the concepts *revolution* and *violence* have been closely linked. This is quite understandable, given the proliferation of technological weapons in this century, but this association is not inevitable and deprives us of the tradition prior to Marx, the tradition that radical social change was possible without resorting to violence, as it was then understood.

The term *nonviolence* calls equally for clarification and careful delineation, particularly since modern dictionaries either omit it entirely or define it in purely negative terms. There is no denying that, as a political concept, it carries—like pacifism—conflicting connotations. For those committed to nonviolence as a way of life, it means positive action to bring about social change, to eradicate various forms of oppression, and to "building a new society in the shell of the old," as the Wobblies put it and as the Catholic Workers still describe it. These various aspects of nonviolence have emerged slowly, particularly over the past century. Prior to that the concept went by other names. In the 1840s, for example, in the writings of Adin Ballou and Elihu Burritt, nonviolence was sometimes called "passive resistance." Burritt wrote of "the irresistable power of passive resistance . . . which any community or country might employ successfully in repelling and disarming despotism, whatever amount of bayonet power [the oppressor] might have at its command." The main point is that nonviolence was regarded even at this time as active rather than passive, as a positive force rather than just as a negative reaction.[5]

In general, nonviolence appears to have had three principal manifestations in America, each represented by a considerable body of writings: (1) *nonviolence as a witness*—holding silent vigils, prayer meetings, and religious liturgies; (2) *nonviolence as protest*—refusing to obey laws that people regard as unjust or to pay war tax, picketing, boycotting; and (3) *nonviolence as a method of bringing about fundamental social change*—initiating and carrying out the abolitionist, feminist, and civil rights movements. The general survey of religious, political, and literary documents that follows includes examples of each of these three manifestations of nonviolence from the seventeenth century to the present. It needs to be emphasized, perhaps, that scholars on political theory and history would do well to read these documents and thereby correct their misuse of and misunderstanding of the term *nonviolence.* The word has a history and a precise meaning, just as "force" or "power" or "authority" do, which any serious treatment of political theory ignores at its own risk.[6]

Although there is a considerable body of material relating to nonviolence in the Colonial period, particularly statements by religious dissidents such as the Quakers, the major direction of the tradition is more clearly observable in four later periods: (1) from 1760 to 1800, in the actions of crowds and the writings of Thomas Paine and others; (2) from 1820 to 1860, in essays and pamphlets by abolitionists and agitators for women's rights; (3) from 1900 through World War I, in songs and poems by labor organizers and war resisters; and (4) since the late 1950s, in extensive writings associated with the civil rights and anti-war movements—the poems of John Beecher, poet of protest and prophecy, quoted above, among them. In each of these four periods, American writers have dealt explicitly and implicitly with the theme of nonviolence, in religious and political documents important to social history and in poems, novels, and essays significant to literary history.

The Colonial and Revolutionary Period

In the period between the landings at Jamestown and Plymouth and the Revolution, several people contributed to the history of nonviolence by their refusal to obey oppressive laws or by their determination to live peacefully among the Native Americans. Roger Williams and Anna Hutchinson, antinomians of the seventeenth century, are commonly associated with the tradition in their refusal, in the face of religious persecution and banishment, to obey "the law." Like the early Quakers, who were ostracized, imprisoned, and killed, Williams and Hutchinson insisted upon freedom of conscience and religious practice, even as the Puritan clergy of Massachusetts tried them and banished them to Rhode Island. Thomas Morton, an Anglican trader and author indirectly "satirized" in Hawthorne's "The Maypole of Merry Mount," probably ran into trouble not because of licentiousness, but because of his friendliness to the Indians.

The close relationship between nonviolence and peaceful coexistence with Native Americans is evident, also, in the Quaker's "Friendly Association for Gaining and Preserving Peace with the Indians by Pacific Measures" and in the life and writings of John Woolman (1720–1772), abolitionist and war resister. "Love was the first notion," Woolman wrote, "and thence arose a concern to spend some time with the Indians, that I might feel and understand their life and the spirit they live in, if haply I might receive some instruction from them."[7] Widely traveled in the colonies and admired by Quakers and non-Quakers alike, Woolman is best known for his *Journal* (1774), the most influential book on Christian nonviolence from the eighteenth century. Benjamin Rush's description of Anthony Benezet, author of *The Plainness and Innocent Simplicity of the Christian Religion with its Salutary Effects, Compared to the Corrupting Nature and Dreadful Effects of War* (1782), suggests the major concerns of another Quaker pamphleteer: "In one hand [Benezet] carried a subscription paper and a petition; in the other he carried a small pamphlet on the unlawfulness of the African slave-trade, and a letter directed to the King of Prussia upon the unlawfulness of war."[8]

A commitment to nonviolent social change is exemplified by many other colonists in the early stages of the American Revolution. Although the movement for independence eventually led to violence, it seems clear that the rebels chose war as a last resort, after failing to achieve their goals by a succession of nonviolent actions. Marvin L. Michael Kay and Dirk Hoerder, in important essays on the American Revolution,[9] describe the various methods of nonviolent protest employed by the North Carolina Regulation and the Boston crowds in the late 1760s–law suits, civil disobedience, petitions, election campaigns, limited destruction of property. And Pauline Maier, in *From Resistance to Revolution: Colonial Radicals and the Development of American Opposition to Britain, 1765–1776,* discusses the various ways in which radicals developed and tested, with growing sophistication, the means of nonviolent social change. Using such terms as "ordered" and "organized resistance," she says, at one point, "while eighteenth-century Whig writers stood ready to challenge anyone who denied the people's right of revolution, they still sought to limit and even deter violence by a series of preconditions that were even more carefully defined. . . . Before any force or violence could be justly invoked, contenders had to try all peaceful avenues of redress."[10] The Sons and Daughters of Liberty did not, that is, simply embark on a path of violence, although they did seek to expose the violence of the other side through skillful manipulation of public opinion. In the "Boston Massacre," for example, they turned public opinion against the British, with the help of Paul Revere's dramatic poster and in various other campaigns in the popular press.

Of some significance to the relationship between nonviolence and the Revolutionary period are the writings and example of Thomas Paine (1737–1809), radical pamphleteer and resident in this country from 1774 to 1787 and, after his involvement in the French Revolution, from 1802 to 1809. Although willing to justify the use of violence in revolutionary struggle and scornful of Philadelphia Quakers who refused to take up arms for the American cause, he consistently argued against abuses of power even by his co-revolutionists. His speeches against the execution of Louis XIV, for example, while a member of the French National Convention, almost cost Paine his head. And a statement he made in support of a French constitution during that long debate, as well as other condemnations of violence, indicate a commitment to nonviolence, in order to allow people time to adapt to major social change.

> There never yet was any truth or any principle irresistibly obvious that all men believe it at once. Time and reason must cooperate with each other to the final establishment of any principle and therefore those who may happen to be first convinced have not a

> right to persecute others on whom conviction operates more slowly. The moral principle of revolutions is to instruct, not to destroy. . . . Had a constitution been established two years ago (as ought to have been done) the violences that have since desolated France and injured the character of the Revolution would have been prevented.[11]

Like Paine, whose writings influenced William Lloyd Garrison and later advocates of nonviolence, John Adams also recognized the role of nonviolent social change and its effect upon public opinion. In a famous letter to Hezekiah Niles in 1818, Adams wrote that the real revolution was not in the American war, so much as it was "in the minds and hearts of the people; a change in their religious sentiments of their duties and obligations. . . . This radical change in the principles, sentiments, and affections of the people was the real American Revolution," accomplished before the violence occurred. As the lawyer who defended the British soldiers involved in the "Boston Massacre," Adams spoke here, perhaps, of his own "conversion" to the radical cause; but he reminds us, too, of what was accomplished nonviolently in the early stages of the movement for independence.

An understanding of the Revolution and its legacy to later generations must recognize its achievements for change through nonviolent means—that is, through direct action, boycotts, civil disobedience, even the destruction of property (burning stamps and tea), rather than the destruction of people. This distinction is important for at least two reasons: (1) it helps to define the peculiar nature of the American Revolution as one in which violence was still regarded as a means rather than an end; and (2) it throws some light on the relationship between radical thought and action during the Revolutionary period and later, when the tactics of nonviolent direct action were developed further and became a permanent part of American political thought.

Between the Revolutionary and the Abolitionist periods, Quakers were joined by other religious groups and some secular societies in the nonviolent quest. Like the early Christians or the medieval religious orders, especially the Franciscans, who took a pledge never to engage in war, they affirmed through visible, however modest actions, that the counsel "Blessed are the peacemakers" was still alive in the hearts of people. Their witnessing to nonviolence included such activities as silent vigils, prayer meetings, and religious liturgies that focused on pacifist teachings. Singing traditional hymns and making pilgrimages, they affirmed, by these and other actions, a belief in the life and teachings of Jesus within a political context. This tradition was maintained by later advocates of nonviolence in the labor and anti-war movements, when they wrote new words to old Gospel hymns, on the picket line, or conducted Good Friday marches "celebrating life in front of institutions of death," as recent demonstrators at the Pentagon put it.

By the early nineteenth century, peace societies existed in several states, the one in Massachusetts numbering 1,000 people by 1922. Six years later, several state societies combined to form the American Peace Society. Two important books by members David Low Dodge, a New York merchant, and Noah Worcester, a Massachusetts Congregational minister, were *War Inconsistent with the Religion of Christ* (1815) and *A Solemn Review of the Custom of War* (1814). Dodge's book argued against war because it wastes human and natural resources and results in hatred and revenge, rather than peace and liberty; Worcester's book maintained that war never rights the wrongs it addresses and kills the people least responsible for the policies that prompted the conflict.

The period from 1820 to 1860 is in many ways the greatest period for American literature in the nonviolent tradition, spanning the early lives and the theoretical and practical essays of William Lloyd Garrison, Adin Ballou, and Elihu Burritt. More generally, it includes the publication of major writings of Nathaniel Hawthorne, Herman Melville, Henry David Thoreau, and Walt Whitman—writers who, although not advocates of nonviolence, nonetheless are crucial to an understanding of the search for alternatives to the violence of American culture.

The Pre-Civil War Period

Between 1820 and 1860, the first extensive writings on nonviolence were the early work of William Lloyd Garrison, beginning with the first issue of the *Liberator,* January 1, 1831, and Henry David Thoreau's *Civil Disobedience* (1848), which, with Martin Luther King's "Letter from a Birmingham Jail," is perhaps the most famous document in American literature relating to nonviolence. In the case of both Garrison and Thoreau, there is a certain irony in the fact that although they contributed substantially to the nonviolent tradition, neither was an absolute pacifist. Garrison, after giving nonresistance "its shape and its drive," as Peter Brock said, eventually embraced the Union Army's cause as a holy crusade for abolitionism; and Thoreau spoke vigorously in defense of John Brown's use of arms in the anti-slavery struggle. Yet, on the basis of their pioneering work and their influence on later apostles of nonviolence—most notably Tolstoy and Gandhi—Garrison and Thoreau are central figures in the tradition, especially in the secularization of nonviolence, in terms suggested by Garrison's statement:

> I am not professedly a Quaker; but I heartily, entirely and practically embrace the doctrine of nonresistance. . . . What is the design of militia musters? To make men skilful murderers. I cannot consent to become a pupil in this sanguinary school.[12]

For many of the abolitionists (Burritt, Ballou, Stephen Symonds Foster), working against slavery and opposing war and violence were the same resistance movement. Out of this community grew extensive writings defining and limiting the concept now known as nonviolence. In addition to

Burritt's "Passive Resistance," published in *Thoughts and Things at Home and Abroad* (1854) and mentioned earlier, there were the extensive publications of Adin Ballou, founder of the Hopedale Community, including *Non-Resistance in Relation to Human Governments* (1839) and *Practical Christian Socialism: A Conversational Exposition of the True System of Human Society* (1854). Stephen Symonds Foster, husband of the famous abolitionist Abigail Kelley Foster and himself the author of *The Brotherhood of Thieves; or a True Picture of the American Church and Clergy* (1846), a popular anti-slavery tract, actively practiced nonviolent resistance on several occasions. During the famous Butman riot in 1854, in Worcester, Massachusetts, Burritt placed himself between a mob and a federal marshall who came to town to arrest a fugitive slave. (The marshall left the city unharmed, without the black man.) The Fosters also refused to pay taxes on their property as a protest against oppressive laws regarding women.

In their writings and in their lives, these people tested their own actions as well as those of the past against an emerging standard, about what was or what was not nonviolence. Two other prolific writers should be mentioned whose central themes are suggested by selected titles from their collected works: C. K. Whipple, *Evils of the Revolutionary War* (1839) and *Non-Resistance Applied to the Internal Defense of a Community* (1860), and Henry C. Wright, *Defensive War Proved to Be a Denial of Christianity and the Government of God: With Illustrative Facts and Anecdotes* (1848). (Not mentioned here are many other writers and editors—Josiah Warren and Benjamin Tucker, for example—who, though they contributed to the tradition through their writings on Christian anarchism, were not as actively committed to nonresistance as Garrison and Burritt.)

It is against this background of agitation and social reform that one may understand the preoccupation among the major novelists of the period, most notably Hawthorne and Melville, both of whom took critical views, generally, toward nonviolence. Melville appears, for example, not to have understood the concept at all; his one treatment of it, as represented by the passive behavior of Bartleby in *Bartleby the Scrivener* (1853), is a caricature, rather than a realistic dramatization of a true nonresistant. In this sense, Hawthorne's portraits of radicals in *The Blithedale Romance* (1851) and *The House of the Seven Gables* (1852) are more authentic. Through the character of Holgrave, the young anarchist in the latter novel, Hawthorne presents an unsympathetic picture of the nonresistance movement. In the famous scene, when Holgrave renounces his hypnotic power over Phoebe, the reader gets some sense of Hawthorne's solution to social problems, implying that, in order for society to heal itself, a personal renunciation of violence must come before any social movement. Only after Holgrave's abdication of his power over Phoebe are the two families united; only then are the two young people able to make a new beginning, unburdened by the weight of old conflicts, old curses, old fears.

Hawthorne, disillusioned by the Brook Farm experiment and allied politically with moderate democrats, including his old friend, President Franklin Pierce, and others who defended slavery, remained skeptical of all reformers throughout his life. He was fascinated, nonetheless, by rebels —Hester Prynne, Hollingsworth, Zenobia—and as preoccupied with the problem of violence in American culture as Garrison and Thoreau were. There is much to be learned about the American tradition of nonviolence in the fiction of Hawthorne and other artists who struggled with the problem imaginatively and conscientiously, just as activists and theoreticians did. For various reasons, in other words, the period between 1820 and 1860 is immensely rich as the seed-time of the nonviolent tradition.

The Civil War divided the movement, however, and it was some time before nonresistance regained its strength or exerted a wide influence in American history and literature again. In part, the leadership had shifted to Russia, through the life and writings of Leo Tolstoy—who acknowledged his indebtedness to Garrison, Ballou, and Thoreau—and his followers. William Jennings Bryan (1860–1925) visited Tolstoy at his home in Yasna Polyana in 1902 and announced himself a disciple; Clarence Darrow, later famous as a criminal lawyer and civil libertarian, wrote a pamphlet, *Resist Not Evil* (1903), based upon Tolstoy's Christian anarchism; and William James' influential pamphlet, "A Moral Equivalent of War" (1910), argued that a pacifist must act, rather than just preach, in order to divert youthful energies away from war-making and toward peace-making.

Early Twentieth-Century Sources

The work of maintaining the nonviolent tradition in the period before and during World War I, however, fell upon people with little or no knowledge that an American tradition of nonviolence even existed. Some activists, such as Big Bill Haywood (1869–1928), co-founder of the Industrial Workers of the World, and Emma Goldman (1869–1940), a popular anarchist speaker and writer, had recommended violent acts to bring on "the revolution," but eventually turned toward nonviolent tactics. Ammon Hennacy (1893–1970), later a Christian anarchist, came to nonviolence indirectly, as a result of his early Socialist politics. The Socialist Party, under the leadership of Eugene Victor Debs (1855–1926), advocated draft resistance, not out of religious principle, but out of loyalty to the workers of the world. Their motto, printed on posters and defined in popular pamphlets, was "Don't be a Soldier; be a Man." As it had during the Revolutionary and Abolitionist period, the sudden increase in writings about nonviolence, between 1900 and 1920, reflected the tumultuous, even rebellious times, in challenges to the dominant political system advocated by significant minorities of syndicalists, Socialists, and anarchists. Responses to this movement included radical periodicals, *The Appeal to Reason, Mother Earth, The Masses,* and the *Liberator,* and organizations committed to nonviolence, founded in these years: Women's International League for Peace and Freedom (1915), Fellowship of Reconciliation (1915), American

Friends Service Committee (1917), and War Resisters League (1923).

The Industrial Workers of the World, founded in 1905, proved to be an important training ground for several advocates of nonviolence. Dorothy Day (b. 1897) joined the Wobblies and wrote for *The Masses* long before she co-founded the Catholic Worker movement in 1933; and Debs and Haywood wrote books and pamphlets describing sit-ins in the labor movement and acts of noncooperation that influenced later pacifists. Jane Addams, who gave her Nobel Prize money in 1931 to the Women's International League for Peace and Freedom, told of her commitment to nonviolence in *Forty Years at Hull House* (1935). Some of the most significant writings during World War I on war resistance and anti-statism are Randolph Bourne's essays, particularly "War and the Intellectuals" and similar writings, published in the *Seven Arts* and *Dial* magazines. Bourne (1886–1918), who maintained that "war is the health of the state," came to be regarded as a prophetic figure in his understanding of the psychological and political effects of the war and cast a long shadow across post-war literature, especially influencing John Dos Passos' novel *1919* (1933). Another exposé of the bureaucratic state is E. E. Cummings' moving memoir about his imprisonment in France, *The Enormous Room* (1922), and his later poem in tribute to a conscientious objector entitled "I Sing of Olaf."

Of the many incidents in the history of nonviolence between World War I and World War II—the sit-ins by the United Auto Workers and the early days of the Catholic Worker—none is more memorable than the action of several brave men in Danbury (Conn.) Federal Prison in 1940. As with some 4,000 conscientious objectors during World War I and some 50,000 conscientious objectors during World War II, these men objected to war and to conscription on religious grounds. Karl Shapiro later described them in a poem, "The Conscientious Objector," written while he was a soldier in the South Pacific, as those whose consciences "we come back to in the armistice."[13]

Unlike many C.O.'s then and now, however, these men were forced to go to jail, and once there found it necessary to resist many of the policies of the criminal justice system. Leading a strike against racial segregation and other repressive practices, the group, which included David Dellinger, soon found themselves in solitary confinement—in the hole. Even there, their nonviolent protest continued. Through a fast, resistance to intimidation, and a personal bribe from the warden—but particularly through the persistence of a man named Benedict, who refused pardon until it was extended to the group—they eventually secured the release not only of their co-resisters, but of all prisoners confined to the hole. Howard Schoenfeld, a survivor of this nonviolent protest, described the return of the resisters, after their release from solitary:

> We straggled across the empty yard, basking in the sun, enjoying our freedom. A spontaneous wave of applause broke out among

> the [regular prisoners] as the first of our group entered the [mess] hall. Surging across the hall, the waves became a crescendo. Six hundred pairs of hands joined in and the crescendo became pandemonium . . . but when the so-called criminals who had been in solitary came in, the convicts literally went wild, beating their metal cups on the tables, and stamping their feet.
>
> We stood in the center of the hall, astounded at the demonstration. It became clear that although they were applauding Benedict, Brooks and all of us who had been in solitary, they were doing something more. A mass catharsis of human misery was taking place before our eyes. Some of the men were weeping, others were laughing like madmen. It was like nothing I had ever seen before, and nothing I ever expect to see again.[14]

Later Twentieth-Century Sources

The fourth, and in some ways the richest, period for literature in the nonviolent tradition is the period from the late 1950s up through the present time—that is the period from the beginning of the civil rights movement to the latest activities of the Clamshell Alliance, the Mobilization for Survival, or the Atlantic-Great Lakes-Pacific Life Community. Under the threat of nuclear war, many Americans have become "nuclear pacifists," contributing to an anti-war movement that builds upon the work of Ammon Hennacy, A. J. Muste, Martin Luther King, Dorothy Day, and Gordon Zahn; is inspired by the poems, essays, and plays of Thomas Merton, Paul Goodman, Daniel and Philip Berrigan; and is informed by theoretical writings by scholars such as Richard Gregg, Mulford Sibley, Gene Sharp, Howard Zinn, and Staughton Lynd, or activists such as David Dellinger, Cesar Chavez, Barbara Deming, Jim Douglass, Dick Gregory, and George Lakey.

Two examples of communal action will suggest the strength of the nonviolent tradition since the 1950s, the first an example of nonviolence as a method of bringing about fundamental social change, during the civil-rights movement, and the second an example of nonviolence as witness, during the San Francisco to Moscow Peace Walk, 1961.

Although generally thought of as beginning with Rosa Parks's refusal to sit at the back of the bus in 1957, the civil rights movement actually began some years prior to that fateful day in Birmingham, Alabama, when one black woman was just too tired to obey the state law that said she had to give up her seat to a white man. Rosa Parks's resistance was an act of personal courage, but it had been prepared for by a potential community of support. James Farmer, later national director of the Congress of Racial Equality, had called it "The Brotherhood Mobilization" in his preparations for effective mass action against segregation; and it had been initiated in 1942, not in 1957. In two memoranda to A. J. Muste, executive director of the Fellowship of Reconciliation, Farmer spelled out the conditions and time plan for such a movement, presenting "a distinctive and radical approach." From these early plans came the freedom rides, often regarded as phenomena of the early 1960s, but actually initiated in April 1947; that year, an interracial group rode Greyhound and Trailways buses throughout the South to test the 1946 Supreme Court decision outlawing segregation on interstate travel. The records of this early organizing and the brief transcripts of the ride by Bayard Rustin and George Houser are among the most valuable writings on the application of Gandhian principles to an American campaign; the leaders stand out as some of the greatest teachers in the history of nonviolence.[15]

The San Francisco to Moscow Peace Walk, 1961—or the later Continental Walk, 1976, described in Charlie King's song, "Do the Continental Walk" ("Stop building H-bombs/And build a better home instead")—stressed the importance of a community's affirming a belief through public and personal testimony. In October 1961, after ten months of walking, thirty-one members of the Committee of Nonviolent Action, including Brad Lyttle, author of *You Come With Naked Hands: The Story of the San Francisco to Moscow March for Peace,*[16] entered Red Square in Moscow after demonstrating for peace at military bases across the United States and Western Europe. As a direct result of this pilgrimage, a series of demonstrations and public pronouncements followed, including the Quebec to Guantanamo Walk, 1963–1964. The history of this action and the confrontation with Laurie Pritchett, police chief of Albany, Georgia, is described in Barbara Deming's moving memoir, *Prison Notes*[17] (1966), as well as in Pete Seeger's verse, added to an old protest song: "No more Pritchett over me./ And before I'll be a slave,/ I'll be buried in my grave,/ and go home to my Lord and be free." As with the civil disobedience of Albert Bigelow, who sailed a 30-foot boat, the *Golden Rule,* into the forbidden nuclear testing area in the Western Pacific in 1958, and Catholic Worker protests that ended the atomic bomb drills in New York City about the same time, the 1961 Walk for Peace brought the problem of atmospheric testing of atomic weapons to public attention. And as a result of a public outcry, that testing was eventually banned by the United States and the Soviet Union. Public witness of this kind may appear a very modest action in the face of major social injustice or danger. Yet in the last year of the Cold War 1950s, many Americans regarded a peace walk as "radical"; at the very least, it kept alive a tradition that post-World War II America had almost forgotten.

In nonviolent movements for social change since the late 1950s—in small actions or large campaigns—the writings of Martin Luther King and Gordon Zahn have proved especially significant. King and his many talented and skilled associates in the civil rights movement reclaimed an American tradition by bringing back to this country an approach to social change that Garrison, Ballou, and Thoreau had helped to initiate. King emphasized, in the Abolitionist and Gandhian manner, the importance of a total campaign and recognized the relationship between war and racial and economic injustice. Zahn, in his sociological studies during the same period, established a link between that tradition and the social teachings of the Catholic Church, uniting two constituencies that had previously remained separate. Later, he pointed out the similarities between the German Catholics' failure to resist Hitler and American Catholics' cooperation with the Pentagon and the war-making state.

Thomas Merton wrote that Zahn's biography of Franz Jäggerstatter, the German war resister, raised not only "the individual Catholic's right to conscientious objection," but also "the question of the Church's own mission of protest and prophecy" in the gravest spiritual crisis in human history.[18] A similar indebtedness to Zahn's writings is acknowledged in Daniel Berrigan's play, *The Trial of the Catonsville Nine* (1972); Robert Bly's essay, "Leaping Into Political Poetry" (1970); and by various "Catholic conspirators against the Vietnam War," as in Philip Berrigan's *Punishment for Peace*[19] and, especially after the founding of the Catholic Peace Fellowship (1964), in the court testimony of numerous war resisters.

This general survey of the literature of nonviolence obviously omits many aspects of the tradition, including any detailed discussion of the subtler implications of the autobiographies, novels, and poems by pacifists and nonpacifists and the historical conflicts that have divided them over the past three centuries. Nor does it deal with the influence of famous anti-war novels such as Ernest Hemingway's *A Farewell to Arms*,[20] Dalton Trumbo's *Johnny Got His Gun,*[21] or Norman Mailer's *Armies of the Night*.[22] But perhaps it does suggest that the literary record in imaginative as well as expository writing is extensive, rich, and distinguished and that nonviolence continues to inform American literary history.

In recent years, in *Rags of Time: A Season in Prison,*[23] the story of an anarchist walk by draft resisters at Allenwood Federal Prison Camp, Jack Cook has written one of the most powerful sustained dramatizations of nonviolent action in American literature. And in "The Peaceable Kingdom," a meditation on the famous painting by Edward Hicks, and in other poems, Marge Piercy describes the experimental nature of nonviolent resistance and the fragile nature of new communities. In her poem, "The 184th Demonstration," a witty reflection on the predictability of protest marches, someone asks, "Tomorrow is the 185th Demonstration/ Will you be there?" And the speaker answers, "Of course."[24]

Like many previous American activists and artists, Cook and Piercy understand that challenges to the violence of the status quo are often tentative, modest, and, at most, partially successful. There is little room for triumphalism in the literature of nonviolence, few happy endings or final victories. Yet the tradition persists, nourished by the writings of pacifists and nonpacifists—carried on by ordinary and extraordinary people—over three hundred years.[25]

Notes

1. John Beecher, *Collected Poems, 1924–1974* (New York: Macmillan, 1974), p. 230.

2. H. J. Hobsbawm, *Revolutionaries: Contemporary Essays* (New York: New American Library, 1975), p. 209.

3. Hannah Arendt's discussion of violence and related concepts appears in "On Violence," *Crises of the Republic* (New York: Harcourt, Brace, Jovanovich, 1972), pp. 105–98.

4. Sheldon Wolin, "Violence and the Western Political Tradition," *American Journal of Orthopsychiatry* 33 (January 1963): 15–28.

5. Burritt's essay is reprinted in Staughton Lynd, *Nonviolence in America: A Documentary History* (Indianapolis: Bobbs Merrill, 1966), pp. 94–108.

6. The standard work on the subject is Gene Sharp, *The Politics of Nonviolent Action*, ed. Marina Finkelstein (Boston: Porter Sargent, 1973).

7. Quoted in *The Power of the People: Active Nonviolence in the United States*, ed. Robert Cooney and Helen Michalowski (Culver City, Calif.: Peace Press, 1977), p. 21.

8. Quoted in Peter Brock, *Pacifism in the United States: From the Colonial Era to the First World War* (Princeton, N.J.: Princeton University Press, 1968), p. 191.

9. "The North Carolina Regulation, 1766–1776: A Class Conflict" and "Boston Leaders and Boston Crowds, 1765–1776" in *The American Revolution: Explorations in the History of American Radicalism*, ed. Alfred Young (DeKalb, Ill.: Northern Illinois University Press, 1976).

10. Pauline Maier, *From Resistance to Revolution* (New York: Knopf, 1972), p. 28.

11. Thomas Paine, "Dissertation on First Principles of Government," in *Common Sense and Other Political Writings*, ed. Nelson F. Adkins (Indianapolis: Bobbs Merrill, 1953), p. 174.

12. Quoted in Brock, *Pacifism in the United States*, p. 529.

13. Karl Shapiro, *Collected Poems: 1940–1978* (New York: Random House, 1978), p. 96.

14. Howard Schoenfeld, "The Danbury Story," in *The Pacifist Conscience*, ed. Peter Mayer (New York: Holt, Rinehart, and Winston, 1966), p. 344.

15. "CORE, The Beginning: The First Freedom Ride," in Mayer, *The Pacifist Conscience*, pp. 362–384.

16. Bradford Lyttle, *March for Peace* (Weare, N.H.: Greenleaf Books, 1966).

17. Barbara Deming, *Prison Notes* (New York: Grossman, 1966; Boston: Beacon, 1970).

18. In the introduction to a superb collection, *Thomas Merton on Peace*, ed. Gordon Zahn (New York: Saturday Review Press, 1971), Zahn traces Merton's own pilgrimage to nonviolence.

19. Philip Berrigan, *Punishment for Peace* (New York: Macmillan, 1969; Ballantine, 1970).

20. Ernest Hemingway, *A Farewell to Arms* (1929), Contemporary Classic Editions (New York: Scribner's).

21. Dalton Trumbo, *Johnny Got His Gun,* reprint of 1939 ed. (Secaucus, N.J.; Lyle Stuart, 1970).

22. Norman Mailer, *Armies of the Night* (New York: New American Library, 1968; NAL Signet, 1971).

23. Jack Cook, *Rags in Time: A Season in Prison* (Boston: Beacon, 1972).

24. A selection of poems by Marge Piercy appears in *Campfires of the Resistance: Poetry from the Movement,* ed. Todd Gitlin (Indianapolis: Bobbs Merrill, 1971).

25. Four indispensable general introductions to the American tradition of nonviolence are the one by Peter Brock and the three edited by Staughton Lynd, Robert Cooney and Helen Michalowski, and Peter Mayer, all cited above. See also David R. Wiber, ed., *Civil Disobedience in America: A Documentary History* (Ithaca, N.Y.: Cornell University Press, 1978).

8
American Catholic Opposition to the Vietnam War: A Preliminary Assessment

David J. O'Brien

For all Americans the war in Vietnam was a searing experience. "While the American involvement in Southeast Asia is materially catastrophic chiefly for Asians, morally it is a catastrophe for the American people," historian Henry Steele Commager wrote in 1972.[1] The speed with which Americans returned to business and politics as usual following the end of their nation's direct military intervention should cause some doubts about the permanence and depth of this moral catastrophe. Nevertheless, for many the war left permanent scars.[2] A continuing struggle to understand the war, its sources, character, and ambiguous resolution would seem a matter of the gravest urgency for those concerned with the moral welfare of the United States. Yet reflection on the Vietnam experience by leaders in the Christian churches has been less than impressive. Apparently embarrassed that their doctrines could be taken so seriously, the churches have not celebrated the courage and dedication of those Christians who resisted the American war effort. Equally important, they have contributed little to a constructive critique of the goals of American foreign policy or to the reformulation of an ethic of power and responsibility regarding weapons and war. Subjected to intense criticism themselves for inflaming passions in what now appears to many to have been a decade of disorder and conflict, church leaders seem to admit their mistake and return to the "proper" concerns of the Church with pastoral care and nurturing faith.

Yet no careful observer of American foreign relations can rest easy with the current state of affairs. Little has been done to limit the arms race, and the hesitant steps which are being taken appear destined to be rendered even less significant by a public opinion resentful at each new evidence of a supposed American retreat from power. Even less has been done to implement the "new international economic order" desired by the member states of the United Nations. Jimmy Carter's heralded policy of human rights has meant little more than some subtle shifts of orientation in southern Africa. Disillusionment, even cynicism, fostered by wartime administrations remains sufficiently widespread to check adventurous militarism and limit presidential freedom of conduct in international affairs, but the result has not been a serious reconsideration of the goals and methods of foreign policy but a seeming inertia and drift which could prove as dangerous to the United States and the world as the militaristic containment policies of the previous generation.

Serious reflection by the Church on the experience of Vietnam could provide one way of clarifying the mission of the Church in the current international scene and testing alternative theologies and pastoral strategies. Such an assessment would have to take account of the whole range of responses to the war, including that of the Vietnam Church,[3] as well as the sources and character of opposition in the United States. Such a full-scale historical analysis cannot be presented here. Instead, we will simply sketch out the parameters of such a study for the Catholic community, suggesting some of the questions which should be considered and indicating some of the directions which a renewed concern with foreign policy and international affairs might take in the days to come.

The Background

Religious activists take it for granted that the American Catholic Church has been an uncritical champion of the government in time of war and that church members have generally been the most militantly nationalist citizens.[4] In fact, the history of American Catholic responses to international events is more complex than that. During the 1930s, for example, the American hierarchy enthusiastically supported Franco's revolution in Spain and opposed American arms shipments to the Loyalist government. When the *Catholic Worker* and *Commonweal* adopted a neutral stance on the war, they were viciously assaulted by major church figures and suffered serious losses of circulation. Yet, public opinion polls indicated that Catholics as a whole had pretty much the same attitude toward the war as other Americans.[5]

In World War II the Catholic bishops certainly gave their moral sanction to the war, ignoring their traditional teaching of the need for moral limits on the use of force. There were a few Catholic conscientious objectors and some theologians questioned the morality of saturation bombing and the use of nuclear weapons, but such dissent was isolated and ignored.[6] Still, the bishops privately expressed to the President their reservations about war-time policies toward the Soviet Union.[7] For many understandable reasons Catholics were early and active cold warriors, but their anti-Communist militance could and did lead them to become very critical of the government and its policies.

Similarly, during the McCarthy era, the Church had a public image of more or less open sympathy with the Wisconsin Senator's crusade against Communist subversion. Like President Roosevelt earlier, many a politician was deeply concerned about the impact of such anti-communism on the Catholic vote. Once again, however, careful studies indicate that Catholics were no more likely than their neighbors to vote for McCarthy or against his enemies.[8] In the natural course of events Catholics rallied behind the nation's cause in time of danger, sometimes dangerously confusing religious imperatives and national interest, but their support was rarely less critical or more emotional than that of most of their fellow citizens.[9]

In fact, recent studies indicate that during the Korean War Catholics were only slightly less inclined than Protestants to express reservations about the war and, like other Americans, they became increasingly dissatisfied with the war and inclined to support a negotiated settlement as the bloody stalemate dragged on in the early 1950s. In the course of the Vietnam War Catholics were somewhat more inclined to support the war than Protestants, considerably less inclined to support withdrawal than Jews. Their opinion changed with events, as did that of other groups; like national opinion generally Catholic opinion crossed the line from war to peace after the Tet offensive.[10] The mild reservations of the American Catholic bishops which began to appear after Tet, rather than leading a change in Catholic opinion, probably reflected such a change. In any case, there is plenty of evidence to support the conclusion that Catholics, like most other Americans, are inclined to form their judgments about foreign policy on a wide range of considerations, most of them far more mundane and sensible than the rhetorical debates would suggest.[11]

The problem of Catholic opinion before the Vietnam War was not its militant anti-communism, so often simplistically interpreted as merely the emotional reflex of an uncritical nationalism, but rather the pervasive parochialism of the American Church. Vigorous debate about the ethics of foreign and military policy did in fact take place. During the decade some outstanding scholars laid out clearly and forcefully a variety of theological approaches to public policy in general and to nuclear war and weapons in particular. Jesuit theologian John Courtney Murray, for example, was forced to cease writing on broad questions of church and state. He turned his attention to issues of public policy and won a respectful hearing outside the Church, but only a miniscule audience within the Church.[12] Sociologist Gordon C. Zahn and theologian Justus George Lawler argued strongly that modern war had become morally unacceptable and that nuclear weapons should not be tolerated by the Christian conscience. While liberal journals like *Commonweal* and *America* editorially accepted the major features of cold-war foreign policy, their pages often provided intelligent discussion of such matters with views ranging across a broad spectrum of ethical positions. Yet the audience for these discussions was very limited; few priests, religious, lay people, or bishops were much interested in the policy debate. When their widely noted anti-Communist statements appeared, they were less deplorable for being emotional and hyper-nationalist then for being simply uninformed and unintelligent.[13]

It was the parochialism and lack of intellectual rigor in the Catholic community that was the problem of the American Church in the years before Vatican II. Yet, that community was generating a discussion of international affairs that would prove invaluable in the 1960s. The small but active and consistent community of the Catholic Worker, the discussion of just war in the Catholic Association for International Peace, the intelligent assessment of the morality of power in Lawler's *Continuum* magazine, the writings of Zahn, Murray, biblical scholar John L. McKenzie and others, all were providing resources for the days ahead.

The Church Universal

Catholics are distinguished from other American religious groups by their loyalty to an international Church whose ultimate authority on earth is the Bishop of Rome, acting on his own or in concert with his brother bishops from around the world. While Catholics believe that the pope's authority is limited, they also believe that they are obliged to give his moral and ethical teaching considerable weight in determining their own position. Increasingly in recent years the popes have devoted considerable attention to questions of world justice and peace. Pope John XXIII's encyclical *Pacem in Terris* received respectful attention throughout the world, while Pope Paul VI spoke out forcefully and frequently on the need for action to alleviate economic and social injustice, end the arms race, and build a stable human community. In October 1965, Pope Paul visited the United States to address the United Nations, pleading "No more war, war never again." His visit symbolized a consistent Vatican support for the international organization, reflecting Pope John's belief that modern technology had created an interdependent human family in need of juridical structures to order its common life.[14]

Perhaps the most important single document for those considering the Vietnam War was the "Pastoral Constitution on the Church in the Modern World" of Vatican Council II.[15] The Council Fathers took up where Pope John had left off, arguing that the whole question of war should be considered "with an entirely new attitude." Drawing heavily on Scripture, the Council seemed to be moving the Church away from its historic reliance on the principles of the just war toward an evangelical stance of prophetic judgment on people and nations. Thus the document contained an explicit endorsement of a position of pacifism and of the right of conscientious objection. Most important from the perspective of the Vietnam conflict, the Council Fathers explicitly condemned "any act of war aimed indiscriminately at the destruction of entire cities or of extensive areas along with their population." For many, nuclear weapons of their very nature would bring about such indiscriminate destruction; thus the conciliar statement seemed to many a condemnation of nuclear weapons and the policy of deterrence. Under pressure from American bishops, however, the Council backed off, allowing participation in the military, legitimate self-defense, and possession of nuclear weapons as part of a deterrence strategy, even while questioning whether such a strategy in the long run could insure peace. The document thus contained directives which could be used to criticize specific American policies in Vietnam, while it also contained sections helpful to defenders of the basic features of American defense policy. While stressing the urgency of action if peace was to be assured, and commending those who refused to participate in war, the Council also reaffirmed the just-war doctrines as a legitimate moral option. Following the Council, this studied ambiguity remained characteristic of Vatican pronouncements, as the Church, in the midst of renewal, attempted to revitalize its sense of mission with reference both to its biblical foundations and to the brutal realities of twentieth-century life.

The Vatican and Vietnam

The teachings of Vatican Council II and of Pope John XXIII and Pope Paul VI provided at least two ethical approaches to evaluating the moral issues involved in foreign policy and war. Yet, these teachings remained abstract; their translation into policy positions involved complex political judgments as well as difficult theological problems. The Vatican's own approach had severe limitations, which the Vietnam War highlighted. Pope Paul took a personal interest in the war and on several occasions launched diplomatic initiatives aimed at the suspension of hostilities, as at Christmastime, or facilitating the start of peace negotiations. In doing so, he was acting partly as moral leader, partly as a diplomat. Unfortunately, in his diplomatic role he was forced to adopt a stance which could only seem biased toward the United States. For one thing, the papacy had no formal diplomatic or ecclesiastical relations with North Vietnam after the Communist takeover of that country and the removal of the Vatican nuncio in 1954. For that reason, the bishops of the North did not seek permission to attend the Council, for to do so would have granted a *de facto* recognition to the government. Rome withheld recognition until a concordat could be negotiated which would guarantee the rights of the Church.[16] It is the nature of diplomacy to take place between recognized governments. Thus the Vatican acceded to any American request for a meeting, and several times American officials made highly publicized trips to visit Pope Paul, apparently demonstrating the American desire to cooperate with the Pope's quest for peace. On the other hand, the frequent requests of the Provisional Revolutionary Government of South Vietnam to meet with the Pope were consistently rejected.[17] While Pope Paul seemed to defend the notion of just revolution in his encyclical *Populorum Progressio*, he later went out of his way to condemn guerrilla war and to reject violence as a means of bringing about even justified social change. To have dealt openly with the PRG would have granted legitimacy to what South Vietnam and the United States regarded as a subversive, aggressive force originating in the North. North Vietnam, on the other hand, could not enter into diplomatic exchanges which implied acceptance of the American contention that the war was one between states rather than internal civil war within the South. Thus Pope Paul's apparent neutrality could only seem biased and onesided when viewed from the point of view of the North.

Similarly, while Pope Paul frequently pleaded for peace in Vietnam, and while the Vatican dissociated itself most pointedly from the extreme nationalist justification of the war made by Francis Cardinal Spellman in 1965, the Apostolic Delegate to the United States went out of his way to publicly indicate his support for the American effort to preserve the freedom and independence of South Vietnam. Again and again throughout the war, Catholic opponents were disconcerted by the manner in which the Vatican, so dedicated to peace and development on one level, engaged in open friendship with American officials and seemed to accept the government's proclamation of its own generous and warmhearted intentions. This position, together with the long-standing presumption of Vietnamese Catholic support for the war, could only reinforce American Catholic reluctance to challenge the U.S. military effort.

Thus while much progress was made in the postconciliar years in advancing Catholic sensitivity to the nature of modern war and the problems of the international economic system, the Vatican did not succeed in detaching itself completely from the Cold War or from association with the Western powers. On the contrary, for many Third World spokespersons, the Vatican still seemed closely connected to those very nations and systems which they regarded as the source of their problems. More importantly, the problem that beset Pius XII during World War II, his immense difficulty in translating his self-image as Vicar of Christ and spokesman for truth in a divided world into an authentic and effective witness, continued to beset his successors. Pius could justify his silence by reference to the safety of Catholics under Nazi rule or by reference to the dangers of Bolshevism, the greater enemy. Yet, as his critics noted, such arguments ignored the safety of civilians and soldiers on both sides, sacrificed by governments and perhaps churchmen to geopolitical strategy. In Vietnam, the Pope's desire to play the role of peacemaker, flawed at the start by the diplomatic approach, could only appear hypocritical to those who believed not simply that the war was evil, but that the primary responsibility for that evil lay with the governments of South Vietnam and the United States. To have accepted that argument, to have played a role like that of U Thant, would have placed the Vatican in a terribly difficult position, to be sure, but for many of the people of the world it might have raised the prestige of the papacy to a new high.[18]

Episcopal Leadership

For better or worse, both Catholics and non-Catholics tend to identify the Church with the bishops. Despite the many changes in Catholic self-understanding occasioned by Vatican II, Catholics continue to depend heavily on episcopal leadership. In any diocese, the degree of openness to dialogue and dissent in the Church, the extent of community reflection on public issues and of institutional involvement in social action is directly related to the personal disposition of the local bishop. On a serious question of public import, one involving political, social, and moral issues of significance, a strong stand by the bishop can excite deep divisions in the Church, greatly encouraging one side of the dispute while perhaps occasioning futility and even bitterness on the part of their opponents. As pastors concerned with the unity and fellowship of their flocks and as administrators concerned with stability, orderly procedure, and respect for authority, bishops are quite naturally inclined to temporize or compromise when faced with divisive issues. Yet bishops are also moral leaders to whom their followers look for guidance amid the conflicting pressures of public controversy. Equally important, in a society where pluralism and separation of church and state inhibit the exercise of moral leadership by the heads of other major institutions, many citizens look to the clergy and its most prominent representatives to articulate moral principles clearly and assist in their application to problems of public and private life.

In the post-World War II years, the race issue sharpened the dilemmas of church leadership causing deep divisions to the point of crisis in many churches. Outspoken advocates of integration were attacked by many church members for ignoring the sensibilities and opinions of their own people, "getting too far out in front," while those who spoke only cautiously to racial questions were condemned for betraying their own gospel mandate. The Vietnam War posed the same problem in even more dramatic fashion.[19]

In the early days of the conflict, few bishops found it necessary to take a public stand. Yet, as early as 1965, when Undersecretary of State George Ball warned that North Vietnam should not consider its capital city, Hanoi, a "privileged sanctuary" from American bombers, a group of nine bishops issued a statement applying Vatican II's condemnation of total war:[20]

> Unlike other clouded issues concerning the war in Vietnam on which there is necessary and justifiable debate, the possibility that either side may bomb any purely civilian center would entail a clear and direct violation of Christian ethics and must be denounced as an immoral action.

Yet these were minority voices. Francis Cardinal Spellman of New York, Vicar for the Armed Forces, was closer to the center when he spoke forcefully in defense of Vietnam policy. In his Christmas message of 1965, Spellman said: "When the freedom and the dignity of people anywhere are challenged, the freedom and dignity of people everywhere stands in peril. When tyranny is allowed to take one bold step in some distant land, it has already begun its terrifying march across the world."[21] A few months later, addressing the United Service Organization, Spellman recognized that "more and more in this modern world of ours, war becomes madness"; nevertheless, he warned that until negotiation could take place without "shameful compromise," "someone must stand and make a defense with arms" of human freedom and human dignity. "Naturally we all want peace," he concluded, but there is a "vast difference between honest negotiation and the abject surrender of the finest values of human freedom and human dignity which remain in our world."[22]

In the summer of 1966, Richard Cardinal Cushing added his voice to Spellman's. Addressing the Catholic Daughters of America, Cushing argued that, while "no one likes war," there are moments in human history when "evil men and evil ways can be met only with force." Referring to American soldiers in Vietnam as "making peace the hard way, but the only way it can be made in a hard world," Cushing concluded:

> Our struggle in Vietnam—like our struggle in Korea—can bring peace because it can prove to the aggressors of the world that wars of oppression will not be won.[23]

Episcopal defense of the war reached its apogee at Christmas 1966, when Cardinal Spellman, visiting American soldiers at the front, called for victory:[24]

> The war in Vietnam is, I believe, a war for civilization. Certainly it is not a war of our seeking. It is a war thrust upon us. We cannot yield to tyranny. We hope and pray that through the valor and dedication of our men and women in our armed forces, we will soon have a victory for which all of us are praying. Less than victory is inconceivable.

Conservative columnists William Buckley and David Lawrence rushed to Spellman's defense, but a wave of criticism from both Europe and the United States swept over the cardinal, long considered the titular leader of the American hierarchy. While San Antonio's aged Archbishop Robert Emmet Lucey publicly defended the war and his friend, President Johnson, in 1968,[25] Spellman's 1966 remarks marked the end of strong episcopal sanction for the war. While criticism and dissent remained muted and isolated, the bishops seemed to realize in the wake of Spellman's controversial statement, which would have been unexceptional in earlier wars, that this was a new war and a new time, and public moral commentary would have to be seriously considered and carefully stated. That, in itself, was progress.

The problems the bishops faced were clear earlier, in the summer of 1966. On June 28, a pastoral letter from Lawrence Cardinal Shehan was read from the pulpits of all parishes in the archdiocese of Baltimore.[26] Intended to provide moral guidance regarding the "patriotic duties of American Catholics," the letter outlined the teachings of Vatican Council II, stressing the Church's support of legitimate patriotism and the Council's affirmation of the "right to legitimate self-defense." Similarly, the Cardinal noted that members of the armed forces "should regard themselves as agents of security and freedom on behalf of their people. They are making a genuine contribution to the establishment of peace." At the same time he was careful to note the Council's defense of the right to conscientious objection. Even the Catholic who supports the war, he argued, "must do all he can to see that this struggle is carried on in a morally acceptable way." He called attention to the Church's explicit condemnation of acts of war aimed at indiscriminate destruction, referring to "some of the suggestions occasionally made about the degree and kind of violence our nation should inflict on its enemies." Citizens have the right to know the facts of their government's policy and the obligation to seek out those facts, Shehan argued. Warning against the dangers of emotion and passion in wartime, he pointed to "harsh voices . . . growing stronger and . . . attempting to pressure our leaders into decisions which the Christian conscience could not endorse." Resisting appeals to unlimited force, Christians should "be responsive to the possibilities of reasonable and honorable negotiations." Concluding that President Johnson "has earnestly sought such negotiations," the Cardinal urged his people to pray that God would provide opportunities for negotiations which could bring a just and lasting peace. In the meantime, "it devolves on each Catholic citizen in every country to weigh political situations in terms of [Catholic] principles and to exert whatever moral and civic influences seem dictated by his conscience."

Shehan's pastoral letter was moderate, reasonable, intelligent and forceful, appreciative of the ambiguity of the war and the conflicting norms provided by contemporary Church teaching. Yet, to his surprise, opponents of the war saw it as a statement of opposition. The newly established Catholic Peace Fellowship printed thousands of copies in leaflet form, while *Commonweal* editor James O'Gara saw it as a word of warning to Washington policy makers.[27] Shehan himself felt it necessary to write the national commander of the Catholic War Veterans, deploring the use made of his letter by anti-war activists. "I made no such condemnation," he wrote. "Our presence in Vietnam and the reasons which have prompted us to involve ourselves there are honorable. I approved of them."[28]

Later in 1966 Archbishop Paul Hallinan of Atlanta issued a very similar pastoral letter. By 1967, such statements had begun to set the tone for most episcopal pronouncements. More and more the statements of individual bishops, and later of the hierarchy as a whole, were characterized by reference to the principles of peacemaking of Vatican Council II and Pope Paul, avoidance of direct challenges to American policy, a presumption of good intentions of American leaders, combined with strong emphasis on the need for moral limits to the conduct of war and the requirement to search for alternatives to force through negotiation and broader actions to limit the arms race, strengthen international organizations, and combat world poverty. As for Vietnam, Hallinan had warned that "a Christian simply cannot approve of indiscriminate bombing, methodical extermination of people, nuclear arms designed for 'overkill' or disregard of noncombatants.''[29] In the years ahead, much of the debate within episcopal circles would center on whether or not these things had come to characterize American policy; insofar as bishops came to think that they had, they could be expected to become critics of the war and advocates of negotiation or, in a few cases, of American withdrawal. In August 1967, for example, Bishops Hallinan, Shannon, Reed of Oklahoma City, and Dougherty of Newark urged the end of the bombing and "Negotiations now."[30]

As a body, however, the bishops were slow to move. Meeting in November 1966, the bishops concluded that, "in the light of the facts that are known to us, it is reasonable to argue that our presence in Vietnam is justified." Nevertheless, they expressed their concern "that the circumstances of the war may diminish our moral sensitivity to its evils."[31] They need not have worried, at least about the active church community, which brought together some twenty-five hundred Christian and Jewish clergy for a mobilization in Washington in February 1967. No Catholic bishops appeared, though all had been invited, and Robert McAfee Brown, in an open letter to the bishops, asked, "How are we to interpret your almost total silence?"[32] For Brown and his colleagues, the time had come to act upon the bishops' statement that "we must clearly protest whenever there is a danger that the conflict will be escalated above morally acceptable limits." Auxiliary Bishop James P. Shannon of St. Paul-Minneapolis responded that independent theologians like Dr. Brown enjoyed greater freedom of action than bishops who, with divided constituencies and less assurance about the exact moral issue at stake in Vietnam, "do not enjoy this perfect liberty of response to social ills." Shannon also argued that demonstrations of public protest were "simply not the style of the Catholic bishops."[33] A more convincing response came from the assembled bishops themselves in November 1967 when they welcomed the growing discussion of the war as "a witness of the ever deepening yearning of the American people for peace" and as evidence "that the moral sensitivity of the American people has not diminished but increased and intensified." On the other hand, they noted that "this longing for peace has been expressed in extreme reactions . . . [and] resulted in considerable division among our people." Concern both for the soldiers and for the people at home led the bishops to plead for "more rational debate and greater solicitude for mutual understanding." They urged the administration, "despite the rebuffs" it had received, to intensify its efforts for negotiation, though noting in conclusion, "We wish it to be understood that we are not pleading for peace at any price."[34]

Such ambivalence was frustrating. Brown had told Bishop Shannon that, if mobilization was not the bishops' style, "offer us some other forms more vigorous than a mobilization and we will follow you in droves."[35] Brown, who had referred repeatedly in his open letter to the peace appeals of Pope Paul VI as a major inspiration of the Christian anti-war movement, was providing evidence of how mainline Protestantism had come to look longingly to the Catholic hierarchy for moral leadership and direction. This longing was even more intense among Catholics. Msgr. Joseph Gallagher spoke for many when he told the bishops that they were not expected to provide political or military judgements but to exemplify "moral passion and evangelical sensitivity during as colossal a tragedy as the Vietnam war."[36] Responding to this need for moral leadership, Shannon and four other bishops urged an end to the bombing in August 1967.[37] Other bishops were also sensitive to the problems, but seemed genuinely puzzled as to how to act without appearing self-righteous or arrogant in dealing with a complex public issue. In 1968 the bishops issued a pastoral letter, "Human Life in Our Day," in which they noted, but did not reaffirm, their earlier conclusion that the U.S. role in Vietnam was justified. Instead, they simply made their own many of the questions regarding means and proportion which were under discussion. In addition, they urged modification of draft laws to allow provision for selective conscientious objection, urged the necessity of peace, and stated their "hope that, in the all important issue of war and peace . . . men will follow their conscience."[38]

Given the neutrality of the hierarchy as a whole, the position of anti-war bishops was not easy. Bishop Shannon had been rebuked for his public statements against the war by the Apostolic Delegate to the United States. In June 1969, he announced that he was resigning from his priesthood. He was followed in June of 1971 by Auxiliary Bishop Bernard A. Kelly of Providence. Both bishops had many reasons for their decisions, but both had been among the leading episcopal opponents of the war. Kelly had even participated in an anti-war demonstration at the naval base in Newport, Rhode Island, and had urged the bishops to take a stand regarding the war at their meeting in the spring of 1971. At that time, the hierarchy debated statements to be presented at the forthcoming Synod of Bishops meeting in Rome, where the assembled prelates were to discuss two topics: the priesthood, and justice in the world. Kelly was terribly upset that at both regional and national bishops' meetings most of the time was spent discussing the priesthood and no collective presentation was prepared on matters of economic justice or world peace.[39]

Yet anti-war statements were becoming more common. The *National Catholic Reporter* counted some 32 bishops, more than ten percent of the hierarchy, who had made public statements critical of the war by the fall of 1971. Most notable was Cardinal Shehan, who had changed his mind and now believed that the war had "become an evil in which the whole country has become involved, and a scandal the Christian conscience can no longer endure."[40] In May 1971, fourteen bishops of northern New England issued a pastoral letter in which they argued that the massive use of air power in Vietnam, "if reported accurately, merits the severest moral condemnation."[41] Active opposition was also building within the staff of the episcopal conference. As a result, the bishops' meeting in November 1971, witnessed their first public debate on the war since the issuance of "Human Life in Our Day" three years earlier. In 1968, they had simply asked the question whether the war had reached the point where its continuation could any longer be considered just. In 1971 they again asked the question and answered no:[42]

> At this point in history it seems clear that whatever good we hope to achieve through continued involvement in this war is now outweighed by the destruction of human life and of moral values which it inflicts. It is our firm conviction therefore that the ending of this war is a moral imperative of the highest priority. Hence we feel a moral obligation to appeal to our nation's leaders and indeed to the leaders of all nations involved in this tragic conflict to bring the war to an end with no further delay.

In the course of debate the bishops had defeated three stronger proposals: a call for an immediate unilateral cease fire; negotiation of a reciprocal cease fire with international verification; and a public statement setting a date for withdrawal of U.S. forces. At a press conference following the meeting, Auxiliary Bishop Thomas Gumbleton, whose appeal for action had been ignored by the bishops in the spring, argued that those who agreed with the bishops "may not participate in the war." Other bishops disagreed, but clearly the hierarchy had come a great distance since 1966.[43] In 1972 they would go even further, condemning continued bombing and terrorism and calling for generous efforts at reconciliation with those who had opposed the war, postwar aid to rebuild Vietnam, and vigorous attention to matters of international social and economic justice.[44]

What had happened was that the bishops, gradually, had begun in 1968 to apply the criteria of the just war to the specific circumstances of the Vietnam War. Bishop Bernard J. Flanagan of Worcester, Mass., for example, said that the 1968 pastoral, coming as it did after long and bitter controversy, caused him to study the war more carefully. Following President Nixon's invasion of Cambodia in May 1970, it "became more and more obvious . . . that this principle [of proportionality] was no longer applicable in the sense of justifying our presence there." For Auxiliary Bishop Dougherty of Newark the continuing demand of sincere anti-war activists that he sign their statements forced him to confront the issue, to study it, and finally to conclude that he could not in conscience remain silent. Bishop Gumbleton, who became the most outspoken advocate of action within the bishops' meetings, attributed his conversion to the experience of counseling young persons in regard to the draft and to the example of serious priests in his diocese who had become actively involved in the anti-war movement.[45] Each bishop undoubtedly had his own story, but by 1971 a majority had concluded that they must seriously consider whether the war violated the teachings of their Church. Yet, it was equally clear that there were no easy answers, and that bishops could not lead in the old way. Even Bishop Gumbleton argued that bishops, in confronting public issues, must work through persuasion and not prescription:[46]

> telling people, yes, you must form your conscience, you must face these issues. I'm not going to tell you exactly how to think of them. I may tell you how I think. And I think that's part of a leader's task, to say, this is how I think. But I'm showing you and I'm trying to confront you with the need to make a decision.

While many bishops could not even go this far, and while the hierarchy as a whole continued to ignore many of the atrocities of the war, the fact remained that the United States bishops had first questioned their nation's policies during the war and finally had concluded that some of those policies were wrong. Given the Church's long record of silence and accommodation in modern war, this was an historic and in its way a courageous step.[47]

Catholic Opinion

As early as 1965 Catholics played a prominent role in the opposition to the Vietnam War. David Miller, a young Catholic Worker, burned his draft card at an anti-war rally in October, and Tom Cornell, a co-founder of the Catholic Peace Fellowship took a similar step in November. Shortly after, Miller became the first Catholic resister to be imprisoned for such acts.[48] The same summer Daniel and Philip Berrigan joined with Rabbi Abraham Heschel and Protestant theologian Robert McAfee Brown to form Clergy and Laity Concerned about Vietnam, and they assisted in the birth of the Catholic Peace Fellowship. Yet the impact of these actions, while dramatic, was limited. The bishops' statements which have been discussed were carefully phrased to avoid identification with anti-war activists. Conservative Catholics still strongly supported the national cause, given a religious sanction for them by their belief that the Vietnamese Catholics were solidly behind the Republic of Vietnam government. Liberal Catholics looked askance at the militarization of the conflict, for they had strongly supported those who saw such struggles in political and social terms. Nevertheless, they found it very difficult to justify opposing a war they believed had originated in Communist aggression against a regime which, whatever its faults, still kept open the possibility of free, democratic development. Only in 1970, when President Nixon extended the war into Cambodia, did Catholic campuses, with their faculty and students, join in a massive way the growing opposition of the young and of the academic community to the war.

Since Pearl Harbor, Christian moralists had generally accepted the position of ethical realism associated most prominently with Reinhold Niebuhr and articulated for Catholics by John Courtney Murray. This position justified the use of force as a last resort, emphasized the need to maintain military strength as a deterrent to aggression, and advocated a disciplined use of economic and political influence to combat Communist expansion. Accordingly, Catholic liberals supported the American intervention in Vietnam until the escalation of the air war and the introduction of large numbers of American troops in 1965 transformed what had been a program of military and economic assistance into a full-scale war, with direct involvement of half a million American troops. The editors and columnists of *Commonweal* and *America* had long accepted the argument that the threat of communism in underdeveloped regions of the world arose from the existence of poverty and deprivation. Peoples determined to overcome these barriers to human development could choose between Communist and democratic roads to development. America's interest, in this view, lay in assisting in the development of democratic political structures and encouraging economic growth. To repress subversion by military means seemed to admit defeat in the primary struggle for the loyalty of the people. Liberals, confronted with the Vietnam escalation, thus were torn between their own belief in the need for social development and the government's argument that only defeat of the external aggression from the North could provide the security and opportunity necessary for peaceful democratic change.

Filled with doubts over the militarization of Vietnam policy, and fearful that it would lead to confrontation among the great powers, liberal Catholics followed such staunch realists as George Kennan and Senator Fulbright in urging a negotiated settlement. Critical of the war, they could not accept the demands of opponents of the war, who seemed to fasten guilt on the United States, rather than on the Communists, and to demand a purity of policy which smacked of sentimentality. When Daniel and Philip Berrigan declared their intention to refuse cooperation with the American war effort, *Commonweal* editor James O'Gara stated his admiration for their Christian witness but indicated his own belief that their position would allow the "triumph of evil."[49] Not only did he refuse to endorse their apparent pacifism, but he argued that, whatever the sources of the war, the fact of U.S. presence created a moral obligation to protect pro-Western Vietnamese from their Communist enemies. While insisting strongly on the obligation to subject the conduct of the war to moral restraints, he renewed his determination to support a policy designed to bring about a negotiated settlement and to resist fastening responsibility on the United States.

Gradually, however, *Commonweal* and its editor changed their mind, reaching the twin judgments that the war was unwinnable and that its conduct had passed beyond moral restraint. In 1968, *Commonweal* declared its support for unconditional American withdrawal. William V. Shannon, an editor at the *New York Times* and a *Commonweal* columnist, continued to support the American war effort and as a result felt compelled to end his association with the magazine. In offering "The Case for the War" in December 1967, Shannon provided evidence of the continued difficulty intelligent Catholics had in finding some middle ground between what seemed a pacifism which refused responsibility for events and a war policy which abandoned all restraints on the use of force.[50] For Shannon, the "great issue in the world" remained the struggle between "freedom and tyranny." The Communist states, he believed, were bent upon unlimited expansion by whatever means were available. The United States, on the other hand, remained the world's "principal defender of freedom." Arguing that since World War II the United States had acted with courage and self-sacrifice to defend the freedom of Western Europe and South Korea, he denied that U.S. abandonment of Vietnam would bring peace to the world. "Vietnam is only one episode in a worldwide political struggle that has been going on for decades and will continue for decades," he wrote. The source of that struggle is "the ideological effort of Russia and China to appear as the vanguard of world revolution." Russia and China, not the United States, insisted on using force, and "we should be grateful that America has the power to defend freedom and the will to use that power." In South Vietnam an armed terrorist minority refused to allow the people to decide their own destiny; Communist guerrilla tactics threatened to achieve a victory which would be repeated in other such situations. Forced by public opinion to find a quick solution, the government had escalated the military stakes and failed. Nevertheless the war was still a political and social as well as a military struggle; it could only be won on the ground. Shannon feared that America lacked the stamina and will to stay the course, and would eventually withdraw, to the great detriment of the cause of freedom in the world. Later, when the conduct of the war had been transferred from Democratic to Republican hands, Shannon would finally become an opponent. His persistence in holding to a pro-war position, however, illustrated the persuasiveness of realist categories and the failure of the peace movement in general to avoid polarizing the question between the realism dominant since World War II and a discredited and apparently irresponsible pacifism.

Nevertheless, the rising tide of opposition in the United States, the continuing failure of military power to force negotiations, and the gradual revelation of the incompetence of America's Vietnamese allies required a moral response. No less than the bishops, Catholic intellectuals had to wrestle with the moral problems posed by the conflict between their ideals and the realities of the war. A few would begin to re-evaluate their own moral position, leading to a clearcut choice of resistance; many more, like the bishops, would begin to apply the tests of the just war, the categories of realism itself, to the facts of the war. In both cases, the result would be a convergence around the need to end the killing.

Perhaps the best barometer of informed Catholic opinion was supplied by the *National Catholic Reporter*. Founded in 1964, *NCR*, highlighting in lively fashion the internal dynamics of reforming Catholicism, quickly achieved wide circulation among educated and articulate Catholics. Publicizing violations of academic and intellectual freedom within the Church, providing informed background stories on internal Church decision-making in Rome and at home, featuring columns and reviews by a "new breed" of Catholic intellectuals and journalists, *NCR* spoke clearly for those who favored the conciliar reforms, wished to see them implemented in the United States, and hoped that those changes would make the Catholic Church a more vital segment of the national community. During the Vietnam War, *NCR*, like so many institutions and individuals, was "radicalized." Specifically, this meant that the editors came to see the country in general and the government in particular as far more malevolent than they had originally thought. Like many others they proceeded from discussion of civil rights as an issue to dissecting the racism of American society; from discussing the wisdom of particular national security policies to decrying violence and militarism; from welcoming Church statements which lent support to Catholic participation in secular life in secular terms to demanding a full witness to gospel mandates for peace and justice. Toward the end of the period as *NCR*'s circulation and influence dropped, its founder editor, Robert Hoyt, was dismissed, to be replaced by Donald Thorman, whose interests were oriented toward a more gradual implementation of Church teachings. The episode was an indication of the divisions which had arisen within the Church's liberal community, a step toward the disintegration of the liberal movement which had long been a coherent and significant feature of American Catholic life.

NCR's role in developing Catholic attitudes regarding the Vietnam War extended beyond its editorial position. It sponsored the work of correspondents Tom Fox and Robert Blackmun, both of whom described the war in ways far different from what was at that time generally available in the media. Their exposures of corruption, defeatism, and oppression in South Vietnam were being printed long before such information became generally known to the public. Equally important, the paper sponsored a trip to Vietnam by theologian Michael Novak, which resulted in a series exposing the links between the American bishops' Catholic Relief Services and government administration in South Vietnam. In this area, as in so many others, *NCR* was trying to make church policy and administration matters of public discussion, and their efforts were not welcomed.

In the summer of 1965, the paper indicated that it shared the widespread dislike for the apparent self-righteousness of clerical opponents of the war. While criticizing President Johnson for failing to clarify American goals, the editors were quick to add that they rejected as well the moralism of opponents like Father George Tavard, whose ringing denunciation of American policy appeared on the same page.[51] Tavard's full commitment to self-determination, even if it resulted in Communist expansion, the editors described as "political naiveté." Rejecting both "extremes" of escalation and withdrawal, *NCR* indicated its willingness to support the use of force as long as it was designed to persuade the Viet Cong and North

Vietnamese to "quit fighting." The editors feared that, if that policy did not work, additional force would be used until there would "come a time when this war will be an absurdity, when there can be no longer any question that it is fought on behalf of the Vietnamese people or for any rational or moral purpose."[52]

By January 1967, *NCR*'s fears had come true. In a blistering editorial: "You make a desert and call it peace," the editors came out for immediate cessation of American involvement. Utilizing the traditional Catholic categories of the just war, *NCR* argued that the principle of proportionality had been violated:[53]

> We believe that the war in Vietnam is now clearly immoral. The commanding reason for this judgment is that the ends for which we are fighting the war cannot be achieved except by the nearly total destruction of our enemy in North and South Vietnam.

In the editor's opinion, the United States was demanding surrender as the price of peace. Conceding the possible viability of defense of the South Vietnam regime, the *NCR* nevertheless rejected "an open ended war for a Saigon victory." Washington was seeking not peace, but victory, and victory in alliance with an unrepresentative, oppressive government. Communists had succeeded in identifying their cause with national independence; in continuing to use any means to prevent their victory, and indeed in demanding that they surrender the dream of freedom and independence, America was not merely fighting an unpopular war. Rather,

> We are casting away a heritage. We are changing the meaning of America, the very sound and symbolism of the word; we are destroying the trust and hope it inspired, we are dissipating the influence America might otherwise wield in the building of a just and stable world order.[54]

The editors went on to confront the responsibilities which rested on those who became convinced that their nation "is doing serious evil." They urged support for Senator McCarthy's challenge to President Johnson and they urged Robert Kennedy to join the fight. They invited young men "to examine very seriously" whether they can in conscience accept military service. "If the choice were ours" they said, "we would refuse." Their conclusion was even stronger:

> To say a war we are fighting is immoral is not a light matter. Our situation is not really comparable with that of the Germans in World War II; our President is not a Hitler, our war does not aim at world conquest. But we are killing people and destroying a culture without adequate justification, without a rationale that meets minimum requirements of morality. That imposes obligations on all of us. We believe that anyone who despairs of a political solution has a right and duty to search for more effective ways, including civil disobedience and tax refusal.[55]

In the years that followed *NCR*'s declaration of opposition, the pages of the paper were filled with news of the war and calls for stronger action to end it. *NCR,* along with other publications which joined it in opposition, helped to create a climate of opinion which invited, indeed demanded, episcopal reaction. By 1971 the paper's editor could join with his counterparts at *Commonweal* and the major Protestant journals of opinion, *The Christian Century* and *Christianity and Crisis,* to issue a "Call to Penitance and Action." By then, the major organs of liberal Catholic sentiment had all but enlisted in the Catholic resistance.

These liberal editors and commentators, then, were led to condemn the war and eventually to all-out opposition not by any revision of their moral approach to questions of war and peace, not by a realization that what was actually happening in Vietnam bore little relationship to official pronouncements. Only when they became convinced that no reasonable end could justify the terrible means which the war-making machine employed, did they announce their support first for a negotiated settlement, then for withdrawal of American forces. Naturally enough, critical assessment of government policy in regard to the war led to an equally critical approach to foreign policy and international issues generally. *NCR* editor Robert Hoyt was personally drawn to an even more radical assessment of both foreign and domestic policy, while *Commonweal's* editors, in the opinion of one of their predecessors, became "shrill" and "harsh" in denouncing the American stance throughout the world. Yet, their views, like those of the bishops, grew directly from the traditional doctrine of the just war. While they would regard pacifism and nonviolent resistance more sympathetically and would depend more directly on religious symbols than on political analysis once the decision was made that the war was unjust, Catholic liberals for the most part remained loyal to the approach and categories of the just war. The position stated by James O'Gara in September 1967, remained typical:

> The war in Vietnam is a tragic and bloody mistake. . . . We have become reckless in our use of power and undercut the goals we seek, so much so that the war cannot be justified morally or politically. If the traditional Christian norms of just means and right proportion mean anything, we should vigorously seek negotiation and get out of Vietnam as quickly as possible.[56]

The Catholic Resistance

In 1967 the American bishops joined Vatican Council II in giving explicit and clear endorsement to the principle of conscientious objection. In doing so the bishops recognized the existence and legitimacy of a pacifist position articulated out of the Catholic framework. At the same time the bishops continued to present their own analysis and evaluation of the war in Vietnam within the categories of the just-war tradition. It was of enormous significance, however, that they did not insist upon the just-war tradition as the only or the authoritative position of the Catholic Church.

Instead, by according the right of conscientious objection, they endorsed the Council's important breakthrough in recognizing the Catholic pacifist tradition as having equal value and legitimacy with the just-war tradition. That pacifist tradition had roots deep in Catholic history, as indicated by Bishop Flanagan's argument that the Church in its first three centuries of existence was "almost exclusively pacifist." The peace witness of those who rejected war and violence as a way to settle disputes was often lost in the Catholic Church and carried on most visibly by the Protestant peace churches. Nevertheless, there had been a pacifist witness within Catholicism for many years. In the United States that witness was upheld most powerfully and influentially by the Catholic Worker movement, founded by Dorothy Day and Peter Maurin in 1933. A small but significant number of Catholics associated with the Catholic Worker movement had been conscientious objectors in World War II, living out that position despite the lack of recognition or support from the bishops or from the Catholic community generally. Throughout the indifferent days of the 1950s, the Catholic Worker and its friends continued to carry on a peace witness in association with other peace groups, achieving considerable recognition for their opposition to civilian defense drills in New York City.

With the outbreak of the war in Vietnam, new life was given to this pacifist witness and the long struggles of the Catholic Worker began to bear fruit. As troubled Catholic priests and lay people looked for guidance in dealing with the horrors of the Vietnam War and through this experience were led to consider the problems of nuclear weapons and international peace they were drawn to the work of such lonely pacifists as Dorothy Day and Gordon C. Zahn. Miss Day, through the continuing presence of Catholic Worker houses around the country and the excellent writing and reflection contained in the *Catholic Worker* paper had long been recognized as an outstanding Catholic leader, while at the same time her message had not been taken with full seriousness. Professor Zahn, himself a World War II conscientious objector, began writing in the late 1950s on subjects of war and peace, achieving widespread recognition for his study of the experience of the Catholic Church in Nazi Germany.[57] In the days to come many Catholic resisters to the war in Vietnam would point to Zahn's books as important landmarks for them in reaching their own conscientious convictions regarding the Vietnam War.

In 1964 two young men associated for some years with the Catholic Worker, Thomas Cornell and James Forest, brought together a few Catholic leaders including the well-known Trappist monk, Thomas Merton, Jesuit Fr. Daniel Berrigan, and his brother Josephite Fr. Philip Berrigan to form the Catholic Peace Fellowship. This new organization was affiliated with and assisted by the older nondenominational Fellowship of Reconciliation, one of the most respected pacifist organizations in the country. Throughout the decade that followed, the Catholic Peace Fellowship encouraged, supported, and assisted the formation of draft counseling offices around the country and Cornell and Forest played an important role in leading Catholics to resist the war.

The Berrigan brothers, in the years that followed, became the most renowned leaders of the growing Catholic anti-war movement. On October 27, 1967, Philip Berrigan and three friends poured blood on draft files in Baltimore, Maryland. On May 17, 1968 Philip Berrigan was joined by his brother Daniel and seven others in raiding draft offices in Catonsville, Maryland, and setting fire to the files in a parking lot outside the building. They were arrested and their trial, which followed, received national attention. By October 1970, over 250 draft offices had been raided, and priests, sisters, and lay Catholics were invariably prominent.[58]

At the time of the Catonsville raid Daniel Berrigan had indicated that he accepted the traditional rationale of civil disobedience and insisted on the necessity to go to jail as a testimony to sincerity and civil allegiance. However, in the summer of 1970, when they were to be incarcerated, Philip and Daniel Berrigan did not appear and instead "went underground." Philip Berrigan was apprehended a short time later in a New York City church, but Daniel succeeded in avoiding arrest for many months, playing a game of cat and mouse with the FBI. During his underground months, Berrigan made public appearances, was interviewed on radio and TV, and published a number of statements of his position. He and his brother had become convinced that the legal system itself was corrupt, and they fled rather than accept incarceration peacefully.

While the Berrigans continued to advocate nonviolence, a few of their followers announced that they were going underground to pursue revolution.[59] Drawing upon the experience of Catholic revolutionaries in Latin America, they argued that the real violence was practiced by the oppressors and "counterviolence" sufficient to end the oppression and open the door to peaceful change could be justified. Whereas the earlier pacifist movement had emphasized the need in each situation to find the fullest expression of love, the resistance appeared to push toward the limits of nonviolence, asking how far one could go without crossing the threshold to violence. The awful immediacy of the war and the sense of urgency aroused by the daily destruction of human life, made them less patient than their predecessors with defeat, more determined to end the war, no matter the cost.

Thus, there were serious divisions within the resistance community. Some, inspired by the witness of the Catholic Worker and by the writings of such advocates of nonviolence as Dorothy Day, James Douglass, and Gordon Zahn, sought to develop a politically relevant pacifism, a political strategy that built upon a theology of the cross but did not retreat from political responsibility. For this segment of the movement, the Church was a community of witness, bearing testimony to a higher truth, risking all, wealth, influence, even membership, in order to be a sign of contradiction amidst the war-making and violence of the age. Rejecting totally the doctrine of the just war, they would not allow force in through the back door of the "just revolution." Consistent and courageous, this wing was the heart and soul of the resistance.[60]

Another wing emerged whose members, like the liberals, were most struck by the failure, not of the gospel, but of American society. Each defendant at the Catonsville trial indicated a personal experience of disillusionment with the United States. In overseas missions and ghettos at home, they had discovered that America's commitment to liberty, justice, and peace was simply rhetorical, a mask for sordid goals of material wealth and political power. The reality of America, they discovered, was racist and imperialist, supported by a public saturated by materialism and selfish nationalism. For this wing, the break with the nation over the war was only a step toward a new commitment to radical social change. However eloquently they might contrast the peace message of the gospel with the realities of national power, they were driven by their conscience to active resistance which could border on violence and by their analysis to a willingness to accept military action to change the *status quo*.[61]

These divisions within the so-called resistance mirrored those in the teachings of the Church itself. One group, who with their tactics of direct action seemed more radical, were in fact closer to the liberals and to the bishops, for they were prepared to justify the use of force as a last resort. Their experience had led them to a more severe criticism of American policy and of American society, so that they no longer could justify any use of American power, which seemed intrinsically immoral. Yet they could justify the use of force by insurgent groups around the world, including the National Liberation Front, and in some cases at least they would have allowed the use of force at home to overcome the "monster" of oppressive government if there was hope of success.

The pacifist wing of the resistance, together with a small but influential group of bishops and scholars, were in fact far more radical, at least from a religious point of view. For this group, there was a new and profound revelation of the gospel's demand for peace as both the means and ends of Christian social action. While their religious faith was undoubtedly no more sincere than that of their critics, people like Dorothy Day, Gordon Zahn, and Thomas Merton were more prepared to trust their faith as a guide to policy, for both church and state. For the Church, they believed that its presence in the world should take the form of courageous and prophetic witness, rejecting compromises and mediocrity. For the state, the need was similar: to understand that policies of war and war-making led not to peace but to destruction, not to the achievement of justice but to the ultimate contradiction of human aspirations for dignity, freedom, and love. For a Church which had begun with Vatican Council II to accept the reality that it was and would remain a minority in the world, the peace message seemed to offer an approach to mission and ministry which made Scriptural sense.

But it also threatened to remove the Church from involvement in the life and death issues of the human community, to turn it in the direction of sectarian isolation from human history.

While many radical Catholics were modest, open, and ecumenical, the implicit sectarianism of the pacifist position was real and found expression in the writings of many of its most courageous spokespersons. Douglass, for example, argued that the gospel offered a single way to peace: "The realism of the Gospel states that the *one way* to make peace is to live peace as if it were already here, by loving men without compromise and then by resisting all illegitimate authority."[62] This position allowed only a strategy of prophetic witness. The calculus of just war "is obviously intolerable," a *Catholic Worker* contribution argued, "because it attempts to shift the concrete center of Christian action in the world from the realm of witness in behalf of absolute values like justice and peace to the sphere of particular stands in favor of a particular military policy," resulting in "the theology of terror, the casuistry of carnage, the morality of murder."[63] Characteristically, then, the ethics of peace were directed primarily to persons, elaborating a theology of personal responsibility and a strategy of personal dissent and resistance, rather than to priorities, politicians, or government which, it seemed, could be changed only indirectly.[64]

For advocates of nonviolence, the just-war rationalizations of force were not only outmoded, but were themselves a source of the contemporary madness of war and weapons. The beginning of a true "theology of peace," according to Joseph R. Fahey, professor of religious studies at Manhattan College, lay in recognition that "by continuing to elaborate conditions in which a just war may be fought in the age of total war," Christian theologians provided an ongoing "theoretical basis" for the anarchy of nation-states and the spiralling arms race.[65] For Fahey and others the entire tradition of just war had been a massive mistake, a betrayal of the gospel. "If one wishes to leave room for the just war and the just revolution," Father John L. McKenzie concluded, "one can do nothing with the theology of the cross except throw it away."[66]

For other sincere Catholics the matter was not quite so simple. Fahey quoted Martin Luther King: "The choice today is no longer between violence and non-violence. It is between non-violence and non-existence." But James Schall expressed the feelings of many when he argued that to reject the choice of the lesser evil was to cut oneself and the Church off from something fundamental about human nature, from the consequences of original sin. "Man's goal is not merely 'peace'" Schall argued,

> but justice and liberty from which peace results. If the religious mind of our time does not allow man to defend what is noblest in him, will there be any future faith which is based on the possibility of freedom?[67]

No one had a clear answer to the question. The Council Fathers themselves, in composing the sections on war in *Gaudium et Spes,* had wrestled unsuccessfully with the problem of reconciling a purely religious ethic of peace with a political ethic of power and responsibility. Robert Tucker, commenting on the result, described the combination of the Council's strong condemnation of weapons of indiscriminate effect with its allowance of deterrence: "The substance of this position is that the means that may never be used and the evil that may never be done may, nevertheless, be threatened." For Tucker this was simply one more proof that the religious conscience could never be integrated with political realities. "Thus does the Council demonstrate that there is no way by which the circle can be squared, that there is no way by which the injunction against doing, or threatening, evil that good may come can be reconciled with the constituent principles of statecraft."[68] Protestant theologian Ralph Potter, commenting on Tucker's remarks, noticed that such realism made an "ultimate end" of statecraft. Realists and idealists produced the same result, the separation of religion and ethics from politics, the realist by denying the political significance of conscience, the idealist by denying the moral significance of politics. Potter, like many Catholics, preferred the messy but necessary effort the Council had made, the work of a Church which "seeks involvement and accepts compromise for the sake of its leavening influence in society.[69]

Theologically, then, the development of American Catholic thought during the Vietnam period mirrored the advances and the ambiguities of Vatican Council II and the agonizing dilemmas confronting the Christian conscience regarding the war. Clearly there was a revival of Christian pacifism, which enjoyed a new prominence and respectability. James Douglass's *The Non-Violent Cross* provided the first careful and systematic statement of Christian nonviolence to issue from an American Catholic. The writings of Thomas Merton recorded the gradual transformation of a sensitive Catholic from a moderate, uncertain pacifist to a militant advocate of nonviolence.[70] The United States Catholic Conference, the bishops' secretariat, whose staff continued to use the categories of just war in most of their policy pronouncements, recognized the legitimacy of Catholic pacifism. The Conference sponsored a debate between advocates of just war and pacifism and, in publishing the results, the editors seemed to side with the pacifists.[71]

The Catholic Worker provided a center for spreading pacifist ideas, and the draft, with its need for decision on the part of thousands of Catholic young men, provided a ready occasion in every community for consideration of the gospel's teachings and modern war. The Catholic Peace Fellowship printed materials and provided expertise and draft-counseling centers. Information programs sprang up around the country, and draft boards gradually began to accept claims to conscientious objector status based on Catholic belief. Yet, the revival of a Catholic peace witness during the Vietnam War should not be exaggerated. All Catholics involved wanted desperately to end the war; but they needed to win an audience for their arguments and persuade others of the war's evil. To do so, they were drawn irresistably to the use of just-war categories. Thus, as early as December 1965, when the Catholic Peace Fellowship sponsored publication of "A Catholic Statement on the War in Vietnam" signed by more than fifty prominent priests, religious, and laity, they based their argument not on Scripture or Church teachings but on three specific objections: "the character of the governments we have sponsored, . . . our failure to explore peaceful means of settlement, and the conduct of the war itself."[72] Careful measurement of ends and means, reliance upon assumed standards of "reasonableness," avoidance of Scriptural categories in favor of less sectarian values of freedom and self-determination, characterized statements of the peace movement addressed to wider publics.

Careful examination of most public statements regarding the war, both from the official Church and from the resistance, demonstrates that very few people had worked out clearly the relationship between faith and politics. Individual bishops and the hierarchy as a whole, reflecting the uncertainity of the scholarly community, tended to move uneasily between just-war and pacifist statements. In dealing with the actual situation of Vietnam, the bishops, with their sense of public responsibility in a divided nation and a divided Church, could find no alternative to the traditional just-war categories for evaluating war policies. Yet, often in the same statements, they would appeal to the radical peace message of Jesus and to the eloquent pleas of Pope Paul for peace. Thus, in Cardinal Shehan's 1966 pastoral letter, in "Human Life in Our Day," in the bishops' statement on the bombing in 1972, both just-war realist and pacifist radicals could claim to find legitimization and support. In fact, only the crusaders, those who would accept no moral limits to violence once war was underway, could fail to find some comfort and support in the messages of the official Church.

The second crucial development of the Vietnam period, then, was that many leaders of the American Church, including eventually its bishops, began applying with varying degrees of precision the categories of the just war to the actual circumstances and policies of the American war effort. Gradually, this process led more and more Catholics to conclude that those policies could not be justified. Once that line had been crossed, it was a short step to conclude that the war had become so intertwined with the policies that the war itself had become immoral. The next question was no easier: what, then, should be done? Naturally and properly many argued for negotiation. When that seemed to prove inadequate, growing numbers became advocates of unilateral withdrawal. Most who reached that conclusion had few illusions about the Communists of Vietnam. Rather, they reluctantly concluded that even a severe Communist regime would be preferable to the seemingly endless violence which offered no hope of concluding the conflict. By the end of the war, the American Catholic community had thus come to face the classic dualism of Christianity in dealing with power, force, and violence: there existed a strong, prophetic, and powerful peace witness, with its sectarian implications, and a more vigorous and honest assertion of the need responsibly to set limits to power.

The dilemma was simple but seemingly insoluble. As far back at least as Hiroshima, Catholic scholars had questioned the validity of just-war categories. Nuclear pacifism, the position that argues that while just-war reasoning was valid in times when the technologies of war were less developed it was no longer suitable under the conditions of modern war, was a well developed alternative prior to Vietnam. Among other things, modern war eliminated the distinction between combatants and noncombatants; the nature of modern weaponry meant that all wars would become disproportionate. No legitimate end could be secured through the use of nuclear weapons. This was clearly stated by Pope John XXIII and restated implicitly in *Gaudium et Spes* and by Pope Paul. Yet neither Pope, council, nor most responsible theologians wished to follow Dorothy Day and Gordon Zahn to the logical conclusion that the church must become a peace church, witnessing in every situation to a Gospel of peace and nonviolence, for they were repelled by the sectarian implications of that position, which would draw the church away from its traditional reliance upon reason and its traditional understanding of Catholic universality.

One way out was offered by some of the more articulate representatives of the Catholic resistance.[73] They argued that indeed the technologies of modern war had rendered the question of justice outmoded as far as the developed nations were concerned. On the other hand, less developed peoples, fighting with more limited technologies and more calculating and precise applications of force, could conceivably be justified in using force to resist the domination of their countries by technologically advanced powers. Additionally, it could be argued that there was a right of revolution, and that some of the categories of the just war could be applied to wars of national liberation. Often this position reflected a romantic view of the benevolence of the rebelling group and underestimated the capacity of such revolutionaries to make a corrupt use of force against innocent persons. Nevertheless, it received wide support in Latin America among Catholics who wished to shift their church to the side of the poor and powerless, and it had great appeal to American Catholics grown disillusioned with their country and its liberal ideals.

More common was a tendency, increasingly marked among bishops, not so much to transcend the categories of just war and pacifism, as to ignore them. Instead of wrestling with the morality of this or that war or this or that policy, or prescribing a position of pacifism fraught with difficulties for individuals and for the Church, more and more bishops, theologians, and activists simply emphasized the need for the Church and the Christian to be peacemakers, leaving the means to achieve peace to individual consciences. Gospel, council, and papal leadership converged in the mandate to devote oneself to the cause of peace. The means to peace, the strategy which would best end particular wars, eliminate the sources of war, and build a peaceful world, involved concrete choices in the realm of politics, economics, and technology, and complex judgments about human nature and social structures. The Church, it was felt, could best contribute to the cause of peace by emphasizing it as a moral imperative, offering a continuing moral critique of public policies, and assisting and supporting its members as they attempted to form their consciences and translate the imperative of peace into their lives, their ministries, their everyday worlds.[74] Already the popes had argued that work for justice was the surest way to contribute to peace. Rather than spend itself in bitter intramural debate about the exact policy positions the Church should adopt, it should seek a more explicitly religious ground, defending human freedom and human dignity, evaluating current policies and actions from its unique perspective, and urging all persons to join in the pursuit of justice and peace. Resistance, witness, work for international organization, efforts for staged mutual disarmament, efforts for a new international economic order, Christians could pursue any or all of these strategies, provided that they conscientiously sought to relate their choices to their faith and to their responsibilities within both the ecclesiastical and civil communities.

By implication, such a stance could remove the Church a bit from its direct involvement in the policy-making process. Many were prepared to accept this, for while the bishops' conference and its committees continued to testify before Congress on specific pieces of legislation, few any longer believed that the bishops could deliver the Catholic vote. Corporate clout in the policy process had already eroded and would not be restored at least until new forms of consultation led to a situation in which significant portions of the Catholic community shared in defining what positions would be taken and how they would be expressed. Undoubtedly the bishops, individually and collectively, would continue to feel compelled to speak out on what they regarded as critical moral issues, but most recognized the need for modesty in challenging or supporting specific pieces of legislation. Through conferences, programs of consultation, and public debate, the bishops sought to define new forms and methods for making an impact on the policy-making process and the formation of the public moral consensus that lay behind it. Preaching, teaching, and pastoral care, the whole life of the Church, must necessarily be integrated into that process. So, while the debate about a theology of peace would go on, the thrust of Catholic action would be toward developing awareness of the moral dimensions of social and political life, educating for peace and justice, and forming lay leaders and ministerial representatives capable of carrying the Christian message into everyday life.[75]

Conclusion

As we move to the end of the 1970s, we begin to gain some perspective on the period of protest and division occasioned by the Vietnam War. As the war and its issues recede from national consciousness and the institutional

Church returns to its natural and necessary preoccupation with faith and community, the question of mission remains. For many, particularly among the Church's various elites, the mission question is critical; the need to be specific about that mission in terms of war, weapons, economic injustice, and political oppression will not go away. The most deeply committed of the anti-war activists continue their work, through the Catholic Worker, or new study/action centers like Philip Berrigan and Elizabeth McAlister's Jonah House in Baltimore. Local and regional justice and peace centers, some established under official auspices, others under the sponsorship of religious communities, have sprung up around the country forming a loose national network, the "Convergence of Justice and Peace Centers." A small group of scholars have organized to promote research and writing on the theme of theology of liberation, while the learned societies of theologians and biblical scholars are devoting more attention than in the past to theoretical problems of social justice and world peace. Educational organizations, particularly those gathered around the National Catholic Educational Association, have made education for justice a priority, and a large amount of educational materials is available for use in classrooms and in CCD programs.

Perhaps most important, many of the nation's religious communities have moved through systematic processes of self-examination and renewal, very often ending with mission statements which give central importance to active efforts to secure peace and justice. Most dramatically, the Thirty-Second General Congregation of the Society of Jesus committed that massive order to the pursuit of "faith and justice." Father General Pedro Arrupe, S.J., was tireless in goading local provinces to reconsider their work and resources in light of world and domestic poverty, injustice, and violence. But the Jesuits are not alone; every American order has considered these matters seriously and those with members engaged in overseas missions or social ministry in the United States have felt daily pressure to incorporate the social mission of the Church into all phases of their work. In 1978 the leaders of men's and women's religious communities met jointly for the first time. After hearing eloquent appeals from Catholics from overseas they expressed their collective determination to work ceaselessly to arouse concern and bring about action to end injustice and build a just and peaceful world.

So there is every indication that, even if the thrust of American life continues in the direction of domestic preoccupations and creeping conservatism, the direction of Catholic Church reform is irretrievably set toward the pursuit of justice and peace. American Church leaders who recognize this have come to understand that translation of that insight into pastoral practice and ecclesiastical policy is complicated. The pastoral task of renewing the parishes and other Christian communities of the United States, and the mission task of sharpening the Church's moral edge in confronting the realities of contemporary life must ultimately be brought closer together. The need for action for justice and peace is urgent and cannot be postponed until churches and Christians have gotten their personal lives and corporate structures straightened out. The problems of faith, personal meaning, and social understanding are too real to be ignored while Church activists rush headlong toward a supposedly prophetic radicalism that turns out also to be self-righteously irrelevant. Serious, intelligent confrontation with the issues and problems which are the Church's legacy from Vietnam, taking place within a community of conscience and mutual respect, is what is needed. And for that to come about, all involved must sincerely and appropriately love the Church, share its faith, and care about its people.

Notes

1. Henry Steele Commager, "The Defeat of America," *New York Review of Books*, October 5, 1972.

2. Among the best accounts of the moral scars of the war is Gloria Emerson, *Winners and Losers* (New York and London: Harcourt, Brace Jovanovich, 1977).

3. On the Catholic Church in Vietnam see Piero Gheddo, *The Cross and the Bo-Tree: Catholics and Buddhists in Vietnam*, trans. Charles U. Quinn (New York: Sheed & Ward, 1970); "Catholicism in Contemporary Vietnam," *IDOC International*, North American edition, 1972. In June 1971, a delegation of American Catholics visited with anti-war Vietnamese Catholics in Paris; thereafter news of Catholic opposition to the war in the South and Catholic life in the North became increasingly accessible in the American press.

4. On American Catholic nationalism see Dorothy Dohen, *Nationalism and American Catholicism* (New York: Sheed & Ward, 1967). The presumption of uncritical loyalty informs almost all the literature of the Catholic peace movement cited below. For a brief survey of episcopal leadership see John Tracy Ellis, "American Catholics and Peace" in James S. Rausch, ed., *The Family of Nations: An Expanded View of Patriotism* (Huntington, Ind.: Our Sunday Visitor Press, 1970).

5. J. David Valaik, "American Catholic Dissenters and the Spanish Civil War," *Catholic Historical Review* 53 (January 1968): 537–555; Valaik, "Catholics, Neutrality, and the Spanish Embargo," *Journal of American History* 54 (June 1967): 73–85.

6. Patricia McNeal, *The American Catholic Peace Movement* (New York: Arno Press, 1978).

7. See, for example, the strong letter of Edward Cardinal Mooney to President Roosevelt, November 28, 1942, expressing "the grave concern of the Bishops over the role which the atheistic and communistic Soviet Government may play in the post-war settlement," Roosevelt Papers, Hyde Park, N.Y.

8. Donald Crosby, S.J., *God, Church and Flag* (Chapel Hill: University of North Carolina Press, 1978).

9. Among other relevant studies is George Q. Flynn, *Roosevelt and Romanism* (Bloomington: University of Indiana Press, 1977).

10. This essay cannot cover in detail the evolution of public opinion in the Catholic community, but several points should be made. According to the American Institute of Public Opinion, Catholics were slightly more inclined to support the war, slightly less inclined to opposition than the population generally:

		Support	*Opposition*	*No Opinion*
Population	May 1965	52	26	22
Catholics	May 1965	59	23	18
Population	October 1968	37	54	9
Catholics	October 1968	42	49	9
Population	January 1971	31	59	10
Catholics	January 1971	36	57	7

The analysis of the Survey Research Center, on the other hand, shows an even more surprising moderation, and a much sharper division than expected.

	Pull Out Altogether	*Stay But Try to End Fighting*	*Take Stronger Stand Including Invasion of North if Needed*
1966 Protestants	8	35	36
Catholics	.10	39	39
Jews	19	44	33
1968 Protestants	18	36	35
Catholics	20	39	32
Jews	36	36	19
1970 Protestants	30	34	25
Catholics	35	30	25
Jews	50	21	14

Figures are taken from John E. Mueller, *War, Presidents and Public Opinion* (New York: John Wiley, 1973), pp. 142–144.

11. This is also true, of course, for at least some of the active participants in the public controversy. The rationale for an essay like the present one is simply to try to understand the ideas used to interpret and influence events, not to suggest that the arguments made fully disclose the motives or even the full range of thought of those who publicly discussed the war.

12. Donald Pelotte, *John Courtney Murray: Theologian in Conflict* (New York: Paulist Press, 1975).

13. "I've often reflected that while Catholics are, in theological and religious matters, the most cosmopolitan and world-minded people on earth, somehow in political, social, and economic matters they turn out to be ultra-nationalistic. On the other hand, those who are so ultra-nationalistic theologically that their very church name reflects the name of their nation—the Church of Scotland, the Church of England, the Boston Unitarians—are, as a matter of fact, usually the most internationally minded in what pertains to politics, problems of peace and war and similar temporal problems of a cultural and social kind." Bishop John Wright, Interview in Donald McDonald, *Catholics in Conversation: Seventeen Interviews with Leading American Catholics* (Philadelphia: Lippincott, 1960).

14. Stephan Verosta, "The Holy See and International Organizations," *Worldview* 15 (July 1972): 31–33.

15. On the American role see Hervé Chaigne, "The Council and Peace," *The Catholic Worker* (July and August, 1966); Archbishop Thomas Roberts, "The War for Peace at the Council," *The Critic* 25 (October and November, 1966); Vincent Yzermans, *American Participation in the Second Vatican Council* (New York: Sheed & Ward, 1967), pp. 183–270.

16. Gheddo, *The Cross and the Bo-Tree,* passim.

17. "Catholicism in Contemporary Vietnam," pp. 88–89.

18. In fact, a study of the papacy and Vietnam might reveal that strong exercise of moral leadership did have some impact, perhaps more than diplomacy. During the Christmas 1972 bombing of North Vietnam for example, the Pope told a public audience, "What has happened during the last few days, and the shocked reaction of human, not to say Christian, consciences, to the horror of this tremendous new tragedy, should convince all responsible persons even more strongly of the necessity, which is moral even more than political, to continue indefatigably in clear and honest negotiations." Citing the Pope's statement as evidence, the *New York Times* editorialized that the bombing "has intensified bitterness and anxiety in world opinion." *New York Times,* December 23, 1972, and January 1, 1973. For a survey of papal response to the war see Dennis Kenny, "Pope Paul VI and Vietnam," *Worldview* 15 (September 1972): 26–31.

19. See Geoffrey Hadden, *The Gathering Storm in the Churches* (New York: Doubleday Anchor Books, 1970).

20. Statement in *Continuum* (Summer 1965), inside cover.

21. *Courier-Journal* (Rochester, N.Y.), February 18, 1966.

22. *National Catholic Reporter,* August 3, 1966.

23. Ibid.

24. *National Catholic Reporter,* January 5, 1967.

25. *New York Times,* September 23, 1968.

26. "Cardinal Shehan on Vietnam, Patriotism and Individual Conscience," Pastoral Letter, June 28, 1966, published as a leaflet by the Catholic Peace Fellowship.

27. "The Cardinal on War," *Commonweal* 84 (July 22, 1966).

28. *National Catholic Reporter,* August 31, 1966.

29. Ibid., October 19, 1966.

30. Ibid., August 23, 1967.

31. Hugh J. Nolan, ed., *Pastoral Letters of the American Hierarchy, 1792–1970,* (Huntington, Ind.: Our Sunday Visitor Press, 1971), pp. 604–606.

32. "An Open Letter to the U.S. Bishops," *Commonweal* 85 (February 17, 1967).

33. "Catholic Bishops and Vietnam," ibid. (March 17, 1967).

34. Nolan, *Pastoral Letters,* p. 618.

35. "Reply" to Bishop Shannon, *Commonweal* 85 (March 17, 1967).

36. Msgr. Joseph Gallagher, "Peace: Sad Orphan of Mother Church," *National Catholic Reporter,* April 10, 1968.

37. *National Catholic Reporter,* August 23, 1967.

38. "Human Life in Our Day" in David J. O'Brien and Thomas A. Shannon, eds., *Renewing the Earth: Catholic Documents on Peace, Justice and Liberation* (New York: Doubleday Image Books, 1977), pp. 421–467.

39. *National Catholic Reporter,* May 14, 1971; Worcester (Mass.) *Catholic Free Press,* June 18, 1971; *New York Times,* June 27, 1971.

40. *National Catholic Reporter,* September 24, 1971.

41. Worcester, *Catholic Free Press,* May 24, 1971.

42. "Resolution on Southeast Asia," leaflet published by United States Catholic Conference, 1971.

43. *National Catholic Reporter,* November 26, 1971; Marvin Bordelon, "The Bishops and Just War," *America* 126 (January 8, 1972).

44. *National Catholic Reporter,* November 24, 1972; *New York Times,* November 17, 1972.

45. "Bishops on Bishops on the War," *National Catholic Reporter,* February 11, 1972.

46. Ibid.

47. In the course of this evolution, however, moral issues of tremendous significance passed by officially unnoticed by the American Catholic bishops. While their eventual, cautious dissent was historic, it nevertheless required little vision and less courage. Failure to recognize their own irrelevance in the national debate, or to understand that silence by implication sanctioned official policy, meant that the bishops were unable to move clearly and forcefully to build a more creative approach to influencing U.S. policy when the war ended. See Gordon C. Zahn, "The Church an Accomplice: Reflection on My Lai," *Worldview* 14 (March 1971).

Shortly before the November 1971 meeting, the bishops' press office issued a misleading "white paper" highlighting episcopal criticism of the war and ignoring pro-war statements and moments of conspicuous silence. See Gordon Zahn, "The Scandal of Silence," *Commonweal* 95 (October 22, 1971).

48. *New York Times,* October 24, 1965, and November 6, 1965; *Catholic Worker,* November 1965.

49. *Commonweal* 86 (September 8, 1967); 88 (May 10, 1968).

50. William V. Shannon, "Au Revoir," *Commonweal* 88 (May 24, 1968).

51. *National Catholic Reporter,* August 11, 1965.

52. Ibid., August 24, 1966.

53. Ibid., January 3, 1967.

54. Ibid., December 9, 1967.

55. Ibid., April 9, 1967.

56. *Commonweal* 86 (September 8, 1967). Most liberal observers, even when they opposed the war, refused to believe that the war, as James Finn put it, was "the result of careful planning guided by sound principles and under rational control." Rather, "accident, ignorance, national pride and faulty judgment played a greater part." "Vietnam Views, Left to Right," *National Catholic Reporter,* January 12, 1966.

57. For a sample of Zahn's writing on peace see *War, Conscience and Dissent* (New York: Hawthorne, 1967).

58. *National Catholic Reporter,* October 2, 1979; among the studies of the Berrigans is William VanEtten Casey and Philip Nobile, eds., *The Berrigans* (New York: Avon Books, 1971).

59. Peter Rohrbach, "From Teresa of Avila to Eldridge Cleaver: The Odyssey of a Radical Priest," *Catholic World* 212 (June 1970).

60. See Gordon C. Zahn, "The Great Catholic Upheaval," *Saturday Review* 54 (September 11, 1971); Zahn, "The Future of the Catholic Peace Movement," *Commonweal* 99 (December 28, 1973).

61. See David J. O'Brien, *The Renewal of American Catholicism* (New York: Oxford University Press, 1972), pp. 194–230.

62. James Douglass, "Can Nonviolence Ride Again?" *National Catholic Reporter,* September 24, 1969.

63. Hervé Chaigne, "The Council and Peace," *Catholic Worker*, July and August 1966.

64. "I am not so much concerned about the need to incorporate principles of morality into law or with the more immediate need to translate them into individual behavior. Unfortunately, too many of our moralists are so transfixed by the glamour of power and power politics that they devote more intellectual effort and energy to the latest strategic concepts, or to tracing all the nuances and limitations of international law, than they do to developing and clarifying guidelines for the Christian who seeks to live and act according to the moral and behavioral implications of his faith" (Gordon Zahn, "Response," *Worldview* 16 [October, 1973]: 47).

65. Joseph R. Fahey, "Toward a Theology of Peace," *Catholic World* 213 (May 1971): 64–68.

66. John L. McKenzie, Review, *Commonweal* 96 (September 22, 1972).

67. James V. Schall, "Religion and War," *Commonweal* 84 (November 18, 1966).

68. Robert W. Tucker, *Just War and Vatican Council II: A Critique* (New York: Council on Religion and International Affairs, 1966), pp. 49–50.

69. Commentary by Ralph Potter, ibid., p. 60.

70. James Douglass, *The Non-Violent Cross* (New York: Macmillan, 1968), and Gordon C. Zahn, ed., *Thomas Merton on Peace* (New York: Saturday Review Press, 1971).

71. James R. Jennings, ed., *Just War and Pacifism: A Catholic Dialogue* (Washington: United States Catholic Conference, 1973).

72. *National Catholic Reporter*, December 8, 1965.

73. See Thomas and Marjorie Melville, "The Catholic Resistance," *New York Times*, April 26, 27, 1971; the best argument for this position was supplied by philosopher Richard Hinners, in a letter to the *National Catholic Reporter*, April 26, 1967 and in "Vietnam: Technology versus Morality," *Cross Currents* 18 (Fall 1968), pp. 221–234.

74. Suggestive comments in this regard are found in Thomas Merton, *Seeds of Destruction* (New York: Farrar, Straus and Geroux, 1964), pp. 93–121; Patrick McDermott, *Christian Tradition and Peacemaking Today* (Washington: United States Catholic Conference, 1970). The bishops' own 1972 resolution, "The Imperatives of Peace," is in a leaflet from the National Conference of Catholic Bishops. I have developed these thoughts further in "The Future of the Catholic Peace Movement," *Origins* 4 (June 1976): 721–31.

75. A good example of the explicit refusal to select either pacifist or just-war alternatives, to insist on a role in the policy process but to speak to the general goals of foreign policy rather than to the specifics of policy is "Pursuing Peace: Working for Justice," a statement prepared by the United States Catholic Conference Committee on Social Development and World Peace for presentation to the Platform Committees of the Republican and Democratic parties, 1972. Recently James Finn noted that the difficulty of conducting the pacifist/just-war debate is not confined to the Catholic community. He quotes Richard Falk, commenting on Michael Walzer's *Just and Unjust Wars* (New York: Basic Books, 1977): "Those who most deeply imperil the human prospect will be pleased to discover their moral vindication in Walzer's book." Finn remarks that such words indicate "how divided we are in this country about the possibility of discussing the justice of war." "The Just War: Reviving an Old Debate," *Commonweal* 105 (August 18, 1978): 532–537.

PART III
THE CHURCH AND PACIFISM

9
Pacifism and the World Council of Churches

Walter G. Muelder

Though profoundly committed to world peace, the World Council of Churches (WCC) has not been an essentially pacifist organization. It is the principal agency of the ecumenical movement, a movement for global Christian unity in and through the churches. It conceives unity both as *given* in Jesus Christ and as a *task* to interpret and manifest this unity in historical form. Since Vatican Council II it has been deeply engaged with the Roman Catholic Church, but this essay will concentrate on the WCC. On questions of war and peace, as on all theological and ethical matters, the WCC cannot commit the member churches. It may and does, however, lead. But it leads a pilgrimage of churches—ancient, medieval, and modern—with heavy historical baggage.

The legacy of the churches to the ecumenical movement on the issues of war and peace has been fourfold: (1) the pacifism of the early church; (2) the "just-war" tradition; (3) the holy crusade and; (4) duty to obey the state. Neither of these legacies dominates officially, though "just-war" and its derivative "just revolution" has tended to be the nuclear practical or allegedly "realistic" position, while pacifism has struggled for recognition and is more appreciated today than it was four decades ago.

This essay will show that there is a potent immanent peace principle inherent in ecumenism itself; that religious liberty and conscientious objection are closely related; that the nuclear age has put in question every "just-war"ethic; that disarmament and international institutions press in a pacifist direction; and that present commitments by the WCC to a just, participatory, and sustainable society involve the churches in a struggle against the cult of militarism and toward recognizing the ambiguities of revolutionary liberation and development.

The present scene was vividly acknowledged at the Fifth Assembly of the WCC in Nairobi, Kenya, in 1975:

> The problem of Christian responsibility in a world of force and violence is as old as the Church itself. It has appeared in ever-

> changing forms through the centuries; in the suffering but triumphant martyrdom of the early Church, in the question of military service from the time of the Roman Empire, in the question of the "just-war," in the justification of tyrannicide, or in the limits of obedience to unjust political authority and the means by which it may be resisted, to mention only a few. In all these forms, the agonizing question is the same: how can Christians, children of God's love and followers of Jesus Christ, live and work in a world where the use of force and violence against the countless forms of human sin seems unavoidable.[1]

Despite the predicaments of history and the present scene, there are at least four immanent and inherent aspects of a growing pacifist development in the ecumenical movement. Firstly, "ecumenical" is in principle different from "international." The latter presupposes the over-againstness of sovereign powers; the former stresses supranational inclusive community. International manifests structural disunity; ecumenical presupposes a given unity in Jesus Christ and the Holy Spirit and the essential theological demand to manifest that unity in visible organic form. Hence, peace as unity calls for a global reconciliation of Christian groups and ecumenism makes the churches the servants of human unity. Secondly, ecumenism shows that national churches attached to national loyalties cannot combat militarism effectively. Hence disarmament, for example, calls for a supranational standpoint and concurrent effort ecumenically. The Church as a global institution must make the demands of disarmament on all the belligerents, while also seeking to resolve the root causes of oppression and hostility. Only a global strategy—not national "just-war" strategies—can fulfill the reconciling requirements of the Church's given unity and the unitive vocation of the Church.

A third aspect of the inherent pacifist tendency of the ecumenical movement is the recently emphasized formula, unity of the Church and unity of humankind. This solidaristic notion that Christian unity does not exist for its own sake and that Christian unity and human unity are one in the purpose of God has the penultimate consequence of giving the Church the task of serving the unity of the whole human race. Programmatically, this insight and commitment by both the WCC and by Vatican Council II require that all secular divisiveness (race, sex, class, nation, domination) be overcome within the churches so that the Church may be a true "sign" of the Kingdom of God in a world struggling for liberation and justice.

A fourth pacifist element inherent in ecumenism is the nonviolent character of the ecumenical process. The churches in the WCC have put the wars of religion behind them. They now know that unity cannot be coerced. Shame marks the situation where religious and ideological violence still prevail. By contrast, ecumenism is a dialogue with two dimensions: *(a)* a horizontal dimension comprising conversation, joint-study, and negotiation among spiritual equals and *(b)* a vertical dimension of dialogue between Christ and the churches through the Holy Spirit. Violent maneuvers are violations of religious liberty. The authority of dialogue is its merit.

There is thus an urge toward pacifism in the ecumenical movement. On the other hand, structures in which militarism reigns disguise the Christ whom Christians and the Church profess. He preached and died for peace, making it a major theme in his work. Therefore, it cannot be given a lesser priority by the churches.[2] This priority is recognized whenever the cult of militarism is identified. Most Christians are agreed on this. Militarism encourages the positive hatred of the enemy; it promotes enmity; it contradicts the most basic interpersonal and intergroup attitudes which Jesus taught his followers to cultivate. Though Christians are expected to adore Christ as lord, military realism denigrates Christian ethics as unrealistic and sentimental. Ecumenism has slowly and steadily raised the moral consciousness of its participants and moved them in a nonviolent direction, as this essay will show. On the whole it has taught that militarism cannot provide security but rather undermines the chance of world survival; it rejects the notion that militarism is good for the world economy; it repudiates the aggressive use of defense forces for national defense and notes that defense forces may even take over countries and wreck them; it has contended that militarism endangers the natural environment; it has pointed out the risks of the misuse of nuclear energy; it criticizes militarism's distortion of scientific development and the lives of scientists; and it abhors the contradiction of the arms trade in relation to the needed new international order.

Pacifism as a Minority Perspective

A detailed outline of the historical development of pacifism within the WCC falls outside the purview of this study, but from the beginning it was a minority perspective. On the eve of World War I the Lausanne meeting of the World Alliance for International Friendship through the Churches was suddenly interrupted by hostilities. In 1925 at Stockholm many of the strains and fears of that war were still evident among the participants. At Oxford (1937) the delegates already sensed the ominous forebodings of World War II and they could achieve no consensus on issues of war and peace, but rather listed types of ethical attitudes noted at the beginning of this essay. Some indeed wish to regard pacifism as a heresy. During World War II the majority of Christians supported their governmental policies, though not, despite Hitler's provocations, with the unqualified zeal that characterized their postures in World War I. There were two criticisms which deserve note at this point. Christian pacifists were lumped together with isolationists and they were accused of moral irresponsibility by so-called Christian "realists." We should turn to these briefly.

There are Christian pacifists whose sectarian commitment to nonviolence is so absolute that the practical effect of their ethics is against all intervention in military action. But this position should not be confused with the isolationism of secular noninterventionists. There were Christian pacifists who were genuine internationalists but who opposed the conflagration of World War II. Many were committed to a responsible world society, a world community established on international justice, undergirded by world law, and guaranteed by a world political authority. They opposed national sovereignty and balance of power as nineteenth-century anachronisms. They wished the Oxford Conference masthead, "Let the Church Be the Church," to be manifested in a truly ecumenical (supranational) witness. Isolationism, on the contrary, was to them anti-ecumenical as was interventionism. Isolationism is often rooted in militarism and national introversion as, for example, with the "America Firsters" in the 1930s and the "Continentalists" in the early 1950s. Isolationism as an ethical principle can hardly be Christian ecumenism or pacifism. Christian pacifism is costly internationalism rooted in the supranational unity of the Church. Ecumenical pacifism affirms world interdependence and the global interpenetration of such issues as racism, imperialism, sexism, overpopulation, economic exploitation, development, and ecology.

The second principal argument levelled against pacifists was that individual persons might forswear violence and mount their individual crosses, but "love of the neighbor" still required a willingness to use violence (war) in defense of a collective neighbor. It was also pointed out that pacifists benefited by the sacrifices which the military made in defense of country and it was argued that acceptance of these benefits compromised the integrity of pacifist behavior. Even the doing of "alternative" service was mocked as falling short of true "love of neighbor." Pacifists have by and large acknowledged the ambiguity of living in interdependent communities, particularly of coercive societies with structural violence deeply entrenched. The dilemma of accepting benefits, however, should not be overlooked when "love of neighbor" is the moral appeal. In conflicts leading to overt violence, whether resulting in international war or in domestic revolution, the national interest, class interest, or other special interests are seldom far removed from interest in the neighbor. Church people closest to the centers of secular power are generally more inclined to see the neighbors' interest and their own in that perspective.

At the Oxford Conference the churches had to confront in a fresh way the relation of church and state and the question of the churches' responsibility to the state. Since Oxford it has become clearer that the Church owes the state a great deal more prophetic criticism than it has exercised. What pacifists and nonpacifists have agreed on is to seek more realistically to deal not alone with symptoms of injustice but with its social causes. Both have sought the "responsible society," a "new international economic order," and a "just and sustainable society." They have together addressed structures and processes. They have not only sought to eradicate overt acts of violence, but have addressed themselves to conditions and social structures which were regarded as equally or more violent in their persistent dehumanization than physical violence. Indeed, systemic violence has engaged the ethical will of the whole WCC.

The minority status of the pacifist position is understandable historically. The politicizing and militarizing of the Church took place as the close relation of church and state developed under and after Constantine. Despite the doctrine of the two swords, the mutual defense of church and state and the appeal to compulsion grew hand in hand. The Church was seen as an institution that could help unify the empire. Emperors presided over ecumenical councils. Augustine, on the other hand, grew to see the institutional value of coercion in dealing with alleged heretics. The interpenetration of the political and the ecclesiastical order developed greatly in the period of the territorial churches during the five hundred years between Gregory I and Gregory VII. It was inherent in the centralizaion of the papacy and the violence of feudalism. Even great mystics like St. Bernard preached a holy crusade against the infidels. Church and state were partners in the age of the medieval Inquisition and this continued as natural in the Reformation. Religious liberty, the separation of church and state, and nonviolence were pushed to the periphery of the theological self-image of the Church and were regarded as sectarian and heretical.

Religious liberty and the separation of church and state are indispensable for the effective development of a peace movement. Dependence of church and state on each other must cease if the one is not to dominate the other. Only a self-reliant church willing to suffer persecution is free enough to reject militarism altogether. From this perspective the "just-war" theory is largely a function of the accommodation of the Church to the interests of the political order. From the outset it was a product of compromise by the imperial Church. Whatever critical functions the doctrine possessed it tended to lose because of its own ecclesiastical and temporal concerns to exercise power. In medieval centuries the bishop was often a feudal prince. At the national level "just war" generally legitimized the military action of whatever states or nations bounded the Church's temporalities. In modern times the Church has usually been dragged along in the wake of the failures of diplomacy of the ship of state. It is difficult to find examples of official Church actions to refuse to sanction the wars of the environing nation-state, even though the Church claimed a universal character. That is, until the Indochina War.

Religious Liberty and Conscience

Religious liberty and the rights of conscientious objection to war are closely related in principle and in history. Both have had slow recognition since the Middle Ages and the Reformation. The Erastian relationship of church and state and the dominance of the "just-war" ethic and the idea of duty to the state as a religious obligation contributed to the halting pilgrimage. Being dependent on the state the churches did not wish to harm the state, and they feared social disorder. Until World War I conscientious objection was virtually identified with the historic peace churches, part of the radical wing of the Reformation. By the time of the Oxford Conference, however, greater emphasis was given to the affirmation, "Let the Church Be the Church." This meant a greater self-consciousness by the churches over against the community, the economic order, and the state. The meaning of history was prophetically examined. Totalitarian states, Fascist, Communist, and National Socialist, threatened the emerging ecumenical witness and world peace. Accordingly, conscientious objection was acknowledged more and given a broader scope of application, particularly in some Protestant countries. Significantly, however, conscientious objection now had a double root, the one the pacifist tradition, the other the ethic of the "just-war" churches. Individuals were seen to have the right conscientiously to evaluate the justice of a war. Not all believers in the rights of conscientious objectors are, therefore, to be counted as pacifists. Many denominations produced young people who were assigned "alternative service" in World War II.

The Church Commission on International Affairs, to be discussed below, and the first three Assemblies of the WCC supported the rights of conscience. A further development took place in the 1960s with the notion of "selective conscientious objection." This principle extends the idea from the universal objection to all wars to objection to a particular war. In the U.S.A. the religious basis for such objection was also broadened. The Fourth Assembly (Uppsala, 1968), influenced by the developments above, by the nature of modern warfare, and by the conduct of the war in Vietnam, formulated a statement as follows:

> Protection of conscience demands that the churches should give spiritual care and support not only to those serving in the armed forces but also those who, especially in the light of the nature of modern warfare, object to participation in particular wars they feel bound in conscience to oppose, or who find themselves unable to bear arms or to enter the military service of their nations for reasons of conscience. Such support should include pressure to have the law changed where this is required, and be extended to all in moral perplexity about scientific work on weapons of mass human destruction.[3]

It should be noted that the last sentence above adds a new dimension to the ecumenical witness, work on war material as well as war itself. Along with J. Robert Oppenheimer many had "experienced sin." In this statement the WCC is still within the "just-war" theory, for, when an amendment at Uppsala was proposed that churches should commit themselves to call on Christians personally to disavow direct involvement in processes of manufacturing weapons of mass destruction and the system that threatens to use them, it was defeated. Thus, on the issue of war as a moral heresy the Assembly was not prepared to go the whole distance of complete Christian pacifism.

The Commission of the Churches on International Affairs (CCIA)

Between 1946 and 1968 the principal official voice of the WCC on matters of war and peace was the CCIA. It was founded as the instrumentality of the International Missionary Council (IMC) and the WCC while still in process of formation. Its work for peace was dominated by a Western orientation to the then colonial powers, who were the sending countries of the missionary movement, and to the purposes of the United Nations. It sought to be relevant to actual international crises, to diplomatic processes, and to the developing tasks and programs of the U.N. In this it continued the majority legacies of the participating churches and their agencies with respect to day-by-day practical international affairs. Among its aims were careful preparation of studies on international problems, guidance and assistance to the churches of the world as they sought to exert their influences on nation states in international questions, and maintaining contact with international bodies. In so doing the CCIA was embedded in the dilemmas of leadership, as close as possible, to deal with those in secular authority and power and involved in balance-of-power and in some cases balance-of-terror.

The Commission functioned with a great deal of autonomy as the representative of the parent bodies. Obviously its personnel did not have a pacifist commitment and its very institutional existence tended to push the pacifist witness to the periphery of serious reflection from the Commission's inception in 1946 until its reconstitution in 1968. In those more than twenty years its very competent leadership and sophisticated board functioned within the perspectives of realistic compromise. In 1951 the CCIA Executive Committee issued a widely quoted statement entitled "Christians Stand for Peace," which was intended to distinguish its position from that of secular agencies serving ideological purposes. It said: "We must neither purchase peace at the price of tyranny nor in the name of justice look on war as a way to justice or as a ground of hope."[4]

As the churches had been very active in helping to bring the U.N. into existence in 1945, so they had a continuing stake in its support and in developing its institutions. The Commission was concerned to maintain such contacts with the U.N. as would help develop and codify international law, promote supranational agencies, encourage respect for religious liberty and other human rights, advance the international regulation of armaments, further international economic cooperation, promote the well-being of dependent peoples and their advancement toward self-government with free political institutions, and forward worldwide social, cultural, educational, and humanitarian enterprises.

The CCIA has sometimes been called the churches' "international civil service." It was hoped that despite the strong differences on war and peace in the churches they could unite on the formulated aims and on the elements of an international ethos. The CCIA helped draft the statement on religious liberty that went into the Universal Declaration of Human Rights and worked closely with the Commission on Human Rights of the U.N. It helped formulate many statements on international crises for the Central Committee of the WCC. Characteristic items included the Netherlands-Indonesia dispute in 1949, the explosion of the first hydrogen bomb in 1950 (condemning it as sin against God), support of the U.N. "police measure" in Korea, the "cold war," disarmament, a test ban of hydrogen bombs, conscientious objection to war, expanding the concept of the "responsible society" to "responsible international society," and spelling out the middle axioms of an international ethos (1954). The competent work of the CCIA on disarmament was endorsed by the Central Committee in 1957 and 1958. They did not press for unilateral disarmament, nor did they identify with either the East or the West on the issues involved, but they recognized the need for nations to defend themselves. Thus the approach was to seek policies that would provide both adequate security and also gradual disarmament. This approach was reflected in the position taken by the New Delhi Assembly in 1961 on the issue of nuclear weapons:

> Christians must press most urgently upon their governments as a first step toward the elimination of nuclear weapons, never to get themselves into a position in which they contemplate the first use of nuclear weapons. Christians must also maintain that the use of nuclear weapons, or other form of major violence, against centers of population is in no circumstances reconcilable with the demands of the Christian gospel.[5]

A positive recommendation at New Delhi was to hold a conference of church persons from East and West at which experts on disarmament would explain their relative positions. This was carried out in Geneva in 1962 under the auspices of the CCIA.

This consultation was one of many which the CCIA has conducted to bring Christians from both sides of a dispute together. Noteworthy also is the role of the churches with respect to the Indochina War. With respect to that tragedy there was concurrent and focal action by the Commission, by the Geneva Study Conference of 1966, by the Central Committee, and subsequent action by the Uppsala Assembly in 1968. The CCIA began consultations on Indochina in 1954, involving regional representations from East Asia, and again in 1965. In 1966 the Central Committee noted that the U.S.A. and its allies faced increased bitter racial and other resentments against the U.S.A. and the West, while the Vietnamese faced vast destruction of their people and resources. The prospect of victory at the end of the conflict does not, they added, justify the inevitable cost.

In the positions taken by the WCC regarding Vietnam not only were disarmament and negotiation stressed, but also the recognition of a great social revolution—a theme which would become explicit in the post-Uppsala study document, "Violence, Non-violence, and the Struggle for Justice." Three of ten measures listed by the Central Committee are of special relevance to the present essay: social revolution, futility of military action, and the U.S.A. policy of "containment" of communism. These measures stated:

> 6. that all the parties recognize the extent to which what is happening in Vietnam is part of a social revolution and that, freed from foreign intervention, Vietnam, both North and South, ought to be in a position to determine its own future, with due consideration of the demands of peace and security in South East Asia;
> 7. that all parties recognize the futility of military action for the solution of the underlying political, social and economic problems of Vietnam and the necessity of massive and generous development programmes;
> 8. that in order to relieve present international tension, the United States review and modify its policy of 'containment' of communism, and communist countries supporting 'wars of liberation' review and modify their policy.[6]

Some changes were made in the constitution of the CCIA at Uppsala. The changes came partly as a result of a criticism that over the years it was too Western in staff and orientation and did not give adequate attention to the Third World. There were also the criticisms that it was not open to the pacifist witness and that the staff tended to dominate and control section meetings on international affairs at Assembly sessions. In its reconstituted form the Commission continues to be a strong influence in shaping WCC positions.

Martin Luther King, Jr., as Event

Despite its central position in the legacy of the churches entering into the WCC, the negative impact of Hiroshima, the futility of the Korean police action, and the moral scandal of American intervention in Vietnam continued to undermine the reliance on a "just-war" theory for Christians. But the event of Martin Luther King, Jr., from Montgomery to Memphis put nonviolence as theological and applied ethics at the new center of creative thinking of the WCC. King put the civil rights struggle against structural racism and the protest against the Indochina War together coherently with his dynamic view of agape, a standpoint which emerged from his pilgrimage into nonviolence while a doctoral student at Boston University. He achieved international acclaim in being awarded the Nobel Peace Prize. Then the WCC invited him to be the preacher in the Protestant cathedral at Geneva during the Church and Society Study Conference in 1966, which, as we have noted, wrestled with liberation and revolution. Though unable to be personally present to deliver the sermon because of the civil rights crisis in Chicago, the eloquence of the vacant pulpit—the sermon was taped, flown to Geneva, and broadcast—fired the moral imagination of many delegates. In 1968 he was again invited to speak, this time before the Uppsala Assembly, but he had by this time been assassinated during the garbage-workers' strike in Memphis, Tennessee. Martyrdom has always had its unique power within Christian tradition.

King had an activist ecumenical conception of the meaning of nonviolent love. As expounded in *Stride toward Freedom*,[7] he showed that it was no abstract principle, but an existential commitment to Christ and a personalistic interpretation of God. Christians must be educated and trained for such a life of love in action. Churches should be proving grounds for supranational efforts to raise up the poor and oppressed from the bottom. Through the churches a new solidarity and a new sense of hope can be communicated to the powerless. King's civil rights campaigns in the U.S.A. became ecumenical events far beyond the borders of Protestants. He argued that agape nonviolence is *(a)* not a method for cowards; *(b)* it does not seek to defeat or humiliate the opponent; *(c)* it is against forces of evil rather than persons who do the evil; *(d)* it means willingness to accept suffering without retaliation; *(e)* it avoids not only external violence but also violence of spirit; and *(f)* it is done out of agape as a way of life, not a stratagem, and trusts in God, the unity of humankind, and objective justice in history.

The Uppsala Assembly resolved to do the following:

> 3. encourage the member-churches to continue to bring his example before their members with the aim of deepening their own Christian witness;
> 4. ask the Central Committee to explore means by which the World Council could promote studies on non-violent methods of achieving social change, bearing in mind that the issue of using violent or non-violent means has been raised in the Reports of Sections III, IV and V.[8]

Two programs developed: the Programme to Combat Racism and the renewed more general dialogue on "Violence, Non-violence, and the Struggle for Justice." Unanimity on this latter issue in a revolutionary age was not to be achieved. Indeed, the struggle has been fervent, beginning at Zagorsk, Soviet Union (1968), between activists for whom nonviolence was integral to Christian obedience and others who saw it as a sell-out to the status quo.

In the ensuing debate still in progress pacifists have tended to make certain points: (1) Too much stress is being placed on structures and not enough on the attitudes of people, though structural violence is a reality in oppression. (2) Without changed consciousness any new political leadership will become as oppressive and self-serving as the old. (3) The idea of changing social structures by the seizure of power is romantic and underestimates the ambiguities of political and social systems unless there is at the outset a concrete idea of what the future society will look like. (4) Changing social structures by violence does not of itself provide for the continuities of social structures, without which chaos intervenes. (5) Changing social structures alone does not recognize the cultural continuities that persist even when political change has been effected. 6. The use of violence tends to overlook the moral relations of means and ends both as process and as resultant institutional outcome. 7. Since violence is instrumental by nature it can be rationally justified only if it pursues short-term goals, for a society cannot be built on violence, but only on power. 8. Since the goal of liberation is development, and development is a long-term process, those who hold power through violence are in a contradictory position.

The Nairobi Assembly and Peace

The Fifth Assembly (1975) was convened on the fiftieth anniversary of the Stockholm Conference. The theme of peace was integral to all Section Reports from "Confessing Christ Today" to "Human Development: Ambiguities of Power, Technology, and Quality of Life." Throughout there was a realistic appreciation of what a peace witness means when the Christian community experiences itself as a minority commissioned to proclaim the gospel of Christ to the ends of the earth and simultaneously "commanded to struggle to realize God's will for peace, justice, and freedom throughout society." Humankind had experienced one hundred wars since the close of World War II. The contradiction that existed between a nuclear confrontation of the superpowers and any formulation of "just-war" ethics was obvious. Gone was the "just-war" dominance in social ethical theory as at Oxford (1937). It would be an error to affirm that Nairobi embraced a Christian pacifism like that of the Church in the first three centuries. Yet, it would be correct to state that the WCC is struggling with Christ's nonviolent way in all human struggles for justice.

The peace testimony of the WCC is activist. This activism transcends both violence and nonviolence:

> We find hope where churches, whatever the cultural context, confess Christ by standing for that which is truly human, where Christians 'bear the marks of Christ' among suffering humankind, where churches address public issues in the name of Christ, and where communities of Christians are radically changing their life style as a sign of their discipleship.[9]

Confessing Christ today means "that the Spirit makes us struggle with *all* the issues this Assembly has talked about."[10] For many, confessing Christ is practically the same thing as involvement in struggles for justice and freedom. Pacifism in such a confession is the opposite of passivism or withdrawal.

Peace relates also to the Faith and Order question of what "unity" requires. Here it was noted that the Church's unity is lived in the tension of political struggle.[11] At the Eucharist all are equal and thus the Church is the place where people with sharply opposed commitments can meet at the foot of the cross within the divine mercy which sustains them all. The company of Christians is under Christ's discipline. Both individual Christians and the Church as a whole are under the discipline of truth, ethics, and obedience, including political decision making.

> To do this is not to 'politicize' the Church. Rather, the Church is politicized when it is so tied to a party or government, a class or an ideology, that it is not free so to speak or act.[12]

When the Assembly turned to the common search of people of various faiths, cultures, and ideologies the element of peace played a prominent role. Whereas in some former periods of history these diverse faiths, cultures, and ideologies had been sources of military conflict, and whereas they are still factors which often reinforce hostility, the ecumenical movement seeks what is common, for a deeper ethos that leads to peace. Christians are a minority in the world, but their vocation is to seek a community which is broader than the Church or their Christian culture. The task is urgent:

> Whether we like it or not, we find ourselves thrown in with all humanity in a common concern for peace and justice. We have been thrown together in an interdependent world, in which the urgency is that of survival or extinction.[13]

A righteous and peaceful society requires dialogue. Cooperation is a necessity. "Authentic dialogue is a human and Christian undertaking in its own right."[14] The starting point for dialogue is often the common concerns of society.

In the search for community that transcends cultures one must come to terms with both what is universal and what is particular, with both the worldview and the way of life of a people. A common concern is the wide-ranging effects of technological culture, including the kind of secularity which dehumanizes as it urbanizes the crossroads of world society. "Though technological culture is international, it is not the final answer to the quest for wider community."[15] The place of Jesus Christ in the tendencies toward cultural imperialism is here worthy of note. Jesus came as an historical person and shared a specific culture. Yet, "no culture is closer to Jesus Christ than any other culture." "He offers us liberation from attitudes of cultural superiority and from self-sufficiency." "Jesus Christ restores what is truly human in any culture and frees us to be open to other cultures."[16]

Among the dialogues that need to take place in a world struggling for justice are the ideological ones, including those between Marxist atheists and Christians and between the multiform socialisms and the plurality of capitalist economic and political ideologies. Although Christians cannot remain neutral in the struggle for justice, they do not necessarily take sides ideologically. They must understand the various kinds of ideology and their functions. Christians everywhere are called to examine the presuppositions of ideology and the relationship of faith to ideology.

One of the aims of such study and dialogue in the interest of a peaceful world community is to remove all caricatures and misrepresentations of other peoples' faiths, cultures, and ideologies so that there can be mutual trust. The WCC Assembly recommended:

> Actual collaboration between people of different faiths, cultures, and ideologies, in commonly organized programmes in a specific area of promoting social justice and human dignity; this may be organized either between people of different religious convictions or ideological persuasions, or both, depending on the circumstances.[17]

Such perspectives and recommendations have profound implications for education, particularly education for liberation and community building. People cannot be truly liberated if they are divorced from the culture which bred them. The way to development which assures peace requires an educational policy that is critical of the strengths and weaknesses of various developmental strategies. The WCC calls attention to the fact that

> education in too many societies is a consciously used instrument of power: designed to produce those who accept and serve the system; designed to prevent the growth of a critical consciousness which would lead people to want alternatives.[18]

The principle that ties such education to the struggles to overcome the structures of injustice and to achieve liberation is the right of all people to participate in their own development. To follow Christ in such a vocation means to be committed to the cause of the poor, oppressed, and rejected. Not only must particular rights be upheld and specific denials of them abolished, but unjust social structures must be reconstructed, e.g., economic exploitation, political manipulation, military power, class domination, racism, sexism, psychological conditioning, and alienation. As part of the contributing factors which inhibit peace and the just and sustainable society are the structures which favor the rich nations' control of a large proportion of the world's resources and markets, the exploitation of poor nations by transnational corporations, and the patterns of exploitative land ownership. A precondition, therefore, of the guarantee of fundamental human rights and the participation of groups and individuals in decision making is the creation of the foundation which is in the interest of all segments of society. Of particular concern are the status of women, industrial and rural workers, and minority groups.

This philosophy of peace holds that the interdependence of oppressive factors must be matched by a strategy of interdependence and coordination of the forces of liberation for a just and sustainable community. This means, inter alia, that since a large proportion of the world's wealth and scientific and technical labor goes into weapons and military technology, the churches must openly work against the increasing deployment of these resources to such destructive purposes.[19] To these ends the Nairobi

Assembly underscored both the importance of the Helsinki Accords on human rights and renewed the call for worldwide disarmament. The cult of militarism must be as sacrificially resisted in the twentieth century as the cult of Caesar was in the early Church; and disarmament is part of that action.

In underscoring the Helsinki Accords the WCC appealed "to the signatory governments to implement it without delay and in all its parts."[20] One of the responsibilities of the churches is to make clear that security and the development of genuinely human relations across frontiers go together. To this end "nonviolent structures are also needed for the settlement of disputes between nations."[21] The churches are to be realistic in recognizing the power of evil seen in individual and collective egotism, distrust, and the search for power; and yet peace demands the willingness to admit one's own faults and the preparedness to give up one's own position. Indeed, the churches should show forth the implications of reconciliation for the relationships of nations in their own interrelationships. Naturally, the ecumenical assembly was particularly concerned about human rights and religious liberty. It was as well "to prevent a new era of 'cold war.' "[22]

Because of the enormous scope and distortion of the armament situation and the need for disarmament in nuclear and conventional weapons, the WCC was particularly emphatic in treating this peace theme. The Church is concerned for the peaceful development of Asia, Africa, and Latin America; and so it contrasted the equivalence of actual world military spending of hundreds of billions of U.S. dollars and the national income of more than a billion people in the developing countries.

> The bulk of this expenditure—82 percent in 1973—is shared by NATO and Warsaw Pact nations. China accounts for about 5 percent. In addition to the monetary expenditures, the figures represent a tremendous waste of the world's natural resources.[23]

The question is not only one of waste but also of military power in the form of maintaining zones of influence by the superpowers in many parts of the world. Within the framework of the balance of power, arms have been used in Africa, Asia, Latin America, and the Middle East. A consequence of this logic of competitive dominance has been the use of military equipment to repress popular forces.

> Thus the cycle is complete: the arms produced in the metropolis (of the great powers) become tools of control and domination, within the respective zones of influence, of the peoples of the dependent countries.[24]

Militarists are playing a determinate role in processes of economic growth and social organization, thus proving not to be appropriate agents for the full liberation of people. Military power is thus the enemy of people's power. Nairobi decried the cancerous growth of military research and development, the shift in the arms race from quantitative competition to a qualitative revolution in weaponry, the failure of deterrence to slow down the arms race, the increased danger of proliferation of military bases, and the alarming militarization of the Third World. "The Third World, China excluded, accounts for 7 to 9 percent of world military expenditure, nearly three times the level of official foreign development assistance."[25] Armaments and militarization have often contributed to shifting development priorities, weakening and stifling economic growth, and checking socio-political strength.

The effect of the present military situation is to intensify the propensity to over-perception, over-reaction, and over-design. This propensity is reinforced by the growing military-industrial-bureaucratic establishments. In these contexts outlined above, three appeals in the strategy of the churches are noteworthy: (1) the churches should emphasize their readiness to live without the protection of armaments, (2) disarmament should be made a major concern of the WCC, and (3) there should be a call for a world disarmament conference under U.N. auspices. The U.N. addressed this latter question in 1977–78.

Taking everything into account over a fifty-year period from Stockholm to Nairobi we are led to conclude that the WCC is not a pacifist organization, but its general positions on questions of war and peace are closer to pacifism today than at any time in its history. The theology and ethic of nonviolent participation in the struggle for liberation and justice are more seriously debated as the distinctive Christian position than at any previous time. There is a convergence of understanding between pacifists and non-pacifists on the interdependence of many factors that make for the resolution of global conflict.

Notes

1. WCC: 1975 Assembly Document, Section V, "Structures of Injustice and Struggles for Liberation, How Does Christ Set Free?" p. 45.

2. See Keith D. Suter, "The Christian and Militarism," *Ecumenical Review* 30 (April 1978): 131.

3. *The Uppsala Report, 1968* (Geneva: World Council of Churches, 1968), p. 64.

4. O. Frederick Nolde, "Ecumenical Action in International Affairs," in Harold E. Fey, ed., *The Ecumenical Advance* (Philadelphia: Westminster, 1970), p. 273.

5. *The New Delhi Report, 1961* (London: SCM Press, 1962), par. 64, p. 108.

6. Quoted in Paul Bock, *In Search of a Responsible World Society* (Philadelphia: Westminster Press, 1974), p. 110.

7. Martin Luther King,Jr., *Stride Toward Freedom: The Montgomery Story* (New York: Harper and Row, 1958).

8. *The Uppsala Report*, 1968, p. 270.

9. *Breaking Barriers: Nairobi, 1975* (Grand Rapids, Mich.: WCC and

Eerdmans, 1976), p. 47.

10. Ibid., p. 48.
11. Ibid., p. 63.
12. Ibid.
13. Ibid., p. 74.
14. Ibid., p. 77.
15. Ibid., p. 78.
16. Ibid., p. 79.
17. Ibid., p. 85.
18. Ibid., p. 89.
19. Ibid., p. 127.
20. Ibid., p. 172.
21. Ibid., p. 173.
22. Ibid., p. 174.
23. Ibid., p. 180.
24. Ibid., p. 132.
25. Ibid., p. 181.

10
The Beatitudes, the Works of Mercy, and Pacifism

Eileen Egan

Christians nod in the direction of the Beatitudes, recognizing that they are, together with the Sermon on the Mount of which they are a part, the very core of the message of Jesus. The followers of Jesus acknowledge that here is found the ideal of the Christian life, the life that is the sign of the reign of God.

The Shock of the Beatitudes

The implications of the Beatitudes for our time are as shocking as they were on that day when Jesus opened his mouth to speak on a hill overlooking the Sea of Galilee. Yes, shocking—because Jesus said happiness was not to be found where most expected it and because it was to begin in day-to-day living, not postponed until some future date. This is particularly clear in the Gospel of Luke, in which Jesus used the expression "rejoice and dance for joy" to describe the reaction of those who might have to undergo all manner of abuse on his account.[1] The word "blessed," used in earlier translations, came to be absorbed almost completely into a finalistic sense, assigning all happiness to a future beyond time. Scripture scholars point out that the Hebrew *baruch* carried the implications of present welfare, seen as the reward for the faithful carrying out of the law; the Greek *makarios* had the connotation of happy and fortunate, of being free from care and suffering, and was thus applied to the gods of Greece; the Latin *beatus* meant happy in the here and now.[2] Among Christians, the word took on the meaning of spiritual happiness, the happiness that flows from abiding in God's law and from the hope this gives of future happiness. In true happiness, the future does impinge on the present, for the Christian lives both in time and in eternity. The term "happy," however, as used in the Beatitudes, is not robbed of its reality for daily living and the later translations beginning with "Happy are . . ." reflect this.[3]

Those who accepted Jesus came to see happiness shining through the "present-future" screen, the holy paradox repeated eight times in the Beatitudes in Matthew's Gospel. Each Beatitude presents a paradox which must be incorporated into the relationships and events that make up the daily lives of Christ's followers. With eyes opened to a new vision of the reign of God, they can see happiness warming the hearts of the "poor in spirit," "the meek," "those that mourn," "those that hunger and thirst after justice," "the clean of heart," "the merciful," "the peacemakers," and those "that suffer persecution for justice' sake."

In dealing with the Beatitudes and pacifism, the focus will be narrowed to those Beatitudes that bear most directly on the issue of pacifism. For the purpose of this discussion, pacifism is used in the root meaning of the verb, "to make peace" and the pacifist as "maker of peace." Catholic pacifists, including this writer, have often omitted the word "pacifist" from their vocabulary because of the common connotation of passivity. Pacifists were seen as persons who surfaced only in wartime, claiming for themselves the right not to defend the society whose benefits they enjoyed in peace time. This was particularly true of the Catholic community, where the role of pacifists was viewed as that of doing nothing at all rather than sharing the dangers of those who were drafted to "lay down their lives" for their country. Pacifism was seen as a form of quietism allowing evils to go unchecked. The active nature of "making peace, " of reconciling differences through creative initiative, has not yet reached large numbers of the Roman Catholic faithful.

This writer's experience indicates that the common misunderstanding of pacifism, as a word and as a position, is also current in European countries and in such Asian countries as Vietnam. Christian pacifists are those who conceive of their vocation as one of reconciliation—after the example of their Master. They actively pursue reconciliation, the settling of disputes and the righting of wrongs by nonviolent means which might involve the acceptance, but never the infliction, of suffering on others. Thus the option of participating in actions calling for the injuring or killing of other human beings is excluded. This would include the legalized killing of criminals called capital punishment as well as the legalized killing of enemies in the social organization of mass killing called war. What aids pacifists in their commitment to accept suffering is the central message of Jesus, that of love which overleaps the usual human barriers of family, tribe, nation, friend, or foe to become universal. While there is basic agreement among Christian pacifists on the matter of the intentional injuring or killing of other humans, there is some difference regarding the use of force as applied to criminals or to the demented. This writer agrees with a large segment of the pacifist community (including, incidentally, Mahatma Gandhi) in the necessity for a police force with its powers of restraint.[4] There are also degrees of absolutism in the pacifist position which cannot be analyzed here.

To return to that day when the Beatitudes were first given to Jesus' disciples—what would be likely to fall most shockingly on their ears? They had followed Jesus from Galilee, the Ten Towns, Jerusalem, Judea, and beyond the Jordan only to hear strange prescriptions for happiness as a beginning of many more hard sayings. The strangest and most shocking of the prescriptions for happiness was surely "Happy are the meek; for they shall possess the land." People, mourning under the occupation of a pagan empire, had lived in the expectation of a Messiah who would come in power and restore the Kingdom of Israel. All around them were the occupation troops of Rome, lording it over them, humiliating them, and executing them when they revolted for freedom. Now they were told that the meek, the gentle, the lowly would possess the land—and they were to be happy about it.

Such an assertion must have assaulted their ears because they, the carriers of the word of God, were ready for a Messiah-king who would put to rout their enemies with consuming fire in a war of liberation. Into such a war they could fling themselves with wild joy. The Messianic war, in which God's wrath would expunge the enemy, was expected as the culmination of the holy-war experience of the Israelites. At a time when the Roman Empire had all the might of arms and soldiery, the intervention of the Almighty through the Messiah would be the climactic point of the history recounted in the Hebrew Scriptures. Instead, they were told of the very opposite of the war of liberation. They were faced with a message that could ensure the continuance of the dreadful, grinding reality of occupation. The occupation might not be lifted in their time at all, but in the mysterious time of the Almighty. If such teaching were followed, the only means of liberation they knew would be withdrawn. Could this Galilean be the Promised One? Even among those who accepted Jesus as the Promised One, the longing for the restoration of the kingdom died hard. After witnessing the crucifixion and the resurrection, the Apostles still placed the question before Jesus, "Lord, has the time come? Are you going to restore the Kingdom of Israel?"[5]

Almost as an epiphany of his attitude toward the occupier, an attitude precluding Messianic war, Jesus followed the Sermon on the Mount by heeding the appeal of the centurion, a good centurion, to be sure. The humility and utter faith of the centurion that Jesus' power could obliterate distance, and that his word alone could heal without his actual presence, caused Jesus to marvel and to contrast such faith with that of many in Israel.

The Beatitudes and Pacifism

For modern Christians, the Beatitudes do not seem to have the immediate shock value that they had in the setting of an occupied country. They are too often accepted, whether the translation be "Blessed are" or "Happy are," as bland openings to a bland sermon. Their implications are not plumbed, since they put in question a specious morality, far from that of Jesus. Two Beatitudes have an especially direct relationship to pacifism, the most obvious being, "Happy are the peacemakers: for they shall be called the children of God."[6] The followers of Jesus have his life as the model of the peacemaker, the one who made peace between humanity and God through the blood of the cross. Jesus' method of nonviolence, of accepting suffering, though innocent, when he could have called on the power of legions of angels, is the method he has left to those who claim to follow him. The last act of healing performed by Jesus was to undo the work of Peter's sword—in restoring the ear severed by Peter. Could there be a clearer disavowal of defense by the sword than the command to Peter to put away his sword although it was raised to protect one about to be unjustly executed? In plumbing the ultimate meaning of this Beatitude, might we not put the question thus: if the peacemakers are the children of God, whose children are the warmakers? Warmakers are surely not the soldiers snatched from their homes to join in organized killing, but those who have the power to plan and declare hostilities and to dragoon others into prosecuting them. Jesus does not tell us whose children the real warmakers are, but he does tell us their end. This we learn in one of his most fateful warnings. After ordering Peter to sheath his sword, he announced that "all who draw the sword will die by the sword."[7] It has remained for the nuclear age to reveal the dread reality of this warning.

The second Beatitude with a direct relationship to pacifism is "Happy are the merciful: for they shall obtain mercy." This fifth Beatitude reaches the heart of the Christian message.[8] Mercy is love under the aspect of need, love going out to meet the needs of the person loved. The person to whom mercy is shown has one identity, as we learn from the parable of thc Last Judgment. Jesus is the hungry one; he is the one who thirsts; he is the naked one; the homeless one, the one suffering from disease, the imprisoned one. Thus, whenever we meet another's need, we meet the very person of the Savior. Why should we be so concerned about having mercy shown us by the Creator when we live ordered lives and attempt to follow the way of Jesus? For the simplest of reasons; we are all beggars before God, all weak, all sinners. Our happiness lies, then, only in the acceptance of our powerlessness and our confidence in the ultimate mercy of God.

War faces the Christian with the question as to whether Jesus taught love, and its expression in the works of mercy, as a sometime thing. Can there be times when Christians are justified in a suspension of the works of mercy for those in need of merciful aid? Can there be a moratorium on feeding the hungry, giving drink to the thirsty, clothing the naked, sheltering the homeless, and visiting the sick and imprisoned?

The answer provided by those who consider warfare, any warfare, acceptable activity for Christians is in the affirmative. Merciful relationships, they believe, between human beings can be set aside from time to time by reason of a state of war. As long as the war lasts, the moratorium on the works of mercy for those who are called enemies is a necessity accepted by most Christians.

War and the Works of Mercy

In the earlier wars that have marked European history, the works of mercy were interrupted for the duration of the conflict. Since battles were conducted by knights and picked or volunteer soldiery, there was some inbuilt immunity for noncombatants. Battles could rage in a limited area while farmers, tanners, weavers, and shepherds went about their daily tasks. Nor were their sons conscripted for battle. Destruction was limited because even lengthy wars were waged between groups of society smaller than the nation-state—between cities, city-states, princely states, and fiefdoms. Even brutal siege-warfare, in which there was no distinction between combatant and noncombatant for the duration of the siege, did not end in the massacre of noncombatants once the siege was lifted. There were in Europe no massacres to match that of the inhabitants of Isfahan, in Persia, by Tamerlane, who put at least 70,000 to the sword and made a hill of their skulls. The works of mercy that were interrupted in European warfare were, of course, feeding the hungry, giving drink to the thirsty, clothing the naked, and caring for the sick.

This writer, in years spent in the physical debris of modern war and among the world's refugees, who could be called the human debris of war, came upon the reality that the works of mercy are not merely interrupted but, in an obscene way, reversed. It is not sufficient, in modern war, to interrupt the flow of food to the hungry among the enemy population; technical means are at hand to scorch the earth that produces food. In World War II this was done by Hitler's armies when they met reverses on the Eastern European and Russian fronts. When peace came to France after World War II, three hundred thousand hectares (about 750,000 acres) of crop-producing land were still mined—a consequence of a Nazi strategy that spread hunger among the civilian population long after all fighting had ceased. Polish farmers and their children, returning to the works of peace in a devastated land, were often killed by buried mines. Many lost hands or feet or were blinded when the earth yielded lethal weapons.

In Vietnam, crop destruction was achieved by spraying with herbicides in "area denial" programs which cut off food supplies to opposing forces. Extensive areas of paddyland yielded no rice, and other crops were lost. A petition for compensation by six Vietnamese farmers, whose farms were sprayed in South Vietnam, explained, "We are people who live by farming alone and have fallen into a deficient, indigent situation. . . . American military performed this by planes spreading chemicals. . . . The effect has made various types of fruit trees lose their leaves, ruined fruit and crops such as green beans, white beans, peanuts, soybeans and black beans lose their leaves and then die."[9] Not only are the hungry not fed, but hunger is prepared for present and perhaps future generations.

When World War II was nearing its end, the Allied Forces trumpeted one of their most important strategic victories, the destruction by bombardment of one of Europe's largest reservoirs. The destruction of the reservoir was not incidental to mass bombing and no effort was made to justify it under the principle of the "double effect" whereby the bombing of military targets has an unintended secondary effect of injuring civilian life. The bombardment was carefully planned to deal a mortal blow to civilian life in the Frankfurt area of Germany and thus hasten the end of the war. The reservoir was a prized target and its bombardment an acceptable mode of warfare. Those who planned it were commended. A whole area was to be deprived of a regular water supply, not only homes, but hospitals and institutions for children, the aged, and the infirm. Rather than give drink to the thirsty, such methods of warfare bring thirst to the many. This bombardment offers itself as a symbol of the reversal of the works of mercy—a reversal to which both sides were a party in World War II and in succeeding conflicts in Korea and Vietnam.

Rather than shelter the homeless, modern war destroys in minutes the shelters that humankind has constructed over generations. Millions more are driven from their shelters to wander the roads of the world as refugees. When the Soviet Union entered eastern Poland in 1939 in the pact with Nazism, it proceeded to deport at least a million and a half inhabitants of eastern Poland to Siberia and Asiatic Russia. The survivors of the trek who found their way out of Soviet territory were scattered around the earth to settle in any country that would accept them. Their part of the Polish homeland was incorporated into the Soviet Union. At the end of World War II, more than fifteen million Germans and ethnic Germans were expelled from their homes in one of the most brutal mass expulsions of history. The people involved in the transfer into destroyed Germany were not soldiers but the civilian population, including large numbers of the aged and children. Since World War II, conflicts in India, China, Korea, Vietnam, and the Middle East have generated at least twenty-five million homeless refugees, tossed about the world like "loose grains of sand."

Rather than clothe the naked, those who participate in modern war have a part in razing the plants where cloth is produced or clothing manufactured; rather than healing the sick, they help destroy the very centers in which the healing arts are practiced. Such medicaments as are needed from the outside for the civilians of the opposing side are blockaded. Rather than visit prisoners or ransom captives, the aim of modern armies is to make captives of as many of the enemy as possible. This applies to civilians who are interned for a war's duration.

Christians are urged to perform a sixth work of mercy, namely to bury the dead. This work of mercy is honored in the Hebrew Scriptures and in other religious traditions. To make the unspeakable cycle of reversals complete, the bombardments of modern war unbury the dead and disinter them from their supposedly "last" resting-places. One of the best-known examples of this was the blasting of the tombs in the cemetery of San Lorenzo-Outside-the-Walls in the Allied bombing of Rome in World War II. In the wake of World War II, the writer visited the village of Pournoyla-Chetive, Lorraine, France. Here, not only was every building smashed through air and ground bombardment by German forces, but the graves in the cemetery were opened and the bones of the dead exposed to the light. Homeless families turned to the re-building of their homes and farms only after they had completed the task of re-burying their forebears.

If Christians turn away from the works of mercy, how can they call with confidence on the mercy of God? If, as Jesus makes clear in the Beatitude, the merciful are happy because their poor mercy is a shadow of the limitless mercy they need from their Creator, is it not a supremely perilous enterprise to interrupt the works of mercy? When the works of war reverse and make a hideous travesty of the works of mercy, how can Christians justify taking part in them?

The remainder of the Sermon on the Mount, following on the Beatitudes, only reinforces the message of love and mercy. Jesus enunciates a break with the morality of the time in saying, "You have heard that it was said, 'Love your friends and hate your enemies.' But now I tell to you: love your enemies and pray for those who mistreat you, so that you will become sons of your Father in heaven."[10] This is only one of the many "contradictions" which serve to buttress the message of love by breaking with contemporary morality, contemporary to Jesus as it is to the twentieth century. These contradictions include: not demanding restitution for wrong, not resisting evil and insult by the usual methods but by turning the other cheek to the striker; not withholding one's coat from the snatcher but relinquishing one's cloak as well, and not refusing to go the forced mile but instead being willing to go two miles.

While the Beatitudes in a direct way picture the "new creature" called for by the Good News, the contradictions delineate the contrast between the "old creature," giving the expected response to evil and unjust deeds, and the "new creature" of the gospel. It is the "new creature," reborn in Christ, and springing from the "old creature" buried with Christ in baptism, who can incarnate the new responses. Imbedded in the contradictions is the Christian way of expunging evil, overcoming it by good in the spirit of love.

How can Christians, knowing that they will be judged on love and on the expression of love through the works of mercy for friend and enemy, be dragooned into massive reversals of the works of mercy? How could they have come to accept and justify a moratorium on the works of love by order of the secular power, whether prince, king, president, or elected body?

Pacifism and Early Christianity

The response of the early Christians to war and bloodshed of all kinds is documented in their lives and deaths as well as in the writings of the Church Fathers. There is hardly a work on Christians and war which fails to give the reason given by Maximilian the Martyr for his refusal of military service.

Conscripted because his father was a Roman army veteran, Maximilian explained his conscientious objection saying, "I cannot serve as a soldier; I cannot do evil. I am a Christian."[11] The Proconsul before whom the case was heard, then pronounced sentence, "Because you have with a rebellious spirit refused to bear arms, you shall die by the sword." Maximilian was twenty-one years old when he was beheaded in 295. His body was taken from the place of execution and buried beside the martyred St. Cyprian in Carthage.

Another young man, conscripted because his father was in the Roman army, became a Christian while in the army. He was Martin of Tours, who remained in the army even after his conversion. It is reported that there were Christians in the Roman army at that date, about the middle of the fourth century. Their function was chiefly that of policemen, guards, and firemen. Martin's decision to break with the army came just before he was to take part in battle against the barbarian invaders of Gaul. His revulsion against the necessity to shed blood moved him to request separation from the service. Julian Caesar, to whom he made the request, accused him of simple cowardice. Martin's reason was, "I am a soldier of Christ and it is not lawful for me to fight."[12] Martin offered to stand unarmed in the battle line and even to approach the invaders alone in the name of Christ. He was imprisoned but was freed after a short time because an armistice was signed with the invaders. The only recorded use of Martin's sword was his renowned act of shearing in two his army cloak to cover with one half the shivering body of a beggar. It is a powerful symbol not simply of Christian charity but of the turning of an implement of war to the use of mercy. The tomb of St. Martin at Tours has become one of the great pilgrimage places of Western Europe.

Lactantius, the North African theologian whose life-span covered the years 240 to 320, condemned not only violence but the legal violence of war and in addition warned Christians against accusing anyone of a capital crime which might result in his execution. In the same section of *Divine Institutes* he describes the duties of the Christian in terms which reflect the fifth Beatitude's reminder that it is the merciful who may expect mercy. "On account of this relationship of brotherhood, God teaches us never to do evil, but always good. And he also prescribes in what this doing good consists: in affording aid to those who are oppressed and in difficulty, and in bestowing food on those who are destitute. For God, since he is kind, wished us to be a social animal. Therefore in the case of other men, we ought to think of ourselves. We do not deserve to be set free in our own dangers if we do not succor others; we do not deserve assistance if we refuse to render it."[13]

The Christian Justification of War

One of the most powerful defenses for the lack of Christian participation in war is offered by Origen, Egyptian philosopher and son of a Christian martyr. This was formulated in his reply to Celsus, a pagan Platonist, who, among other things, accused the Christian community of enjoying the benefits of Roman order without accepting the obligation of defending it by arms. The Christian abhorrence of bloodshed evoked from Origen many strong arguments, one of which adverted to the exemption of pagan priests from the duty to shed blood. In *Against Celsus,* we read: "And to these enemies of our faith, who require us to bear arms for the commonwealth and to slay men, we can reply: 'Do not those who are priests at certain shrines, and those who attend on certain gods as you account them, keep their hands free from blood, that they may with hands unstained and free from human blood offer the appointed sacrifices to your gods; and even when war is upon you, you never enlist the priests in the army. If that, then, is a laudable custom, how much more so that while others are engaged in battle, these too should engage as the priests and ministers of God, keeping their hands pure, and wrestling in prayers on behalf of those who are fighting in a righteous cause. . . . And none fight better for the king than we do. We do not indeed fight under him, although he require it; but we do fight on his behalf, forming a special army—an army of piety—by offering on his behalf our prayers to God."[14]

Many Catholic apologists for war participation by the faithful have attempted to explain away the pacifism of the early Christians by attributing their refusal of soldiery to the fact that idolatry was involved in the taking of a military oath and in participation in sacrificial rites or by the argument that the Christians expected an early end to the world and therefore could not be concerned with the defense of an earthly kingdom. Other apologists for the role of the Christian soldier attribute the pacifism of these Christians to the fact that Rome persecuted them and they therefore could not defend so unjust a state. Such apologists do not deal with the reasoning of individuals such as Lactantius and Origen, whose arguments rise above the circumstantial and rest on the bedrock of the gospel of Jesus.

A time was soon to come, however, when Christians would be allowed by the Church to cross over from the special army, the army that shed no blood but prayed for a righteous cause, to an army that killed and died for a righteous cause.

It was a fateful turning point in the history of Christianity, and like many such turning points, it happened quietly and entered Christian life as if by stealth. The changeover owed much to the influence of classical Roman philosophers on Christian thinkers as well as to the improved situation of the Christians within the Roman Empire. Three Church Fathers reflect the crucial changeover: Eusebius, the Greek church historian; Ambrose, born in Trier in the Rhineland and renowned bishop of Milan; and St. Augustine, the great North African Doctor of the Church who became bishop of Hippo. Eusebius lived during the era of Constantine; Ambrose and Augustine lived under the successors of Constantine.

Eusebius, in 313, asserted that the Christian might engage in a just war, and listed it as one of the pursuits of the righteous life, including a pure marriage, farming, trade, or civic tasks. The "two moralities" enter here, since the clergy are barred from the bloodshed of a just war as they are from marriage and the concerns of the world.[15]

What a contrast this is to the answer given by St. Justin the Martyr to the Emperor Antoninus Pius in the second century. He asserted that Christians accepted the obligations of citizenship and of productive work while continuing to abide by the Christian rule that "it was not right to answer fighting by fighting." "It is our special care," Justin explained personally to the Emperor, "to be the first of all to pay our taxes and dues to those whom you have commissioned to receive them. . . . Further though, we adore God alone; but in other matters we gladly serve you, we acknowledge you as kings and rulers of men, and we pray that you may be found to have health of mind together with royal power."[16]

The clear record is that the Christians of the early centuries attempted to live an ethic of love, a positive teaching which commanded the works of love and mercy and abjured the works of war. They made the distinction between the Old Covenant, with its divine sanction of war, and the New Covenant of Jesus Christ. Origen adverts to this in the answer to Celsus, who had evidently familiarized himself with Mosaic law. Admitting that the Jewish nation had been permitted to kill its enemies, Origen adds: "But that Providence which once gave the Law, but now has given the Gospel. . . ." He emphasizes the universal mission of Christianity saying, "And because God desired the doctrine of Jesus Christ to benefit all nations, all the counsels of men against the Christians have been brought to nought; and the more emperors, rulers of nations and peoples persecuted them, the more has their number increased."[17]

The persecution which had struck at Origen's own family broke out again between 303 and 313 from one end of the Roman Empire to the other. The Christian community suffered one of the bloodiest onslaughts ever inflicted on a group of people until the mass murders of the twentieth century. The decrees began with the burning of the Scriptures and Holy Books which the Christians were ordered to hand over; they next called for the destruction of places of worship and ended by inflicting on the Christians every form of torture known, including being thrown to wild beasts and being burnt alive. The aim was to have a unified Empire in which there would be no one who had not sacrificed to the gods of Rome.[18] The humanity of Constantine, who brought the persecution to a close by the Edict of Milan in 313, earned the gratitude of the saved remnant. Many of them had only survived by fleeing to the lonely forests around the Black Sea, to the deserts of the Middle East, and to Armenia and Persia. The memory of this holocaust haunted Christians and the examples of those who had resisted to the death were part of the lessons at liturgical services.

The toleration of Christianity by Constantine, who was baptized on his deathbed, was continued by his successors and Christians became more numerous and many obtained positions of importance within the Empire. The safety of the Empire now had meaning for the future of Christianity. Threats to the Empire by barbarian invaders, many of whom were Arian heretics, called for an ethic by which Christians could resist by arms, by which they could be simultaneously Christians and soldiers. Living the Beatitudes, being merciful to enemies, feeding, clothing, sheltering them and curing their ills—while at the same time joining with others in injuring and killing them: this was the dilemma raised by war's violence. No undergirding for a reconciliation of the opposed modes of conduct could be found in the words of Jesus, in the Christian Gospels, in the experience of early Christians, or in the early Christian commentators.

Ambrose and Augustine went to another source, to the good pagan Cicero. In his treatise *On Duties,* Cicero stated that there are two ways to settle a dispute, "first, by discussion; second, by physical force; and since the former is characteristic of man, the latter of the brute, we must resort to force only in case we may not avail ourselves of discussion. The only excuse, therefore, for going to war is that we may live in peace unharmed; and when the victory is won, we should spare those who have not been bloodthirsty and barbarous in their warfare." Cicero drew on Roman tradition with its requirement that the priestly Fetiales make the declaration of war. He asserted that "no war is just unless it is entered upon after an official demand for satisfaction has been submitted or warning given and a formal declaration made."[19] Righteous grounds for going to war included preserving the faith or safety of a city, protecting the innocent, avenging wrongs, and honoring pledges to allies.

St. Ambrose of Milan had been governor of a northern Italian province before the striking example of his righteousness and justice caused him to be raised to the bishopric by popular demand. Writing in prose similar to that of the great philosopher and politician Cicero, Ambrose took over the concept of the "just war." His borrowings from the Stoic tradition of Cicero are frequent, including the assertion, "He who does not ward off injury from his comrade, when he is able to, is just as guilty as he who does the injury."[20] He praises the virtue of fortitude in a manner vastly different from that of such earlier Christians as Justin, Origen, or Lactantius: "For fortitude, which in war preserves the country from the barbarians, or helps the sick at home, or defends one's neighbors from robbers, is full of justice."[21]

It would be an injustice to Ambrose not to point out that his rich treatment of fortitude rests on the Christian conception that the truest fortitude consists in the conquering of self, in containing anger, in accepting adversity and in becoming an "athlete of Christ." The fortitude proper to war is not the fortitude proper to the clergy "who must be more intent upon the duty of the soul than of the body." The "two moralities" are again stressed, since only the laity are to take part in battles, the life of the clergy being directed "to the business of peace." Ambrose does not hesitate to use examples from the Hebrew Scriptures to justify resort to war under certain circumstances. He wrote, ". . . in the matter of war, care must be taken to see whether the wars are just or unjust. Never did David declare war unless he had first suffered injurious attack."[22]

The great Augustine of Hippo, though he did not write a unified treatise on war and military service, confronted the issues in many of his writings, and particularly in his mammoth *City of God*. The pacifism of the gospel is preserved in Augustine, who is considered to be founder of theology. The Christian who is attacked must prefer to suffer death rather than kill the attacker. The Christian must also obey the command to love the enemy, even attempting to love the enemy more than friends—who, after all, ingratiate themselves by flattery and other actions that may lead to damnation rather than salvation. The personal enemy, on the other hand, causes suffering and thus may bring Christians closer to salvation if they accept the suffering willingly and without hatred or revenge.

Augustine, whose life as bishop of Hippo, near Carthage, was a glorious example of Christian poverty and communal life and whose care for the poor of his diocese was an extraordinary witness to the gospel of his Master, preserved intact the pacifism of the gospel, for Christian clergy as well as for the individual Christian. The clergy, who "occupy a higher place in relation to God" in abandoning all secular employments, fight against invisible enemies by their prayers. They are not to take part in bodily warfare but keep their hands unstained by blood. Thus the "two moralities" are enshrined in Catholic theology.

The Beatitudes and the Sermon on the Mount are to be preserved in the personal life of the Christian at whatever cost. In the *Letter to Marcellinus* Augustine stresses how much concord it brought into daily life by the precepts of the Sermon on the Mount. "That to him who smites us on one cheek we should offer the other to be smitten; to him who would take away our coat we should give our cloak also; and that with him who compels us to go one mile we should go twain. For these things are done only that a wicked man may be overcome by kindness, or rather that the evil which is in the wicked man may be overcome by good, and that the man may be delivered from the evil."[23]

The problem presented to the Christian who goes to battle as a member of an army is resolved by preserving an interior disposition of love. In the *Letter to Boniface,* Count of Africa, who had written to Augustine for advice on giving up the life of the soldier for the religious life, Augustine attempts the reconciliation of the Beatitudes with warmaking: "Therefore, even in waging war, cherish the spirit of the peacemaker, that, by conquering those whom you attack, you may lead them back to the advantages of peace; for our Lord says: 'Blessed are the peacemakers; for they shall be called the children of God.' If, however, peace among men be so sweet as procuring temporal safety, how much sweeter is that peace with God which procures for men the eternal felicity of the angels! Let necessity, therefore, and not your will, slay the enemy who fights against you. As violence is used towards him who rebels and resists, so mercy is due to the vanquished or the captive, especially in the case in which future troubling of the peace is not to be feared."[24]

Thus mercy is to be withheld from the enemy until he is vanquished.

The *Letter to Boniface* was written when North Africa was threatened by the Vandals—invaders whose depredations are so dreadful that the word "vandalism" lives on in the language to perpetuate their infamy.

But the great divide had been crossed. Christians, when it became a question of defending the threatened commonwealth, could take up arms with good conscience.

Augustine accepted from Cicero that war is fought to secure peace and that it must be declared by lawful authority, "for the natural order which seeks the peace of mankind, ordains that the monarch should have the power of undertaking war if he thinks it advisable and that the soldiers should perform their duties on behalf of the peace and safety of the community." He asserts that a righteous man may serve an ungodly king and may even carry out an unrighteous command and still remain blameless "because his position makes obedience a duty."[25] Justice is a basic concern of Augustine and thus wars may sometimes be required to restore justice and to avenge a wrong. "Just wars," he writes, "are usually defined as those which avenge injuries, when the nation or city against which warlike action is to be directed has neglected either to punish wrongs committed by its own citizens or to restore what has been unjustly taken from it."[26] Given the special situation of Christian citizens in a society that had become a bulwark against barbarian onslaught, one can view the introduction of the "just-war" ethic, with its warrant for participation in the military defense of that society, as a response of "situation ethics."

Augustine's pain in confronting evil and war, and the evil of war, bursts through from time to time, as in this section from *City of God,* "For it is the opposing party which compels the wise man to wage just wars, and this wrongdoing, even though it gave rise to no war, would still be a matter of grief to man because it is man's wrongdoing. Let every one, then, who thinks with pain on all these great evils, so horrible, so ruthless, acknowledge that this is misery."[27]

The Christian abhorrence of bloodshed shines through a letter on war and peace written a year before his death to Darius, an officer of the Roman army who negotiated a truce with the Vandals. The aged saint had lived through the sacking of North Africa and the wanton destruction of churches by these Vandals. He tells Darius: "These features of your character are joyfully seen both by us, and through the mercy of God by yourself also, as in a mirror in the Holy Gospel in which it is written in words uttered by him who is truth: 'Blessed are the peacemakers; for they shall be called the children of God.' " After giving recognition to the bravery of warriors, he says, "But it is a higher glory still to slay war itself with the word than men with the sword, and to procure or maintain peace by peace, not by war. For those who fight, if they are good men, doubtless seek for peace; nevertheless it is through blood. Your mission, however, is to prevent the shedding of blood."[28]

To maintain peace by peace is a foreshadowing of a peace motto attributed to an American pacifist leader of the twentieth century, A. J. Muste, "There is no way to peace. Peace is the way."

Augustine's crucial discussions on war and peace reached all the faculties of law of the early Middle Ages through Gratian of Bologna, a Master of Canon Law. About 1148, he incorporated them in the *Decretals,* which became part of Canon Law. Thus they reached St. Thomas Aquinas, who cites Augustine in his seminal treatment on war in the great *Summa Theologiae*. St. Thomas points out the three conditions for a "just-war," namely, it must be declared by the authority of the prince; there must be a just cause, and the intention should be right. The last point indicates that the intention must be to effect a good or avoid an evil.

In commenting on the argument that war is a sin, being contrary to the divine precept, St. Thomas reminds the Christian about the right disposition of soul: ". . . man ought always to be ready, if necessary, not to resist or not to defend himself. But sometimes we must act otherwise for the common good, and even for the good of those we fight."[29] Here we have a central concept of St. Thomas, an immensely fruitful one in bringing morality into such fields as economics and politics—the common good. We also have the often questioned principle of showing our loving concern for others by opposing them with material weapons. Of three other aspects of war treated by St. Thomas, namely the licitness of fighting on feast days, the use of ambush, and the licitness of engagement in warfare by clergy and bishops, only the last point will be touched on here. The chief reason that bishops and clergy are forbidden to take part in war is that their "clerical Orders are directed to the ministry of the altar on which the Passion of Christ is represented sacramentally according to 1 Corinthians XI:26: 'As often as you shall eat this bread and drink this chalice, you shall show the death of the Lord until he come.' Wherefore it is unbecoming to them to slay or shed blood. And it is more fitting that they should be ready to shed their own blood for Christ so as to imitate in deed what they portray in their ministry."[30] St. Thomas goes on to explain that when their flocks are attacked, bishops must rely on weapons that are not carnal.

Nonviolent response to attack is thus a "counsel of perfection," reserved for those in religious life, bishops, clergy, and monks. For the ordinary faithful, shedding blood in warfare is not against the laws of God since it is done in the spirit of obedience, in pursuit of peace and the common good, and presumably with the right disposition.

Criteria of a Just War

Building on Ambrose, Augustine, Gratian, and Thomas, other theologians, both Catholic and Protestant, have erected a "just-war" edifice, in which seven criteria should be met before a war can be considered "just." These criteria, in addition to the three conditions stated by Thomas, are: war must be the last resort and only means of securing justice; only right means must be employed in the conduct of the war; there must be a reasonable hope of victory; and the good to be achieved must outweigh the probable evil effects of the war.

Theologians have often been termed "merchants of abstraction," and this seems particularly apt in the case of the "just-war" criteria. To be termed "just," a war had to meet every one of the criteria. Since there is no supranational power to hand down a decision on whether a given war is "just," every war declared by every nation is announced as a "just war." Religious hierarchies have associated themselves with the "just wars" of the nation-states to which they belong. In passing, it might be mentioned that an important break with the tradition of having the hierarchy serve as the moral arm of a warring nation occurred when the United States was six years into the Vietnam conflict. The American Catholic hierarchy announced their "moral obligation" to urge an early end to the war since "continued involvement in this war is now outweighed by the destruction of human life and moral values which it inflicts."[31] Applying the seventh condition of the "just war" cited above, the American hierarchy judged that the Vietnam conflict was not a "just war." For the first time in the United States, and possibly in history, a national hierarchy announced as unjust a war being waged by its own nation. It is well to give thought to the fact that in a nuclear war, moral authorities would not have six years to come to such a decision, but would have to make a determination in minutes.

History shows that "right" or "appropriate" means refers to the latest and most lethal weaponry available to the warring nation, from the crossbow which tore the vitals of the individual enemy to the nuclear bomb which cremated alive chiefly noncombatants. It is worth noting that the Catholic Church in the Lateran Council of 1139 did make a moral judgment on means by condemning the crossbow.

This ban fell into disuse as war escaped all moral restraints. The next condemnation of a means of warfare by the Catholic Church came in 1965 when the bishops of the world at Vatican Council II issued the ban on indiscriminate warfare. Without dignifying conventional or nuclear instruments of mass destruction by the name of weapons, the bishops stated in the single ban of the entire Council, "Any act of war aimed indiscriminately at the destruction of entire cities or extensive areas along with their population is a crime against God and man. It merits unequivocal and unhesitating condemnation."[32]

Any war initiated in the era after Hiroshima and Nagasaki, after the fire-bombing of Hamburg and Dresden and the destruction of such cities as Coventry, will be one in which "just-war" criteria are irrelevant and inapplicable. Even so-called limited wars, such as those that may explode in the Middle East, may sooner or later involve the powers who possess conventional weaponry whose use is indiscriminate and nuclear instruments whose power is genocidal. Mercy is annulled. Even those Christians who accepted the "just-war" expected to bring mercy to the vanquished. On our side of the mushroom cloud, it will be impossible to bring the works of mercy to human beings who are incinerated along with their cities, or who, by the even more sophisticated neutron bomb, may perish while their cities remain standing. A recent report from a peace research institute estimates that the world's nuclear arsenals contain tens of thousands of nuclear instruments with a total explosive power equal to about one million Hiroshima bombs.[33] By their cost, these arsenals pre-empt the works of mercy for the needy of humanity.

It can now be seen that the adoption of "just-war" concepts, allowing Christians to take part in warfare, has had fateful results since that turning point in the late fourth century. Some of these effects could hardly have been foreseen before the advent of the great secular states and the power of war technology. Four of these results can be singled out here. First, as already mentioned, the changeover from the pacifism of the early Christians allowed the Christian laity to participate in a suspension of the works of mercy for the duration of wars. The reversals of the works eventually assumed monstrous proportions. Second, the "just war" allowed sovereigns and sovereign states to "rent" their Christians for any of their wars. Christians thus found themselves in the opposing sides of most wars. Even if one side could be considered "just," it was hardly possible for both sides to be so. What was more likely, since the possibility of meeting all the criteria of the "just war" was so remote, was that neither side was just and that Christians were engaged in unjust mutual slaughter. Third, through the "just war," morality in matters military was given to the political power which alone had the right to declare and conduct wars. The power of the nation-state has been immeasurably increased since the comparatively recent institution of universal military conscription. The Christian conscript has been expected to surrender his conscience into the keeping of the state, for as a soldier, his abdication of conscience must be complete. Fourth, the most tragic aspect of the operation of "just-war" thinking is that it effectively displaced love from its centrality in the Christian message and robbed Christianity of its most distinctive teaching, love of enemy. As St. Justin the Martyr enquired in his first *Apologia* on behalf of Christians, "If you love merely those that love you, what do you do that is *new*?"[34] The enemy, who could be expunged for an intermediate, finite, and political end, even where some moral aims were involved, was not seen and loved in his true light, as a being of infinite and ultimate value and a repository of the divine spirit.

Cicero, the good pagan, whose thinking entered Christianity at a crucial and threatening time, has had an immense influence on the entire history of Christianity, and, in fact, on the history of the world. What we see in the wreckage of the planet from past "just wars" in which Christians had a part, and in the threat to its future from the stockpiles of armaments, is the ultimate failure of the "just-war" tradition to bring peace or to right wrongs. What we see is that man who took the sword against his kind, has now perfected a nuclear sword which is anti-creation. The wielder of such a sword can in no way escape its lethal effects. Thus what we are seeing as a result of Christian involvement in the wars of the world is the good pagan's failure.

The only exception to the influence of "just-war" thinking has been the witness of the Christian communities known as the "peace churches" and the witness of the minority of conscientious objectors to war in the Catholic and other Christian churches. Support for such objectors has not been the brightest page in the history of the Catholic Church.

A Return to Origins

Where can Christians turn in the "post-just-war" age? The answer would seem to be a return to the witness of the "pre-just-war" age.

In that age, the Beatitudes were a reality of daily life for the followers of Jesus. They took to heart the call to perform the works of mercy for friends and enemies—and the enemies were not across some far border but all around them in the form of brutal persecutors. It would seem to be the time to return to the "pre-just-war" ethos when human beings must be tender with their kind if their kind is to persist. This return will involve a turn-about in thinking as revolutionary as was the original turn-about from the pacifism that sustained Christians in the age of persecution.

Christians who achieve this turn-about will not allow the nation-state to declare (along with the declaration of war which is not in their power to prevent) a moratorium on the works of mercy. It is hardly necessary to point out that such a stance would invite the same accusations as were made against the first Christians by Celsus and others. The charge of lack of patriotism might even be a prelude to some form of persecution. An insistence by greater numbers of Christians in serving as agents of God's mercy, coupled with the refusal to serve as agents of wrath in violence and war, will have its effects. The cost of discipleship will rise and Christians must be ready to pay it. The rejection of what the Apostle Paul called "carnal weapons" will strengthen the conviction that the kingdom toward which Christians move is one which cannot be defended or won by such weapons.

Above all and after all, Christians will not be torn between "two moralities," neither the "two moralities" which forbade bloodshed to one part of the Christian community while enjoining it on another part, nor the "two moralities" whereby the soldier-citizen may participate in actions morally repugnant to him as a Christian. The one morality is that of love brought to all by Jesus in the incarnation, a love memorialized for Christians in the Eucharistic celebration where the union of communicants with Jesus and with each other is a mystery of completion. The one morality would make imperative the search for practical alternatives to the violence of war. Training for the skills of reconciliation, for nonviolent resistance, and for civil disobedience as responses to injustice and oppression, would become necessary constituents of gospel teaching. The readiness of civil disobedience and resistance on a scale paralleling that of Gandhi's followers would be a feature of Christian living in time of coercion by injustice and military conscription.

At the end of the Sermon on the Mount, Jesus taught the crowd to pray, "Thy kingdom come. Thy will be done on earth as it is in heaven." The coming of the kingdom is related to doing the will of the Father, a kingdom where human wills are united with the divine will. What of the other kingdom—or as St. Augustine called it "the earthly city"—which sporadically demands bloodshed and the suspension of love and mercy? Christian citizens, while realizing that they are "strangers and pilgrims" in it, can and must serve the purposes of love and justice for fellow citizens and for humankind. The orders of a nation-state which they refuse are those that carry with them denials of the life and teaching of Jesus Christ. They know that their salvation is not linked with the victory or survival of any nation-state.

The much-desired turn-about to the "pre-just-war" age, while it might be slow in coming and while it might have its *lapsi* (as the Christians called those who fell away in those early persecutions), would preserve and proclaim the one morality of the gospel. Christians would again see that "Happy are the peacemakers" is a Beatitude meant for all members of the Christian community. Do not all members of the community wish to be called "children of God?" Christians would see themselves as "other Christs" serving all and reconciling persons to each other and to God. If more and more Christians become active peacemakers, uniting their wills with the will of the Creator who sent them the message of peace through Jesus, they might yet fulfill their task as the reconcilers of humankind.

Notes

1. Luke 6:23, *Good News for Modern Man: The New Testament in Today's Modern English* (New York: American Bible Society, 1966).
2. *Encyclopedic Dictionary of the Bible* (New York: McGraw-Hill, 1963), pp. 215–217.
3. Matthew 5:3–10, *Good News for Modern Man*.
4. M. K. Gandhi, *The Science of Satyagraha*, ed. A. T. Hingorani (Bombay: Bharatiya Vidya Bhavan, 1970), p. 94.
5. Acts 1:6, The Jerusalem Bible.
6. Matthew 5:9, The Jerusalem Bible.
7. Matthew 26–52, The Jerusalem Bible.
8. Matthew 5:7, The Jerusalem Bible.

9. *Christian Science Monitor,* November 15, 1967; quoted from *In the Name of America: The Conduct of the War in Vietnam as Shown by . . . .* (New York: Clergy and Laymen Concerned About Vietnam, 1968; Annandale, Va.: Turnpike Press), p. 284.

10. Matthew 5:44–45, *Good News for Modern Man.*

11. Albert Marrin, ed., *War and the Christian Conscience: From Augustine to Martin Luther King* (Chicago: Regnery, 1971), p. 88.

12. Roland H. Bainton, *Christian Attitudes towards War and Peace* (New York: Abingdon, 1960), p. 88.

13. Quoted in Marrin, *War and the Christian Conscience,* p. 39.

14. John Eppstein, *The Catholic Tradition of the Law of Nations* (London: Burns, Oates & Washbourne, 1935), p. 43.

15. Bainton, *Christian Attitudes,* p. 84.

16. Eppstein, *Catholic Tradition,* p. 32.

17. Ibid., p. 42.

18. Giuseppe Ricciotti, *The Age of Martyrs,* trans. Anthony Bull (Milwaukee: Bruce, 1959), pp. 46–149 passim.

19. Marrin, *War and the Christian Conscience,* p. 51.

20. Eppstein, *Catholic Tradition,* p. 59.

21. Ibid., p. 58.

22. Ibid., p. 59.

23. Ibid., p. 76.

24. Marrin, *War and the Christian Conscience,* p. 67.

25. Ibid., p. 61.

26. Eppstein, *Catholic Tradition,* p. 74.

27. Marrin, *War and the Christian Conscience,* p. 55.

28. Eppstein, *Catholic Tradition,* p. 79.

29. Ibid., p. 84.

30. Marrin, *War and the Christian Conscience,* pp. 72–73.

31. *Resolution on Southeast Asia,* U.S. Catholic Bishops, November 19, 1971.

32. "The Church in the Modern World," voted at Vatican Council II, December 7, 1965, n. 80.

33. Statement by Frank Barnaby, Stockholm International Peace Research Institute, at U.N. Special Session on Disarmament, June 12, 1978.

34. Bainton, *Christian Attitudes,* p. 77.

11
The Civilian COs

Paul Hanly Furfey

The concept of "conscientious objectors" is familiar enough. It means those who, for reasons of conscience, refuse to be inducted into the military service or to bear arms. However, there is another sort of citizen who, also for reasons of conscience, refuses to participate in his or her country's war effort, but does so in other ways than by refusing induction. Thus citizens may write articles or make speeches against the war their country is waging. They may bring political pressure to bear on their congressional representatives. They may refuse to pay taxes that aid the war. They may join in anti-war demonstrations. They actively oppose the war even if they merely spread their ideas in their private conversations with friends and neighbors. In this chapter, those who oppose the war effort in these various ways will be called "civilian COs" to distinguish them from the conventional draft resisters.

The Role of Civilian COs

Civilian COs can have an extremely important effect on national policy, particularly in a democracy like the United States. This fact was dramatically illustrated during the Vietnam War. Successive administrations strongly supported the war. At first, the bulk of the civilian population apparently also did. However, dissatisfaction gradually grew and it became organized. There were dramatic demonstrations. On October 21–22, 1967, thousands of protestors marched on Washington. The following year, during the Democratic National Convention in Chicago, police and troops clashed with ten to fifteen thousand anti-war demonstrators. Activity grew until the largest such demonstration in history took place on November 15, 1969, when some 250,000 participated in Washington. On May 4, 1970, the dramatic Kent State incident occurred. Only four were killed, but the incident had a profound effect on the national conscience. Finally, on May 3–5, 1971, Washington police arrested 12,614, a record high for arrests in a civil disturbance. All this protest proved politically effective. President

Johnson, who had tried to win public approval for his escalation of the war effort, realized that the country was not with him, and he announced, on March 31, 1968, that he would not seek or accept another term. His successor, Richard Nixon, was left with no choice but to phase out the war.

The fact that civilians joined with draft resisters to oppose the Vietnam War and that their combined influence was effective enough to bring the war to an end is certainly an encouraging fact. However, the question remains whether these civilians were literally *conscientious* objectors to the war. For some of them other motives might have been predominant. If the war had been escalated, as Johnson wished, this would have brought higher taxes. Also, escalation would have brought the temptation to use the atom bomb and this might have precipitated another World War.

There is no doubt about the duty of Catholics in case of war. Catholics are bound to consult their consciences. If they are morally certain that the war is unjust, they must refuse participation. They must become COs, military or civilian. Surely some Catholics did precisely that during the Vietnam days. Yet this conscientious examination of military issues seems to be far from universal among Catholics. Even theologians and the bishops seem remiss in this respect. We tend to concentrate on the sins of the individual—lying, stealing, sins of impurity—and to forget about the sins of society and our obligation to oppose them actively. We may forget about economic injustice, about interracial discrimination, and the great, great evil of war.

Catholic Support of War

The consequences of all this are exceedingly tragic. Catholics seem ready to support the slaughter of their fellow humans whenever their national leaders command them to. It would be easy to fill a book with horrible examples. However, only two examples will be given here, two examples that illustrate rather different circumstances.

The first example will be the German Catholic support of Hitler's policy in World War II. The war itself was preceded by the annexation of Austria and a large part of Czechoslovakia; these raise obvious moral questions which will not be considered here. However, when German armies invaded Poland on September 1, 1939, this was war indeed. German Catholics, almost unanimously, supported the war; yet there can be little doubt that this war was unjust. This fact will be readily accepted by the many Catholic moralists who contend that all war is unjust.[1] However, even the most conservative moralist can surely not justify Hitler. There was no vestige of an excuse for his invasion of those vast areas of Europe. His only reason was a lust to dominate. This is obvious; yet Catholics supported him.[2]

The moral judgments of German Catholics are most officially expressed in the statements of their bishops. At the very outbreak of the war, in September 1939, at their national meeting in Fulda, the bishops said they intended "to encourage and exhort our Catholic soldiers to do their duty in obedience to the *Führer,* ready for sacrifice and with the commitment of the whole being."[3]

There were many other significant episcopal statements. A noteworthy one was the joint pastoral issued by the eight Bavarian bishops in 1941. It was to be read from the pulpit on the First Sunday of Lent that year. The date has significance; for this was after the German armies had overrun Poland, France, and the Low Countries and it was before the war with Russia, which some might have considered a holy war against atheistic communism. Yet at that particular time the bishops emphasized "how vitally important" it was "for everyone to fulfill his duty fully and willingly and loyally, to maintain a calm presence of mind and a firm trust in God, not to begin to waver or to complain." The bishops said they were "directing a word of exhortation to you in our fatherly love and concern, that it may inspire you to devote your full efforts to the service of the Fatherland and the precious homeland in conscientious fulfillment of duty and serious awareness of your mission."[4]

Of particular importance was the attitude of Bishop Franz Josef Rarkowski; for he was the bishop in charge of the military chaplains and was thus, in an official sense, the man responsible for the moral decisions of all Catholic soldiers. As Zahn rightly said: "It follows that the German Catholic who came to the army troubled by moral misgivings as to the justice of the war or any of the actions involved in that war (or who may have developed such misgivings in the course of his military service) would be expected to turn to his chaplain and the Military Bishop for authoritative guidance and direction in solving his problem."[5] There is little doubt as to what such guidance and direction would have been. Rarkowski was most extreme in defending the justice of the war, as Zahn shows by abundant quotations.

The most troubling aspect of the bishops' attitude was their utter silence on the morality of the war. "Nowhere in these episcopal statements does one encounter the question, or even a hint of any question, of whether or not the Hitler war effort met the conditions set for a 'just war.' "[6] It is precisely this attitude that constitutes the essential evil being discussed in this chapter. One might forgive those who in the heat of wartime passion convinced themselves that a certain war was just, even though it would seem clearly unjust to a dispassionate observer. But even this hypothetical war supporter had at least the decency to raise the question of morality. The German bishops did not even go so far. As we shall see, this attitude has not been confined to Germany.

This lack of any criticism on the part of the hierarchy concerning the morality of Hitler's war is particularly unfortunate because a strong and united Catholic opposition would at least have dulled the intensity of Hitler's war operations and might even have prevented the war. In 1939, at the outbreak of the war, it is said that 40.3 per cent of "Greater Germany" was Catholic.[7] It was part of Hitler's political skill that he did not take extreme measures until he had whipped up massive popular support. This fact is illustrated by his treatment of the Jews. From the outset Hitler hated them savagely; yet after he came into power, his persecution of them grew only gradually. It was not until 1942 that he felt secure enough to put into effect his "final solution," the systematic massacre of the Jewish population.

The German bishops dared to oppose Hitler on some matters. Indeed, as Zahn remarks, it amounted to "a truly heroic resistance." Often, indeed, their opposition met with considerable success. However, this resistance dealt with "assaults upon Church rights and property" or with certain policies which the hierarchy considered immoral. The astounding fact remains, however, that the bishops did not examine their country's war policies on moral grounds. These policies were exempt from moral criticism and were thus not hampered in the least by Catholic moral doctrine.[8]

Now we shall turn to our second example of the lack of civilian conscientious objection to the injustice of war, namely, the official silence during American participation in World War II. For some, our situation in the United States might seem entirely comparable to that of German Catholics in Hitler's war; the hierarchy simply supported an unjust war. Personally I opposed the war on the ground that it was simply taking sides in the confrontation of two evils. Given the choice, we sided with the Communists instead of with the Nazis. This opinion of mine however, was not a popular opinion.[9] It will not be assumed in this chapter.

There was, however, one feature of American participation that must be unequivocally condemned, namely, the deliberate bombing of noncombatants. There cannot be the slightest doubt about this. It is the traditional teaching of Catholic theology. Even while the bombing was going on, Father John C. Ford, the distinguished Jesuit moral theologian, put it this way: "I do not believe any Catholic theologian, in the face of conciliar and papal pronouncements, and the universal consensus of moralists for a long time, would have the hardihood to state that innocent non-combatants can be put to death without violating natural law. I believe that there is unanimity in Catholic teaching on this point, and that even in the circumstances of a modern war every Catholic theologian would condemn as intrinsically immoral the direct killing of innocent non-combatants."[10]

The immorality of obliteration bombing is so clear that it needs no argument. However, it may be worthwhile to cite the solemn declaration of Vatican Council II which was included in the constitution *Gaudium et Spes,* n. 80, issued December 7, 1965: "Any act of war aimed indiscriminately at the destruction of entire cities or extensive areas along with their population is a crime against God and man himself. It merits unequivocal and unhesitating condemnation."

The first striking instance of the aerial bombing of non-combatants was the bombing of the Basque town of Guernica during the Spanish Civil War. In World War II Germans began to bomb London and some provincial cities in the summer of 1940. The Allies were slower to develop a bomber offensive; but once they did develop it, they did so much more effectively.

On the night of May 16–17, 1943, the British bombed the Ruhr dams, and some 12,000 civilians were drowned in the ensuing flood. However, it was only with the development of fire bombing that the Allied air raids reached the climax of their hellish effectiveness. By dropping a number of incendiary bombs, the raiders could start so many fires simultaneously that they could not be controlled. The separate fires would merge into one great holocaust so that tens of thousands of civilians would be burned to death. Thus between July 24 and August 3, 1943, the British bombed Hamburg four times and the Americans did so three times. The loss of lives has been estimated at over 30,000. In 1945 the slaughter reached a climax. At Dresden some 135,000 were killed in February of that year, and some 84,000 in the slums of Tokyo.

Then came the atom bomb. About 68,000 were killed at Hiroshima on August 6, 1945, an act which Pope Paul VI called "an infernal massacre" and an "outrage against civilization."[11] Then followed Nagasaki with some 38,000 dead. It was only with the end of the war that the massive slaughter ceased.

The atom bombs added a new dimension of horror to obliteration bombing. Like the older bombs, they could kill by explosive force and by fire, but they could also kill by radiation. Radiation could kill directly, at once or within weeks. It could cause delayed injuries. And it could cause genetic defects, so that the children of those bombed, or even later generations of descendants, could be affected.

It is hard for us to realize what a nuclear explosion meant to those attacked. The following is a description written by a Hiroshima survivor: "It was a horrible sight. . . . Hundreds of injured people who were trying to escape to the hills passed our house. The sight of them was almost unbearable. Their faces and hands were burnt and swollen; and great sheets of skin had peeled away from their tissues and hung down like rags on a scarecrow. They seemed to move like a line of ants. All through the night they went past our house, but in the morning they had stopped. I found them lying on both sides of the road so thick that it was impossible to pass without stepping on them."[12]

In the official history of the Army Air Force, we are told that the crew of the plane which bombed Hiroshima attended "religious services" just before they took off.[13] The massive killing at Hiroshima was the largest murder by a single act in the whole history of humankind. Cumulatively, more people were killed at Dresden, for example; but the bombing of Hiroshima was a single act. It says something for the incredible moral blindness of the chaplains that they could invoke God's blessing on such a hellish crime. Yet their blindness seems to have been typical of the whole ecclesiastical establishment.

The blindness of the military chaplains was indeed typical. They were merely following the lead of the bishops. On November 14, 1942, the American bishops had issued an official statement "on victory and peace" in the course of which they stated: "At times it is the positive duty of a nation to wage war in defense of life and right. Our country now finds itself in such circumstances." This statement was not withdrawn or modified when the bombing of noncombatants climaxed at Hiroshima. They apparently approved the slaughter of tens of thousands of innocents as a legitimate "defense of life and right."

The German Catholic support of Hitler's wars and the American Catholic support of our bombing of noncombatants are two striking examples of a failure to apply moral principles to the overwhelmingly important problem of war. It is to be remembered that in these two cases the bishops, the moral leaders of the People of God, were as silent and as compliant as anyone else. It is also to be remembered that the two examples given are very far from being isolated. Indeed, these merely illustrate our typical attitude.

The Failure to Examine the Morality of War

What is the reason why Catholics fail to examine the morality of particular wars and, if they judge a war unjust, to raise conscientious objections? Two reasons may reasonably be suggested. One is the confusion now surrounding the theology of war. The other reason—a very scandalous one—is that many tend to put loyalty to country above loyalty to God and his law.

The nature of war has changed so rapidly and so completely that treatments of the subject soon get out of date. St. Thomas devotes four pages or so to the morality of war in his *Summa.*[14] He is still often quoted, but war in his day was something quite different from modern war. He and we are talking about two different things. He could not have imagined the destruction of an entire city or of a large part of a city in an instant by an atom bomb. Our problems are something quite apart from his world. Of course even more recent theologians, who wrote before 1914, had little idea of what a modern war could amount to.

In spite of the efforts of contemporary moral theologians to bring the matter up to date, there still seems to be a general confusion among ordinary, intelligent Catholics. Although the present chapter is explicitly concerned with civilian COs, perhaps some light may be shed on current Catholic opinion by examining Zahn's study of the reasons why the military COs he studied felt that American participation in World War II was wrong. If any group of lay Catholics should be well informed on this moral problem, surely it should be these resisters.

The impression we receive from Zahn is one of confusion.[15] He placed six of the men he studied in a "miscellaneous" group including those who thought the United States was fighting "on the wrong side" and those who claimed to have had a special revelation on the subject. A second group, numbering thirty, which Zahn calls "humanitarian," apparently based their stand on ethics rather than theology. This, of course, was legitimate.

Natural reason can prove that murder is wrong, even though theology can show the horror of this evil more convincingly. There were only nineteen men who followed the theory of just *vs.* unjust war, "the orthodox treatment of the morality of war," as Zahn calls it.

The largest group, fifty-six, were the "evangelicals," so called by Zahn. "These men avoided formal theological arguments, preferring to state their objections in terms of an antithesis between 'the spirit of war' and 'the spirit of Christ.' " Finally, there were sixteen "perfectionists." Their position was "based upon a literal interpretation of the Counsels of Perfection and the insistence that these Counsels must govern the life of the individual Christian."

This is not the place to discuss the relative merits of these various anti-war positions. However, certain points are immediately clear. First, even in this small group of men who agreed on an anti-war position, there were striking differences in the arguments they gave for this position. Secondly, conventional moral theology furnished a moral basis for the positions of only a few of them. Thirdly, it may be fair to say that probably most of them reached their conclusions less on the basis of logical reasoning than on the basis of a sort of Christian instinct, a consciousness of evil, a direct insight into the injustice of the war. There was obviously much confusion among this very select group of men whose protest was no less than heroic. Therefore it is easy to understand that ordinary Catholic citizens would find it very difficult to make firm moral judgments on the morality of their country's war. There was obviously no clear Catholic position. This confusion may help to explain, without at all justifying, the failure of the hierarchy to oppose America's conduct of the war.

The lack of a satisfactory, authoritative moral theology of war is indeed a serious defect. Yet there is something infinitely more important, something that is probably the chief reason for the lack of any very widespread and very serious opposition to a war by Catholic civilians. This is the utterly immoral notion that loyalty to country takes precedence over loyalty to God. It is hard to believe that such a notion should exist among Catholics. Yet there is much evidence for this tragic fact. Here is one horrible example.

On December 23, 1965 Cardinal Spellman was in South Vietnam on a Christmas visit when news reporters asked: "What do you think about what the United States is doing in Vietnam?" His answer was: "I fully support everything it does." Then, paraphrasing the words of Stephen Decatur, he added, "My country, may it always be right. Right or wrong, my country."[16]

The Cardinal was very explicit. He would follow his national leaders, even when they were morally in the wrong. Given a choice between Lyndon Johnson and Jesus Christ, he would unhesitatingly turn his back on Jesus Christ. Such a statement of position was scandalous enough, but possibly one might charitably try to explain it on the theory that the

Cardinal was perhaps becoming senile or perhaps for some reason he was a bit paranoid on this point. One might have expected that there would be an immediate storm of protest, statements by other bishops, editorials in Catholic papers, outspoken repudiation by lay leaders. But there was no such storm of protest. Nor did the Cardinal seek to modify his own words. It is hard to avoid the disheartening conclusion that Catholic thought throughout the country agreed tacitly with the Cardinal.

There is one more charitable explanation for the Cardinal's position. It perhaps never occurred to him that his country *could* be wrong. Our theology of war is so fuzzy and our concept of patriotism is so overpowering, that perhaps the Cardinal felt certain that his country's international policy would be inevitably correct morally. To say that he would support his country even if it were wrong would therefore be a meaningless statement. It concerned something that could never actually happen. It was merely rhetorical and it sounded impressive. Perhaps it was thus that the Cardinal rationalized his attitude.

This attitude could also explain the attitude of the German bishops. They opposed Hitler, even courageously, when certain church-state issues were involved. But opposition to their country's war? Impossible! Our country is always and inevitably right. The same attitude could explain the attitude of the American bishops during the World War II bombing of noncombatants. Whatever the theologians said, our country simply could not be wrong. Whatever theology taught, whatever the Holy Father said, the bombings at Dresden, Tokyo, Hiroshima, or Nagasaki must somehow or other be justifiable.

So there were not many civilian COs during Hitler's wars or during our bombing of noncombatants. This particular moral blindness is part of a larger phenomenon, namely, our lack of concern about the sins of society. The theology of liberation which has been developing particularly in Latin America has been much concerned with sins of this sort. In many Latin American countries there is a particularly sharp and visible distinction between the luxurious affluence of the ruling economic oligarchy and the distressing poverty of the multitudinous poor. The liberation theologians have called attention again and again to the immorality of this situation. They have asserted, and very convincingly, that the Church should be as much concerned about the sins of society as about the sins of the individual. Many bishops have agreed. They have agreed so emphatically that they have stirred up the wrath of their governments. There have been many incidents to illustrate this fact. To mention just one example—in the summer of 1976 a bishops' conference in Riobamba, Ecuador, was broken up by soldiers armed with machine guns because the government suspected that the bishops might be concerned about the injustices suffered by the poor.

The liberation theologians have been chiefly concerned about economic injustice; but of course the same principles would apply to an unjustified war. It is a social sin. Citizens must react against it. This they can do particularly effectively in a democracy. In other words, those not drafted are bound to be civilian COs, just as those drafted must be COs in the usual, military sense. Good Christians cannot cooperate, even passively, in the evils of their country.

The Duties of Civilian COs

The duties incumbent on civilian COs vary, of course, with their position. Probably the most serious duty rests on the bishops because of their official position of moral leadership. It took the Latin American bishops a long time to realize their duty of opposing economic injustice in very specific ways. (Some, indeed, have not yet realized this obligation.) Can we hope that the American bishops will follow suit where the morality of war is concerned? Dare we hope that there will some day be an American equivalent of Riobamba?

It is of course the duty of moral theologians to work out the details of the duties of civilian COs. A great deal needs to be done in their field. As was pointed out above, there is much confusion among Catholics on the morality of modern war. Our war theology is out of date. Even those theological propositions that are universally accepted are not emphasized. As was stated earlier, the bombing of noncombatants is immoral. All authorities agree. Yet how seldom ordinary, intelligent Catholics seem to realize this! Again, it is certainly wrong for a soldier to obey a clearly immoral order given to him by a superior. Yet this clear principle is so little emphasized that the airmen who bombed noncombatants probably felt no twinge of conscience. They were simply obeying orders.

Religious educators obviously also have a very special responsibility in teaching the average Catholic to distinguish between right and wrong. In the past these educators have taken their duty more seriously where the rights and wrongs of everyday life were concerned than in the realm of public policy. This reflects a mistaken attitude. Education should prepare students for good citizenship. To be good citizens they must, among other things, be conscious of this duty to judge the morality of a war. It is therefore dismaying to recall that Zahn found so few of the COs he studied influenced by the standard Catholic teaching on war and peace. Probably this means that they had heard little about the subject in the classroom. The small Catholic Worker group has probably affected Catholic moral judgments on recent wars more than the sum total of all our parochial schools, colleges, universities, and seminaries. This is appalling.

It should be clear, then, that it is primarily the duty of the bishops, moral theologians, and religious educators to take the initiative in stirring up civilian COs to oppose an immoral war or immoral policies in any war. However, past experience has shown that these natural leaders have often been remiss in displaying their leadership. Does this remissness on their part excuse the ordinary lay Catholic from taking some initiative? Obviously not! We must all do whatever we can. This is particularly true of citizens in a democracy. Fortunately, experience has shown that ordinary people can do a lot.

One thing ordinary citizens can do is to write letters to their congressional representatives and senators. This is important. In Washington, clerks keep careful tabs on mail concerning controversial issues. If the mail runs clearly in one direction, it is a rare member of Congress who will dare to take the other side in a floor debate.

Some individuals have special gifts for influencing public opinion. A skilled writer may publish an article on the war or write a letter to the editor. Another may bring the matter up within some organization and have it discussed at a meeting. And of course all citizens should examine the positions of candidates for public office; thus they will be able to make their vote count.

Each citizen should talk about the war with friends and neighbors, or with fellow employees or with fellow students at school or college. Thus people who share a common point of view on a war question get to know one another. In this way groups are formed. Such a group may be very informal at first. But later it may become organized, either as an entirely independent group or as a local affiliate of some national organization. For example, during the Vietnam War some young people and I rented a small house that we called Emmaus House and we lived there as a community. We were recognized by the Catholic Peace Fellowship as their local Washington branch. We found this connection very helpful.

There is a great deal that small local groups can do. They can hold meetings. Probably these meetings will be small at first, just a group gathered in some private house. Even such meetings may have a significant influence. Then perhaps larger meetings may be held in public halls. Perhaps a prominent peace activist will consent to be the speaker. Such meetings may attract newspaper coverage.

Picketing is a common group activity. Even half a dozen pickets attract attention. For instance, if a war rally is being held, the presence of some pickets may dramatize the fact that support of the rally is not unanimous in the community. Picketing is a strategy that has endless possibilities.

Various small peace groups may develop specialties. For example, at Emmaus House we did a good deal of draft counseling. A young man, drafted for military service, may feel strong moral misgivings, and yet not know how to go about applying for classification as a conscientious objector. But the counselors at our house were familiar with the system and we were able to help quite a few attain classification as conscientious objectors.

Groups more or less like ours did a variety of different things. Perhaps the best known and the most effective of such groups was that led by the famous Berrigan brothers. They did sensational things such as burglarizing draft offices, stealing draft records, and burning them. Such actions gained very wide publicity.

As small groups like the ones described multiply throughout the country, they gradually coalesce into a national anti-war movement. Leaders appear. Then large and striking protests take place which strongly affect national policy. At the beginning of this chapter the enormous civilian protests against the Vietnam War were described. These protests finally put an end to the war. National leaders could not defy such massive demonstrations of public opinion. They had no option but to end the war. However, let it be remembered that these wide national protests were simply the sum total of individual reactions. They came into being and had their effect because individual civilian COs recognized their obligation to act on their individual judgments that the war was immoral. These individual COs were effective even though their natural moral leaders, ecclesiastics, moral theologians, and religious educators acted so little and so late.

Notes

1. I cannot accept the opinion that all war is wrong. There have been instances of just wars. For example, the Barbary Wars (1801–1805; 1815) were waged against pirates; but since these pirates were manning official naval vessels of the Barbary States, the suppression of this piracy by the United States was a war in the strict sense. I admit, however, that under current conditions it is hard to conceive a just war waged between major states.

2. In what follows, the writer depends heavily on Gordon C. Zahn, *German Catholics and Hitler's Wars* (New York: Sheed and Ward, 1962).

3. Quoted in ibid., p. 64.

4. Ibid., pp. 60–61.

5. Ibid., pp. 44–45.

6. Ibid., p. 68. Another indication of the indifference of the Catholic clergy to the morality of the war is shown by their lack of counseling for those who refused military service. Zahn, after diligent search, could find only seven Catholics "who openly refused military service" (p. 54). He made a very thorough study of one of these cases, *In Solitary Witness: The Life and Death of Franz Jägerstätter* (New York: Holt, Rinehart and Winston, 1964). In this book Zahn says (p. 161): "Every single one in the long series of spiritual counselors to whom Jägerstätter had turned, from his pastor to the chaplain who called his attention to the paper lying before him in his death cell, regarded his action as an imprudent, foolhardy, and unnecessary sacrifice."

7. Zahn, *German Catholics and Hitler's Wars*, p. 54.

8. Ibid., pp. 77–78. In this connection it is interesting to read Gordon C. Zahn, *The Military Chaplaincy* (Manchester, England: University Press, 1969), a study of British Royal Air Force chaplains which points out a similar weakness in the applications of Catholic moral principles to war.

9. Gordon C. Zahn, *War, Conscience and Dissent* (New York: Hawthorn Books, 1967), p. 150, states that 11,950 men were given the IV-E classification as full conscientious objectors and assigned to Civilian Public Service. However,

Zahn could contact only 135 Catholics among them on whom to base his study. This may give some measure of the small Catholic opposition to the war on moral grounds.

10. John C. Ford, "The Morality of Obliteration Bombing," *Theological Studies* 5 (1944): 261–309, quotation on p. 273. See also P. H. Furfey, "Bombing of Noncombatants Is Murder," *The Catholic C. O.*, July-September, 1944, pp. 3–4, and the same author's *The Mystery of Iniquity* (Milwaukee: Bruce, 1944). I have not found any other American Catholic theologian who opposed the bombing policy during the war itself.

11. In a discourse at Castel Gandolfo, August 8, 1945.

12. Michihiko Hachiyo, *Hiroshima Diary* (Chapel Hill: University of North Carolina Press, 1955), p. 14.

13. U. S. Air Force Historical Division, *The Army Air Forces in World War II* (Chicago: University of Chicago Press, 1948–58), vol. 5, p. 716.

14. *Summa Theologiae,* II-II, q. 40, "de bello."

15. Zahn, *War, Conscience and Dissent,* chap. 9, "Catholic Conscientious Objectors in the United States."

16. Dorothy Dohen, *Nationalism and American Catholicism* (New York: Sheed and Ward, 1967), chap. 1, "Right or Wrong, My Country." The book contains many other instances of excessive nationalism among the American hierarchy.

12
The Catholic Church and Witness Against War

Tom Cornell

Witness of, for, or to the Church? Gordon Zahn has posed this question about the Catholic pacifist movement in America. That the Catholic Church is searching for and finding its proper witness in regard to peace and justice is one of the elements of its Christianization and renewal in our day. But the witness that I am called upon to survey is a witness to and for rather than of. Although we are all "the Church," the pacifists are at best an *ecclesiola*. And if I restrict the witness to Christ's peace to those who take the absolutist, pacifist position and neglect others who do not hold so firm a position but who have contributed to peace from a more traditional posture, it is not to deny their contribution, but to keep to what I know.

Background of the Catholic Pacifist Movement

The antecedents to the present Catholic pacifist movement and to the "great Catholic peace conspiracy" of the 1960s would be discrete, unconnected, fragmented, and as a whole unintelligible if it were not for the force of one personality, that of Dorothy Day, co-founder of the Catholic Worker movement in 1933. From the start the movement and the monthly journal it publishes took an uncompromising pacifist stance. This was due to an instinctive aversion on Dorothy Day's part to the institution of war and all that causes war and supports it. Nowhere in her writings will you find a clear, definitive statement of principles against war, neatly synthesized into a new theory. That is not her way. Others attempted that in the pages of *The Catholic Worker*, to whatever degree of success. Dorothy didn't need any more than her own experience as a journalist on the Left, a text of the New Testament, and the history of the Church to convince her of the blasphemy and the lunacy of war, for whatever purported reason. The root of war is sin, plain and simple, and we are to turn away from sin, as the baptismal rite puts it, from Satan and all his pomps, blandishments, or allurements—whatever the current translation says. The horror of defeat at war cannot match the horror of being guilty of what it takes to win. Theories of nonviolent defense, of popular noncooperation with invading or tyrannical regimes support the original conviction. That Dorothy Day's pacifism has an affinity with perfectionism, that it hovers close to a Jansenistic view are observations that many have made. But the results of her long adherence to her insight have proven something of its value.

During the Spanish Civil War only *The Catholic Worker* consistently opposed it and any U. S. intervention. *Commonweal* and the Chicago archdiocesan journal, *New World*, changed their positions, the former against, the latter for. *The Catholic Worker* lost about one-third of its 150,000 readers for this stand.

World War II was all but devastating to the *CW*, as it continued its pacifist stand against all odds. More than half of the remaining readership cancelled. Almost all bulk orders ceased. The paper was banned from parish literature racks and reading rooms. For years thereafter readership of the *CW* was *prima facie* evidence for lack of a valid priestly or monastic vocation. CW houses of hospitality across the country were closed as the men who staffed them either went to war, to Civilian Public Service camps, or to prison. Some houses dissociated themselves, to one degree or another, from the CW movement, by refusing to distribute the CW monthly paper, by deleting reference to their origins in their promotional literature, and by refusing a platform to pacifist speakers from the New York center. It is necessary to remember that the CW movement has no organization, even to federate itself, one house, farm, or project to another. All are autonomous. There is no party-line either. But in the case of World War II and CW pacifism, Dorothy Day took a hard position. She wrote to each house early in the war and declared that those who would publicly associate themselves with the movement in a leadership capacity would have to refrain from attacking the pacifist stand against the war. Those unwilling to do this were told to dissociate themselves from CW leadership. Many left embittered. Some came back. Jack English, who had established the CW house in Cleveland, with the help of George Ribar and Carlotta and Monica Durkin, joined the Royal Air Force, in anticipation of U.S. entry into the war. He later transferred to the U.S. Air Force, was shot down over Ploesti and spent the rest of the war in a POW camp in Germany. After demobilization he joined the CW staff in New York City, then joined the Trappists at Conyers, Georgia. After fourteen years he left to re-join the New York Catholic Worker group, and went back to his monastery to spend the last few years of his life. John Cogley, of the Chicago CW group, left to join the army, pained by his separation from the CW movement caused as he saw it by Dorothy Day's intransigence, and was never thereafter quite capable of giving the pacifist argument of later years the hearing he might have given it.

Through a benign front, the Association of Catholic Conscientious Objectors, the CW sponsored a camp for Catholic conscientious objectors near Warner, N.H., as part of the Civilian Public Service program. (It should be noted that Dorothy Day did not really approve of Civilian Public Service as an option for COs and urged total noncooperation with the war system.) COs were to be given work of national importance so that they might contribute to the common good in a nonviolent manner and witness to their beliefs in a credible way. They would be able to prove their sincerity by "going the second mile," by working for no pay under the direction of representatives of their own religious communities rather than under the military. There were a number of things wrong with the plan. The ultimate authority in CPS was Selective Service, and that, although technically a civilian office, was headed by a general of the army, Louis B. Hershey, and served the purposes of the military as its prime objective. Lack of financial remuneration was bad enough, especially for those with dependents. But the COs and their supporting agencies had to finance the camps. And the "work of national importance" often served no identifiable purpose, i. e., the clearing of hurricane damage from a wilderness.[1] Zahn identifies this camp as the first corporate witness for pacifism in American Catholicism, and as a source of some roots or antecedents of the very visible Catholic movement against the Vietnam War. Since Zahn does not identify himself as part of that system of roots and antecedents, others must in justice do that.

During the immediate postwar years the CW movement gained momentum. In the dislocations of that time more talented young men and women were drawn to the movement as schools and the army ushered them into a society not yet geared to engage them. The Cold War, clamping down on us in 1947, gave the CW an opportunity to stand with those persecuted for political reasons, radical socialists and Communists. Not that the CW entertained a Marxist philosophical conviction, far from that! But out of simple fairness it seemed to CW activists that government persecution followed the Communists because they attacked the same social and political problems that vexed themselves. During the pre-war years Catholic Workers and Communists often met each other on the picket line, and sometimes in the police van. (During one demonstration of support for a strike a CW contingent joined strikers and Communists, to be hauled away by the NYC police. An officer, who appeared to be an Irish Catholic, was remonstrated with by a CW, "I'm not a Communist, officer, I'm an anti-Communist!" "I don't care what kind of Communist you are, lady, get in the wagon!") It is to be remembered too that the CW had its conception due to a Communist Party sponsored "hunger march" in Washington, in December 1932. Dorothy Day, a convert who had yet to find her niche in the Church, covered the march for *Commonweal* magazine. Viewing the thousands of unemployed workers marching on the Capitol to demand jobs and justice, she felt a great surge of pride for them, their courage and determination to bring about a more just system for all, and she felt isolated, alienated from them as a Roman Catholic. She had joined the Church partly because it was the working people's church, the church of the immigrants. Watching the marchers, organized and led by Communists, she longed to find a way to march with them to find a way to work for social justice and peace in a working-class movement as a Catholic.

At the crypt of the National Basilica in Washington on the Feast of the Immaculate Conception she prayed for an "opening." On her arrival home in New York, at her brother and sister-in-law's apartment which they shared, Peter Maurin was waiting for her. He, a French peasant intellectual, would indoctrinate her. Together they founded the Catholic Worker movement. From this it can be seen that Dorothy Day and the CW did not fear the Communists as most Americans and nearly all Catholics did. And when it came time for people who were "clean" to stand up against an unjust persecution founded upon lies, the liberals disappeared, but the CW and a very few secular radical pacifists made it clear that they would not go along with the national hysteria.

When the Communist Party, driven underground by the trials that imprisoned its first and second string national leadership, surfaced in 1956 for a national convention, it was held by chance around the corner from the CW house of hospitality on Chrystie Street, in the Bowery. Dorothy Day was invited as a non-Communist observer, along with A. J. Muste and a few others. Elizabeth Gurley Flynn and a few CP leaders made it around the corner to take a look at the feeding of the poor and the derelict, several hundred a day, at the CW soup kitchen. The *CW* had attacked the Communists for their subversion of some democratic unions, in the 1930s, and had been attacked in the *Daily Worker*. But when it came down to lies and unjust persecution, when the Communists became in a sense "the least of these my brethren," then the CW knew where to stand. For their annual May Day demonstration in Union Square, the CP organizers always called upon the CW to send a speaker. Ammon Hennacy, the old American anarchist and recent convert to Catholicism, went one year and chastized the CP organizers for using a front committee to obscure the nature of the event, and for singing the *Star Spangled Banner* as at a baseball game to open proceedings. "Why don't you just say who you are, and why don't we sing *The Red Flag* like we used to in the old days," he chided. For years during that bad time a CW would be there, reminding the crowd of about 2,500 Communists and their sympathizers that the *CW* was first distributed to the public at the May Day Communist rally at Union Square in 1933, and of the efforts of the Church, and the papacy in particular, for peace. One reason why CWs took active part was that if the FBI were to slander all the people who took part they would have to slander the CW too.

Of course the CW opposed the Korean War, but organized pacifist manifestations were not yet possible in the chilled climate of the times. The intellectual life at the CW, though, was at its most intense. Michael Harrington lived at the CW in the early 1950s. Robert Ludlow, Edmund Egan, Ciaran Duggan, Ammon Hennacy, Tom Sullivan, Eileen Fantino, Charlie McCormack, and many others assured that the Friday Night Meetings for

Clarification of Thought provided the most stimulating platform in New York at the time. No gratuitous assertions allowed! No speaker could get away with a thing, but he or she would be challenged in a demanding atmosphere, not of debate but of honest searching. It was far better than college, any college. Discussions centered around the nature of the East-West conflict, the unmet social needs of the city and the country, efforts to organize the unorganized, migrant workers, etc., the development of Church teaching on social justice, peace and war, prayer, the sacraments and direct personal responsibility for addressing the immediate needs of people as they come into our lives and for personal responsibility in forming a basis for a new society in which "it will be easier for men to be good." It would have been easy for the Worker to become a sect, to develop an ideology and a manner of operating that would alienate it from the vast membership of the Church and from society in general, as happens so often with radical groups. But the daily work of feeding the hungry, clothing the ill-clothed, caring for the sick, and burying the dead kept the CW grounded in reality and filtered out the more idiosyncratic elements.

Nonviolent group civil disobedience wasn't in the political lexicon in the immediate postwar period. Since the days of labor militancy in the late 1930s there had not been any advance in the technique. But in 1955 the National Civil Defense program was in high gear. Its principal reason for existence, so Catholic Workers were convinced, was to make the idea of nuclear war "thinkable," to prepare, psychologically, for war with the Soviet Union. Civil Defense units were organized on a local basis, and although they sometimes performed worthily in "normal" disaster situations such as floods and the like, many operated as vigilante squads, maintaining dossiers on suspect persons in local communities and intimidating local meetings where anything that local C.D. leaders considered subversive might be said. An annual mock drill in case of nuclear attack was instituted on a nationwide basis. The individual states were left to determine the degree of compulsion upon citizens to participate. New York State decided to make mandatory the taking of shelter in subway tunnels and designated buildings during the spring mock attacks. The first was in the spring of 1955. Ammon Hennacy remarked to Dorothy Day, casually, that pacifists ought not to participate, and that they should do something public rather than just stay home. Dorothy suggested that he take the idea up with the War Resisters League staff nearby. He did, and the WRL co-sponsored a sit-out at City Hall Park the day of the drill. More than two dozen people, including A. J. Muste, Dorothy, Ammon, Jim Peck, and Ralph DiGia, sat quietly on park benches, bedecked with signs indicating that there is no defense against nuclear attack, that peace is our only defense, etc., waiting for sirens to signal their legal obligation to take shelter. The sirens sounded and the group remained on the benches although ordered to leave by the police. Upon their repeated refusal the group was taken to jail.

By chance I happened to be driving from New Haven to the Bowery that day, proselytizing a group of Yale students who were interested in the CW movement. While listening to the news on the car radio, we learned that a group of pacifists had just been arrested in City Hall Park for refusing shelter during the drill. The thought crossed my mind that the Yalees might be in for a more exciting day than I could have planned for them because some of my friends would be likely to have participated in the demonstration. So it was. The Chrystie Street St. Joseph House of Hospitality was bedlam, the telephone ringing off the wall. Friends of the Worker, priests and bishops were calling one after the other to inquire. It was true: Dorothy, Ammon, Eileen Fantino, Pat Rush, and Mary Ann McCoy were in jail, Dorothy for the first time since the 1920s when she was caught in a raid on an IWW house and charged with prostitution, the other women for the first time. (Ammon had the longest arrest record in the movement, any movement almost.) When a telephone call came in announcing that Dorothy and the women were released pending a hearing, most of us decided to celebrate at the White Horse Tavern in Greenwich Village, where we discussed Eric Gill's theory of aesthetics.

The next spring many of the same people sat in City Hall Park, and the next year, and the next. Jail sentences ranged from 30 days to suspended terms. One judge gave tickets to the reviewing stand for the St. Patrick's Day parade to the Catholics. But even her most fervent admirers were beginning to show signs of irritation at Dorothy's insistence on her annual pilgrimage to jail. "Why does she bother? She's made her point! Why go through this over and over again?" "Upsetting our consciences," they might have added.

The band of civil disobedients became smaller each year, until the absurdity of the Civil Defense program became more evident to more people, and the political potential for mass civil disobedience began to dawn on people. In 1961 the demonstration was well prepared for. An estimated 2,000 people showed up at City Hall Park on Civil Defense Day, too many to arrest. The police nabbed 52 apparent leaders. Similar demonstrations were mounted at campuses around the city, involving perhaps another 2,000. Not only was the state law requiring participation nullified, but the national program was drastically curtailed and no more nationwide drills were conducted.

The demonstration begun so casually by the CW in 1953 can now be seen as a watershed. Civil disobedience on a mass scale was not new, but as a manifestation consciously rooted in a philosophy of nonviolence it was new to the U.S. Martin Luther King in 1956–1957 led a mass legal nonviolent boycott of the Montgomery bus system. In 1959 A. J. Muste and a small group including Carl Meyer of the Chicago CW House climbed over a small fence bordering the Strategic Air Command Headquarters outside Omaha, Nebraska, in an act of civil disobedience. In these three actions the movement of nonviolent mass civil disobedience was launched.

Efforts at establishing another kind of Catholic corporate witness for pacifism centered around the Catholic Worker, as the first had in World War II. One could say that the CW was itself that, except that the movement always had within it those who did not accept pacifism, and the movement prided itself on its lack of organization. There had been established in the mid-thirties in England a Catholic peace organization, the Pax Association, by figures such as E. I. Watkin, Eric Gill, Fr. Vincent McNabb, and the left wing of the Distributist movement associated with Hilaire Belloc and G. K. Chesterton, neither of them pacifist. In 1960, a nineteen-year-old conscientious objector just released from the Navy, a Catholic convert, the son of an imprisoned second-string Communist Party leader, James H. Forest, newly arrived at the CW, gathered a meeting at the home of Eileen Egan, an administrator at Catholic Relief Services and a CW adherent, with Ed Rice of *Jubilee* magazine, Anne Marie Taillefer of the CW, and a few others to float an idea insinuated by John Heidbrink of the staff of the Fellowship of Reconciliation. The idea was to form, within the interreligious pacifist FOR, a Catholic unit which would dedicate itself to the study of the peace traditon within Catholicism and give it visible manifestation in a membership group which would operate on pacifist principles and try to stimulate the growth of pacifism within the Catholic community.

Catholic Pacifism and the FOR

In those preconciliar years it seemed inappropriate to the group summoned to organize within the FOR. "The bishops might think we are laboring under a Protestant logic of personal interpretation of Scripture," as one participant put it. Better not to give any reason to think we are other than orthodox Catholics attempting to develop our work within the confines of our own tradition. So the decision was made to form an independent group along the lines of Pax in England, and once having done that, to affiliate with the Pax Association. So it was done. Gordon Zahn was an initiating force. The work of the Pax Association was nevertheless dovetailed into that of the International FOR at the Vatican Council, since IFOR's travelling secretaries were Roman Catholics already involved in pre-Council planning: Jean Goss and Hildegard Goss-Mayr, of Vienna. Dorothy Day, Gordon Zahn, James Douglass, Eileen Egan, and the Goss-Mayrs lobbied the bishops in their own countries and on board ship to Rome. A special issue of the *CW* was published with material designed to educate the bishops on peace issues, and each Council Father was mailed a copy. The results were that the Council documents authenticate conscientious objection for Catholics, and that one of the two condemnations decreed by the Council was against acts of indiscriminate warfare.

The encyclical *Pacem in Terris*, published by Pope John XXIII on April 11, 1963, was another watershed, of different proportions. This was a witness of the Church through its supreme pastor, and became the cornerstone of subsequent teachings.

In 1964 John Heidbrink tried again to form a Roman Catholic pacifist body within the Fellowship of Reconciliation. FOR was a fifty-year-old membership organization, with highly developed structures and about 20,000 members across the U.S. Its membership included leadership elements in most of the Protestant churches. There were a few individual Catholic members, but no impetus from them to gather together for a corporate witness. Jim Forest was by now married and father of one, and had left the CW staff for a job in trade journalism. With encouragement and the public endorsement of Thomas Merton, Dan and Philip Berrigan, Eileen Egan, Gordon Zahn, and others, Forest set up the beginnings of a Catholic Peace Fellowship within FOR, to be completely integrated into the FOR structures. Jim opened an office in space sublet from the War Resisters League in New York City on January 1, 1965. I joined him on staff in the spring. FOR executives were understandably dubious about our ability to attract members to the FOR and to mount programs on the expectation of financial return from them. But the war in Indochina was growing, and U.S. involvement was becoming more serious. FOR put us on salary.

Catholic Pacifism and the Vietnam War

The first demonstration against U.S. involvement in the Vietnam War was in the summer of 1963. Thich Quang Duc of the An Quang Pagoda (Unified Buddhist Church) in Saigon had immolated himself. The Buddhist opposition to the Diem regime was underway. The U.S. supported Diem, had set him up in office, and then Diem invited U.S. troops in to fight the Viet Cong on his behalf. I was managing editor of the *CW* paper at the time. It seemed to some of us that it was necessary to mount some kind of protest against our country's increasing involvement in what looked then like a quagmire of violence. It also occurred to us that demonstrations against the Diem regime might easily stimulate anti-Catholic sentiment, since Diem, a Catholic, was being accused of preferential placement of his co-religionists, and that therefore Catholics ought to be prominent in the protest movement in order to obviate that possibility. Bob Steed, a former editor of the paper, suggested a picketing of the South Vietnam offices in the city. There were none, neither a consulate, nor a U.N. Mission, nor an airline. There was an official observer from South Vietnam accredited to the U.N., and he lived in a luxury apartment house in mid-Manhattan. So one Monday morning Chris Kearns of the CW staff and I appeared at his apartment house door with signs reading "No U.S. Support for Diem Tyranny." The observer came out to photograph us. The next day I went alone for a noon vigil at the apartment house door, the next day Chris, and so on. On some days we were joined by others from the house. One day we had a pleasant contingent of young ladies from Manhattanville College who had come to visit the Worker and came along for the demonstration. We let it be known that there was a daily demonstration conducted by the CW at the observer's address and that all were invited to come with us on the last day to manifest widespread protest over the deepening U.S. military involvement. Dave McReynolds at the War Resisters League alerted the WRL network and we had about 250 for the final demonstration, and most important, network television coverage. The Vietnam protest was underway. Again, it was the Catholic Worker that gave witness *for* an unwilling Church.

Daniel Berrigan, S.J., was first known to us as a poet. He had won the Lamont Poetry Award for his first volume of poems, *Time Without Number*. Jim Forest had gained his friendship, and Berrigan had supplied many of the program ideas for the Catholic Peace Fellowship. For a combination of reasons, not excluding his public stance against the war in Vietnam and the Church's complicity in it, Berrigan was "exiled" to Latin America, by order of his provincial and at the instigation of the Archbishop of New York and Military Vicar for the United States Armed Services, Francis Cardinal Spellman, in 1965. This was rather like tossing Br'er Rabbit into the briar patch. Dan loved it. He toured Latin America searching out poet radicals and revolutionaries. In the meantime this high-handed treatment by his order and by the Church in New York could not go unanswered by the Catholic pacifist community. We demonstrated against Dan's exile in front of the Chancery Office on Madison Avenue, and we sat-in the office, to no immediate effect. Of course Dan came back to his job at the end of his Latin America tour, but protests had been prominently displayed in *Commonweal* and other journals, and we had borne our witness *to* the Church.

In the spring of 1965 Chris Kearns, still on the CW staff, joined a small group of draft protesters at Whitehall Induction Center near Wall Street in downtown Manhattan. He rather casually burned a draft card. We had done it many times before. A photograph appeared in *Life* that August, next to a photograph of a large mass of people marching down the Mall toward the Capitol from the Washington Monument. Counter-demonstrators had thrown red paint at the front ranks of the marchers. Dave Dellinger, Staughton Lynd, Bob Moses, and others looked in the photograph to be spattered with blood. Several Catholic Workers were in the second rank, swabbing the paint from Staughton and Dave's eyes. The full-page photographs made a sensation, especially in the Senate barbershop. Righteous indignation ran very high, indignation over the effrontery of the demonstrators in New York for burning draft cards and thus saying that they would not go to Vietnam, and at the marchers who would take the U.S. Capitol for an "Assembly of Unrepresented Peoples." With no debate in either house, legislation was rushed through making it a specific felony to mutilate willfully a draft registration or classification card. This was understood at the Catholic Worker headquarters to signify the government's intention to stifle anti-war dissent in an unjust and illegal manner. And so the *Catholic Worker* of September 1965 suggested that the best response to this law was to confront it, by destroying draft cards publicly.

In October, David Miller of the CW staff did just that, during a relatively small anti-war demonstration set up by Dave Dellinger at Whitehall Induction Center. Miller was asked to speak on behalf of the CW. He climbed atop a carry-all upon which was mounted sound equipment and said, "I'm not much at giving speeches, so I'll let this speak for me." He then set fire to his draft card. The journalists, who ordinarily seemed to resent having to cover our boring demonstrations, started clawing at each other to get to David, scrambling up the fragile stairs to the top of the carry-all. We had to clear the place, and I cannot remember clearly how the demonstration ended. Press coverage was universal, and radio and television. Never had the CW or the anti-war movement such instant and intense exposure. We decided to plan carefully for a group draft-card burning, which took place in Union Square on November 5. Participating were Dave McReynolds, Roy Lisker, a non-Catholic associated with the CW, Marc Edelman of WRL, Jim Wilson of the CW staff, and myself. Again, the demonstration, which was carried out with great seriousness and dignity, made a national sensation. A photograph was carried in all the newspapers in the area, and throughout most of the country, on the front page of the Sunday editions. About 2,500 came to witness the draft-card burning and it was well recorded. The prominence of Catholic Workers in the demonstration, the presence of Dorothy Day who addressed the congregation, made this another brief but very powerful witness for the Church, and, to a degree, to it, because the attention focused on Catholic pacifism could not have been foreseen by chancery officials. How they were taken by it is unknown.

The Vietnam War still had general support in the country. The hysterical atmosphere generated by the draft-card burnings had a galvanizing and a polarizing effect. Three days later, Roger LaPorte, a Catholic Worker staff volunteer who did not approve of the draft-card burning plan when it was under discussion, set himself ablaze before the United Nations at 5:30 in the morning. He had sat on the landing of the Isaiah stairway on First Avenue across from the Secretariat building, poured a two gallon container of gasoline upon himself and ignited a flame. A Ghanaian guard posted at the U.N. entry saw the fire, thought it was burning trash, then saw flailing limbs. He ran over to Roger and somehow moved him to the middle of First Avenue where the flames melted the asphalt. Ambulance attendants quoted Roger as saying, "I am a Catholic. I am against all war. There's so much hatred. . . ." Roger died in the late afternoon.

There was some feeling that the CW might have put Roger up to it somehow. That was far from the case. Had any one of us known that Roger was contemplating such an act we would not have let him out of sight. Thomas Merton saw in this a sign of demonic influence and that the peace movement was just as apt to turn crazy as any other element or the whole of society. The popular media did not respond to it in these terms, but rather reported on a young and sensitive, good-looking Catholic boy who had aspired to the religious life and who gave his life in protest against the war. The experience was very hard on Dorothy Day and the rest of us. We called for prayer and fasting.

After exhausting all appeals in an attempt to overturn as unnecessary, redundant, and unconstitutional the law against burning one's own draft cards, the defendants from the 1965 draft-card burning did their time in prison, only six months. We had expected more severe sentences similar to the ones meted out to draft resisters at the time, from two-and-a-half to three-and-a-half years. We were spared the worst, and we were not in Vietnam. And we were continuing our witness from prison. It is most important to take the punishment—and easier to say so after it is over.

Philip Berrigan, then a priest of the Society of St. Joseph, poured blood on draft records in the Selective Service System's offices in Baltimore in 1967. He and his co-defendants were tried and found guilty. While awaiting sentence, Phil appeared at the Catonsville draft board in Maryland, with Daniel Berrigan, S.J., his brother, several others and a packet of homemade napalm. They seized the draft records from the files of the Selective Service office, carried them outside to a safe place and incinerated them. From this emerged, with media-hype, the "great Catholic peace conspiracy of the 1960s." Between court appearances the Berrigan brothers and a few others from a small circle of intimates traveled the country holding "retreats," closed in the sense that recruits were supposedly trustworthy, for the purpose of planning and executing raids on other draft centers. Raids occurred all over the country. The recruiters went first to the Catholic Worker group, if there was one, in a given city. Their success in recruiting draft-board raiders from Catholic Worker houses was slender. Only Michael Cullen, director of Casa Maria in Milwaukee, joined the conspiracy. He later thought better of it.

Although *The Catholic Worker* was initially enthusiastic about the raids as an expression of nonviolent resistance to an unjust war, Catholic Workers became increasingly uneasy about the secrecy involved in planning the raids. It is self-evident that such activity cannot be carried out in sight and hearing of the police. But essential to the Gandhian idea of nonviolence is "openness and truth," which means that nonviolent action must not depend to any great degree on conspiratorial, secretive activity. Reasons for this are two: nonviolence must invite the participation of ever larger numbers in all levels of planning and execution—it is democratic and participative in authority structure; and the political purposes of nonviolent action must be fully available to scrutiny by any and all—no hidden agendas. Dorothy Day wrote simply: "These actions are not ours." Nevertheless during the most severe trial of the Berrigan group brought about by a federal charge that Phil and others had conspired to kidnap then Secretary of State Henry Kissinger and to blow up the underground heating tunnels serving federal buildings in Washington, D.C., all who could came to the defense of the accused.

Zahn has written appreciatively of the Berrigan phenomena. In an article in the *Saturday Review* he pointed out, however, that the attention drawn to these extraordinary events may detract from wider awareness that the Berrigans were a "tip of the iceberg," that in fact there has been a glacial change in attitude among Catholics in the U.S. in regard to the war-making authority of the state, and that there is in the mass of Catholics the potential for a yet more powerful witness for peace.[2] This, it seems to me, depends on how successfully Catholics continue to resist assimilation to the dominant WASP culture.

The Catholic Peace Fellowship was under heavy pressure to follow the Berrigan lead throughout the period. The Berrigan brothers had in fact supplied much of the energy, many of the ideas, and a lot of the funding that pushed CPF through its first years, and there were bonds of personal loyalty. When I was serving time in Danbury Federal Correctional Institution, I was visited one day in September by Jim Forest, who swore me to secrecy in the crowded and buzzing visitors' room. There would be a raid on draft boards in Milwaukee and he was planning to participate in it. Jim was jailed immediately after the raid in October 1968, and for several weeks both co-secretaries of the CPF were behind bars. Not long after I returned to the CPF, our office manager, Maggie Geddes, and Jim's wife, Linda Henry, raided draft boards in Rockefeller Center, New York City. They were never prosecuted.

While all this was going on, CPF kept to its business of relating the organized Catholic peace constituency to the larger anti-Vietnam War movement, the Mobilization to End the War, the New Mobe, the Student-Moratorium, etc., and to draft counseling on a large scale. Our involvement in the mass Mobilization began in its initial phases. The first planning meeting was to be held in a Howard Johnson's motel near Case Western Reserve in Cleveland. A.J. Muste, who shared office space with us, urged me to participate for CPF. Thereafter the CW and CPF members helped recruit for and to organize the mass demonstrations leading to the Moratorium-Mobilization of November 1969 in Washington. CW groups offered logistical support, feeding protesters and offering hospitality. At about this time the U.S. Catholic Conference, the bishops' organization, declared the war unjust by reason of the violation of proportionality, a condition in classic "just-war" theory, and urged recognition of conscientious objection to particular wars, never allowed in U.S. law.

It is difficult to measure what proportion of CO claimants were Catholics. Patricia McNeal Dolan cites 7 percent, but this seems low to me. Prisoner Visitation Service, a voluntary agency supported primarily by Protestant groups, once told me that their visitors served more Catholics than any other group. This may be because many Catholics did not know of the legitimacy of their claim within the moral framework of Catholicism and acted on their own in resisting conscription. CPF had an extraordinarily high degree of success with its CO applicants, partly because the men who came to us for counseling had to be more aware than their contemporaries, better educated, just to know of our existence.

By the end of the war CO counseling was available through many Catholic institutions, schools, and parish churches. Paul Frazier of CPF, a student at Manhattan College, pioneered in training draft counselors. Draft counseling centers were set up in many cities, serving all who came, with referral to physicians and psychiatrists where that was indicated, and to lawyers willing to take cases *pro bono publico*. In my travels I often found CO counseling going on after Mass in the sacristy in churches scattered around the country.

The emergence of Pax Christi U.S.A., affiliated with Pax Christi International, the "official international movement of Catholics for peace," signalled another legitimization of the peace witness within Catholicism in the U.S. Organizationally, Pax Christi is the successor to the Pax Association with roots in England. Gordon Zahn was one of the principal organizers and conceptualizers of Pax Christi U.S.A., and serves on its executive board today. Pax Christi counts among its purposes to address the institutional structures of the Church and to stimulate their use for furtherance of peace and nonviolence. Pax Christi, unlike the CW or CPF, is not explicitly pacifist although many pacifists sit in its councils. Its ability to grow and to mature is now being tested. Its promise is great, and crucial, if the Church in the U.S. is to become, as many of us hope, a peace church. Not a pacifist church, but a peace church. The distinction is that in a pacifist church pacifism is normative. Not even the Quakers have been able to maintain normative pacifism; only very small perfectionist sects have been able to do that, and the vocation of the Church is to be a church and not a sect. But in the realities that confront us now, and in the next years of the nuclear age the distinction will probably become more and more narrow and less helpful.

It must be admitted that the Church has not used the full weight of its power and prestige in the cause of peace in our time, that its witness against war and for peace and justice has not been adequate to the needs of our day. Dorothy Day, Thomas Merton, the Berrigans, Gordon Zahn, Eileen Egan, Jim Forest, and many others have made the witness, however well or badly. The Church has failed many times in the past and we cannot afford to be scandalized at its human element. What is of importance is the direction the Church has taken in the era of renewal in the process of becoming the church of Christ's peace. When that is accomplished it will be largely because Gordon Zahn kept us from the schismatic impulse that afflicts perfectionists, kept us rooted in tradition and the Christian humanist rationalism that has been a saving characteristic of Catholicism since the scholastics.

Notes

1. See Gordon Zahn, *Another Part of the War: The Camp Simon Story* (Amherst: University of Massachusetts Press, 1979).

2. Gordon Zahn, "The Great Catholic Upheaval," *Saturday Review* 54 (September 11, 1971): 25ff.

13
The Role of the Peacemaker

Thomas J. Gumbleton

Peace: A Gift Brought to Life

A friend of mine gave birth to a baby girl recently. She had been looking forward to the birth for quite some time with fear and trembling, with excitement and tenderness, with all the emotions common to new mothers. When the baby was finally born her joy knew no bounds. Afterwards, we talked about the long process involved in bringing forth this new life, about how intimate is this relationship between a mother and the child within her, and about childbirth itself. I found myself wanting to know more.

"Was it as painful as they say?"

"Yes."

"But you're glad now?"

"Oh, yes! But during the labor I felt as if I were being torn apart; I felt like I was dying. In fact, a part of me died in giving birth to Catherine. It's the whole passion, death, and resurrection again, but it's worth it. She's beautiful!"

I reflected on her words for some time. ". . . a part of me died . . . but it's worth it." And then: "She's beautiful!" That's what most mothers would say of their newborn child. The casual observer might not reach the same conclusion; in fact, the casual observer might have a difficult time distinguishing one newborn baby from another. They all look alike. Tiny and pink and wrinkled, and so utterly helpless. But a mother is not a casual observer. To her, the little one is a pearl of great price, precious beyond measure.

How quickly all the pain and inconvenience of the months before birth diminish; how easily the agony of labor is forgotten. It would almost seem that the infant deserves punishment for bringing about so much violence to the mother's body, for all the strain and worry inflicted on her. The mother might even welcome the opportunity to "get even," to get revenge of a sort. All that this would require is a slight insensitivity to the baby's needs, a coolness, an unresponsive touch, an absence, invisible to an observer's eye, of tenderness. The baby would suffer without anyone knowing.

Barring mental illness or emotional distraction, a mother is not like that at all. No matter the inconvenience of the past, her baby is the flesh of her flesh, a gem radiant and precious beyond measure! The very way she touches the little one, fondles it, showers it with her love tells the baby how very valuable it is. A mother sees her own reflection in the face of her child. Maybe she even sees the reflection of God there.

What has all this to do with peacemaking? There is a place deep within us, at the core of our being, where we are called to be the bearers of light and truth and love. And peace. The peace that surpasses all understanding does not just happen. Its seeds are planted in the center of our being. We have to let it grow and develop there; we have to allow it to be born within us. We have to look upon it as something precious beyond measure, something we are willing to nurture along by love and constant attention.

If there are violent and spiteful tendencies at our center, then it follows that we have become negligent toward the peace that should flower within us. Maybe we have not been as attentive to its needs as we might be. Maybe we have not recognized it as a pearl of great price. Maybe we have not seen clearly enough the change that has to take place within our hearts before we can become peacemakers. The birth of peace within our own hearts requires a certain amount of dying to ourselves. It is as tragic as it is ironic that the whole world today wants peace, yet there is hardly a spot on earth that is not a witness to brutality and turmoil. Part of the problem is that everyone wants peace on his or her own terms, terms which usually prove to be self-centered and narrow. Pope Paul spoke of peace in terms of justice and truth and harmony. But justice and harmony do not grow and thrive without care and responsiveness on our part.

The Scriptures have much to say about this matter. God teaches how peace comes to life in the heart of the individual and then grows into a love that brings this promise of peace to all. There was a lot of violence in the world during biblical times, so much so that we can recognize in that era the mirror image of today. The behavior and the attitudes of people in the age of the prophets are comparable to the situation now: apathy, injustice, greed. The flaunting and abuse of power by the powerful were widespread thousands of years ago; they are widespread now.

Israel, of course, was a nation constantly trampled underfoot by her neighbors. Its people were carried into captivity, their faces pushed to the ground. God's chosen people had a rough time of it. No wonder they clung to the hope that Yahweh would take revenge on their oppressors. No wonder they wanted a show of power and might and protection from their God. Their pleas that he might, in the idiom of that era, make footstools of their enemies are very understandable.

No one can deny the presence of force or aggressive, militaristic tactics in the Old Testament, even on the part of Yahweh himself. But God used his power and might only to suppress the actions of peoples who had shown the most callous disregard for basic human decency, for disobedience to his law, and who had not infrequently treated others with shameful cruelty.

If we really want to understand what the Scriptures are trying to express, we cannot be content with reading only isolated passages; we must try to understand where the passages lead, what the imagery signifies, why certain themes bear repeating.

The Old Law did not start with turning the other cheek but rather demanding an eye for an eye and a tooth for a tooth. Yet the Old Law represented an improvement over the barbarism of the past, where a person who had stolen a few sheep from a neighbor might come home to find his house razed and his family killed in retaliation. Under the law of "an eye for an eye," at least the wrong inflicted would be proportional to the wrong suffered. The concepts of justice and peace grew and developed as history unfolded. Tempering some of humankind's aggressive tendencies took time; it wasn't until a century or two before Christ that a new spirit began to emerge: "Do not resent [or punish] your neighbor's every offense" (Sir. 10:6).

For those of us who would be peacemakers, it is only natural and even inevitable that we work our way through the Scriptures to follow the development of the understanding of justice, harmony, and true religion, because it is out of these that true peace flows.

Justice is a central theme running all through the inspired Word of God. As we read through the words of the prophets we begin to understand that the concept of justice merges closer and closer to the concept of compassion.

In the poetic words of Isaiah 32, the kingdom of justice is compared to a shelter from the wind, to a stream of water in a dry country, and to the shade of a great rock in a parched land. The wind, the dry country, the parched land describe the setting of the foolish and the wicked who let the hungry go empty and the thirsty remain without drink, who use tricks to plan crimes and lie to the poor. The passage concludes optimistically with the triumph of the kingdom: "Integrity will bring peace, justice gives lasting security" (Isa. 32:17).

The Book of Wisdom (14) describes a period marked by injustice and evil, with no tranquility, no integrity anywhere. The people have strayed so far from the truth, however, that they think they live in a time of peace. Adultery, murder, theft, idolatry, and corruption thrive like advanced diseases. In the midst of it all Wisdom puts her finger on the heart of the matter. Her words of condemnation could have been proclaimed today:

> Soon it is not enough for them that their knowledge of God should be at fault; in the great struggle to which ignorance condemns their lives they next give such massive ills the name of peace [Wis. 14:22].

In Jeremiah we draw still closer to the spirit of true religion, of justice, of righteous living.

> Your father ate and drank like you,
> but he practised honesty and integrity,
> so all went well with him.
> He used to examine the cases of poor and needy,
> so all went well.
> Is not that what it means to know me?
> —it is Yahweh who speaks [Jer. 22:15–16].

"Is not that what it means to know me?" The question is prophetic of words spoken in a later time. We are told that the just person is one who does right, who treats the poor and the weak with compassion, and in doing so comes to know the Lord.

This theme repeats itself in the books of the prophets: the importance of caring for the poor and the needy, for widows and orphans, for the oppressed. Justice and compassion are interwoven throughout the Scriptures; they become a single expression of God's will and of the spirit of true religion. They become, truly, a peace offering.

> A man multiplies offerings by keeping the Law;
> he offers communion sacrifices by keeping the commandments.
> By showing gratitude he makes an offering of fine flour,
> by giving alms he offers a sacrifice of praise [Sir. 35:1].

It remains for the Book of Micah to provide us with that point at which the Old and the New Testaments converge. It announces the One who will link together the Old and the New Law, the Messiah. The words of Micah in Chapter 4 describe a time in which the Lord promises to establish peace and harmony among nations, a time of reconciliation. "They will hammer their swords into plowshares and their spears into sickles. Nation will not lift sword against nation, there will be no more training for war" (Mic. 4:5). When is this time to come? Not yet.

Micah introduces an image that is depicted repeatedly throughout the Old Testament in the dialogue between Israel and Yahweh, the image of Israel as the bride of the Lord. Here it is the image of a woman in labor (Mic. 4:9), one used frequently in the Scriptures, particularly when the enemies of Israel are about to overcome her. She is perpetually in pain and sorrow, about to give birth. For a while, the Lord appears to have abandoned her. Nations gather against her to see her downfall, but "they do not know Yahweh's thoughts." The Lord will deliver her, says Micah, from the hand of her enemies. Israel, the bride of Yahweh, is to bring forth the Messiah.

"He himself will be peace." This is the promise. For so very long, Israel had waited for the Prince of Peace, the Holy One of God who would bring justice and glory and security to the nation. Long abused by her oppressors, she looked forward to a powerful leader, strong, courageous, a great king from a prominent land, a mighty warrior. He would win peace for the chosen people by crushing their opponents once and for all. So Israel dreamed.

> But you, (Bethlehem) Ephrathah,
> the least of the clans of Judah,
> out of you will be born for me
> the one who is to rule over Israel;
> his origin goes back to the distant past,
> to the days of old. . . .
> He will stand and feed his flock
> with the power of Yahweh,
> with the majesty of the name of his God . . .
> from then on he will extend his power
> to the ends of the land.
> He himself will be peace [Mic. 5:2–4].

He himself will be peace. He will be the bearer of justice, of compassion, of truth and light and goodness. All along the Messianic promises led up to and gradually took hold of that realization. But who at the time understood their meaning? And who at this time understands now that we too must become the bearers of peace by coming to life in him who is peace?

"He came to his own domain and his own people did not accept him" (John 1:11). The chosen people were not ready to welcome *this* Prince of Peace. But are we any more ready than they? Are we any more willing to recognize that the first step in building peace must be taken in our own hearts? Jesus is a challenge to everyone (including the oppressed) to undergo *metanoia,* change of heart. So radical is this change, it requires that we must die—at the very center of our being—so that new life, true peace, can begin to grow. This is the first and constant task of the Christian peacemaker: to bring to life in the center of his or her own being this true Peace who is Jesus the Messiah. The role of the Christian peacemaker begins with this. To begin anywhere else leads to failure.

Peace: A Gift Shared

"Blessed are the peacemakers," Jesus said. Why not "blessed are the peaceful, the tranquil and secure?" Isn't it enough for us to enjoy interior calm? Perhaps our Lord saw in the peacemaker something more than could be found in the merely tranquil. Perhaps the latter, in fact, do not possess true peace at all. We could never find perfect peace in ourselves, surely, but we could find its seeds there. We could allow it to grow and nurture it along. Is it not rather a starting point, something which is at once calming, reassuring, loving, and growing, dying, fluctuating, evolving; something we continually strive to nurture in ourselves and in society? Are we not asked to let whatever little peace there is growing in our hearts motivate us to bring peace to our brothers and sisters, to try to be the makers of peace the best we can? Or more correctly, is not the Lord asking those of us who would be peacemakers to allow his peace to work through us, to be born within our hearts, taking root in us, coming to life in us, growing, loving, flowering, recreating, healing not only ourselves but those whom we touch as well?

Our Lord blessed the peacemakers rather than the peaceful in order to tell us that it isn't enough to be easy within ourselves, to calm the storms raging within our hearts. If we really want to carry out the Father's will we can't stop there, sunning ourselves with inner peace. We have to go about calming the raging storms that put people at odds with one another, that threaten to push them farther apart, that leave them divided, discontented, jealous, cruel, indifferent to each other's needs. Surely this is why the Lord blesses the peacemakers and calls them the children of God. To reconcile enemies, to bring about justice and harmony among all people, to bear witness to truth and goodness: this truly is the work of the Lord, doing through his children what he would do himself. This truly is the will of the Father. This is what has been offered, urged, developed over thousands of years of Scriptures and finally revealed in Christ the Lord. This truly is the work of the peacemaker.

In the course of human history there have arisen men and women who dedicated themselves totally to the betterment of humankind; these people found the peace of the Lord deep within the core of their being. And when they began to externalize what was within them the human family was better for it.

Several people in our own era have seen what the Father asks of us and have answered generously. They are the ones who have given witness to truth and goodness and those of us who would become peacemakers could learn from them. They are the ones whom our Lord certainly would have called the children of God.

> There is an immense task incumbent on all men of good will, namely, the task of restoring the relations of the human family in truth, in justice, in love and in freedom.
>
> (Pope John XXIII, *Pacem in Terris,* 1963, n. 163)

> . . . I have the audacity to believe that people everywhere can have three meals a day for their tired bodies, education and culture for their minds, and dignity and equality and freedom for their spirits. I believe that what self-centered men have torn down, other-centered men can build up . . .
>
> (Martin Luther King, Jr., Acceptance Speech of the Nobel Peace Prize, Oslo, Norway, 1964)

> We are sure that all Christians, our brothers, will wish to expand their common cooperative effort in order to help mankind restrain selfishness, pride and rivalries, to overcome ambitions and injustices, to open up to all the road to a more human life, where each man will be loved and helped as his brother, as his neighbor.
>
> (Pope Paul VI, *Populorum Progressio,* 1967, n. 82)

The quotations above represent the hopes and promptings of three such men. Their words flow from the firm belief that the human family is not now all that it can be, but that those who are other-centered can summon and inspire us. Because they were vitally concerned about the well-being of our troubled world, these three men thought about the matter and came to similar conclusions. Their statements reflect their dedication to peace on earth, a peace that requires nothing less than an immense cooperative effort to promote justice and truth and love among all peoples of the earth.

Pope John's encyclical, for example, affirmed the positive side. He could have directed his words largely to a discussion of the forces of fear, oppression, and militarism that make peace impossible. He could have chosen to condemn, step by step, the build-up of all the hatreds and weaknesses that make for war and that contribute to the confused and dangerous state of our world. But the Pope chose not to write on peace by condemning what was choking it. When speaking of the arms race, he simply stated that it was very hard to believe that anyone would deliberately unleash the "monstrous power" of modern nuclear weapons. To John XXIII it was completely obvious that they must be done away with.

> Justice, then, right reason and humanity urgently demand that the arms race should cease; that the stockpiles which exist in various countries should be reduced equally and simultaneously by the parties concerned; that nuclear weapons should be banned.[1]

His words challenge us dramatically. Those who wholeheartedly desire what is right and good for our world know that the important thing is not merely to protest new weapon systems (though that is necessary) but to actively construct world peace through truth, justice, and love. A few years after Pope John XXIII spoke the above words, Pope Paul VI repeated this message:

> Peace cannot be limited to a mere absence of war, the result of an ever precarious balance of forces. No, peace is something that is built up day after day, in the pursuit of an order intended by God, which implies a more perfect form of justice among men.[2]

Building such peace is not easy. It demands a continual effort to overcome our self-centeredness. It may ask of us more than we want to give. But the encyclicals of Paul VI and John XXIII urge us to respond positively. It would be easy, of course, to put off doing anything, and wait for others—the government, the Church, the wealthy, the powerful, the gifted, the interested—to do something about building a better, more just world. But we are not being coaxed into considering whether we would like to do anything. We are being asked, each of us, what we intend to do. Isn't the promise of true peace something all of us are willing to sacrifice for, something precious beyond measure?

Or think of Martin Luther King, Jr. Who among us better echoed the words of Gandhi: "It is my firm faith that we can conquer the world by truth and love"?[3] Surely our own nation was blessed to have such a man among us, even for a short time. King's life offers insight into what can happen when one is willing to speak and live in truth and goodness. He chose to give witness with great patience and perseverance, embracing the way of nonviolence. Because of him the spotlight of the whole world focused upon the cruel reality of racism. All that was ugly and inhuman and brutal, as well as all that was long-suffering, loving, and forgiving was uncovered by that light.

Often the peacemaker must begin to build peace by resisting evil. And this is not an easy task.

In a very small town in Europe, alongside a river separating Austria from Germany, lies a church graveyard. In one of the graves are buried the ashes of a peasant farmer, a man who, like Martin Luther King, gave witness to the truth at great cost. Unlike King, this man did not move thousands of people to look into their hearts for what was right. At the time of his witness, Franz Jäggerstätter did not soften the heart of anyone, really. He simply refused to do what he saw was wrong. He refused to participate in the army of Hitler because he believed that the war was unjust and evil, and he couldn't reconcile his participation in it with what he felt the Lord would have him do. In his order of priorities, the Lord's will came first. He was one of the very few who refused to serve. And because of his refusal, he was beheaded.

One reads the story of Franz Jäggerstätter, if not with admiration, then at least with amazement. During all of the time that he had to change his mind, he was urged and advised to do so. Everyone—his wife, his friends, his parish priest, his bishop—tried to get him to take the sensible course and agree to serve. After all, it was necessary to trust the leaders of one's nation to decide whether a war was just or not.

Gordon Zahn, who brought the story of this peasant farmer to the world's attention, took note of how other Germans saw the matter and recorded their outlook toward the position he had taken. "A waste, his death. A tragedy. A totally senseless position," his lawyer said.[4] What possible good could come of it, when he had a family to support and no one quite agreed with his thinking? The war would continue just as well without him anyway. Foolish man. So thought the people who knew him, even after the war was over and its true horror and injustice were revealed.

Unfortunately, not many saw the issue quite as Franz saw it. We are told not to render to Caesar what does not belong to Caesar. Caesar has no right to demand our participation in gross evil. To Franz's way of thinking, the decision was not really so very complex. It was simply whether to become the bearer of untruth, injustice, and evil, as Caesar asked, or to abide in truth, goodness, and peace. The choice wasn't easy, but it was compelling. Shortly before his death he wrote:

> Just as the wholly secular man will do everything to make this life easier and more pleasant, so must we who still believe in the eternal kingdom do everything so that we may some day find a great reward there.[5]

Franz Jäggerstätter's decision to live and to die in truth and righteousness was applauded by no one. His was a solitary witness.

Two decades ago a Trappist monk began to reflect on the role of the contemplative in the world and, in fact, the role of all those who take upon themselves the name of Christian. His reflections, in articles and books have been truly disturbing to all who read them. In Thomas Merton we find a man who left behind him greater insight into some of the most pressing social issues facing us today. His thoughts on the search for peace in our troubled world are, even now, ten years after his death, invaluable.

He once wrote that a contemplative is one who should refuse to be a part of the world's delusions and activities; he or she should not feel at home in a society that promises happiness to those who drink Coke and Seagram's, and promises protection because it has the bomb. I hope that we might all find a little of the contemplative within us. Being true to our highest calling cannot depend on doing what society expects. Because sometimes what is expected is trivial, meaningless, absurd, or much worse. Sometimes what is expected is evil, as what Franz Jäggerstätter stood against.

There have been times in the history of humankind when society counted on its members to participate in actions so wicked as to be hardly imagined, as in the massive extermination of people during Hitler's regime. As Merton pointed out, Auschwitz was built and managed by dutiful, obedient, persons—citizens who loved their country and proved it by hating their country's enemies. In our own country it was through the minds and hands of dutiful, responsible citizens that the atomic bomb was born—Original Child Bomb the Japanese named it—bringing with it the peace of death.

Thomas Merton recognized that we should be a little more critical of the assumption that church and state are linked together in the pursuit of the common good. He questioned the relationship between church and state, suggesting that individuals ought to be more perceptive about the acts and demands of secular rulers, more sensitive to the possibility that they often ignore ethical and religious responsibilities. Some people feel that the preparation for World War III is the most critical dilemma facing ethical and religious persons today. In confronting this dilemma Merton said:

> There are activities which, in view of their possible consequences, are so dangerous and absurd as to be morally intolerable. If we cooperate in these activities we share in the guilt they incur before God. It is no longer reasonable or right to leave decisions to a largely anonymous power elite that is driving us all, in our passivity, towards ruin. We have to make ourselves heard. Christians have a grave responsibility to protest clearly and forcibly against trends that lead inevitably to crimes which the Church condemns and deplores. Ambiguity, hesitation or compromise are no longer permissible. War must be abolished.[6]

Ironically, some of those who recognize and condemn the nuclear arms build-up as morally intolerable are not necessarily the expected ones. The sociologist C. Wright Mills, an atheist, did not hesitate to denounce the arms race; like Merton, he went straight to the heart of the matter:

> The key moral fact about this situation is the virtual absence within ourselves of absolute opposition to these assumptions by our ruling elites, to their strategy, and to the policies by which they are carrying it out. And the key public result is the absence of any truly debated alternatives. In some part the absence both of opposition and of alternatives rests upon or at least is supported by, the fact of moral insensibility.[7]

We have to begin questioning ourselves, each of us, as to whether we too have been guilty of moral insensibility. Or perhaps the question rightfully ought not to be "whether" but "how much?" Is it not true that the national policies which have brought the whole world to the brink of nuclear annihilation have come about precisely because we have been, almost all of us, morally insensitive, silent when we ought to have voiced objections, and indifferent when objections have been given? Have we not viewed the entire nuclear arms escalation as too remote and too complex for us to judge? Some people think humankind may well go the way of the dinosaur, the great beast with monstrous power but little control, who in the end was destroyed by its own monstrosity. The military build-up taking place in the world right now is apparently using the most powerful instruments on earth to ensure peace. But these very weapons could yet lead us to the fate of the dinosaur: extinction.

Among the many individuals who have challenged military escalation and all of the moral compromises and insensitivities and rationalizations involved therein, none has done so with more perseverance, careful analysis, and dedication than Gordon Zahn. For more than three decades his writings have challenged the beliefs and assumptions of those who take for granted a divine sanction on all our military preparations. For Gordon Zahn it was far too much of an exaggeration to say that the maker of war can consider himself or herself the maker of peace. In a talk entitled "Religion and War" Zahn pointed out that the just-war theory, when applied to nuclear war, leads clearly and necessarily to pacifist conclusions. But in practice our value system gives enough flexibility to the just-war formula to permit the annihilation of the world.[8]

And it is precisely here that we approach the heart of the problem. The issue lies much deeper, Zahn insists, than the limits and conditions under which we may kill, supposedly, without sinning:

> What is really at fault is a terrifying increase in what we might call the "inhumanity potential" of modern man. Auschwitz and Hiroshima are equally evidence of this, not so much in the fact that these were possible (which is bad enough) but that the human mind was able to develop justification for them.[9]

Perhaps those of us who would be peacemakers ought to address ourselves to precisely this dilemma: that we human beings are continually reaching for the sword, for physical power and force to establish peace on earth once and for all, that we still want to think we can insure peace if only we are able to crush our enemies.

But one of the special blessings of our time is the clear guidance we have received from the teaching of the Church. There is perhaps nowhere a more forceful and clear teaching on the immorality of our present course of action than in Catholic social teaching of the last fifteen years.

The whole world took notice in May of 1963 when Pope John XXIII issued his plea and program for peace on earth. The encyclical, *Pacem in Terris*, came as a voice crying in the wilderness, words of peace spoken in a world inflamed with military escalation. Nations all over the earth were beginning to look upon nuclear armaments as a coveted prize in the scramble for more "security." Our own leaders, whom we trusted to make rational, intelligent decisions, were in fact deciding to build more and more of these weapons. Atomic weapons, they reasoned, would safeguard our rights. They were not inclined to listen to words of peace spoken by the most prominent spiritual leader in the world. "In an age such as ours which prides itself on its atomic energy," Pope John wrote, "it is contrary to reason to hold that war is now a suitable way to restore rights which have been violated."[10]

Not long after these words were printed, Vatican Council II was pleading with us to look at war "with an entirely new attitude." In its "Pastoral Constitution on the Church in the Modern World," the Council declared the arms race "an utterly treacherous trap for humanity" which "injures the poor to an intolerable degree."[11]

The encyclical of Pope John XXIII and the position of Vatican Council II began to give us the clearest possible indication of the Church's evaluation of war and the arms race in the nuclear era. But it remained for Pope Paul VI to provide the strongest condemnations ever issued by the Holy See. In his 1976 Peace Day statement, Pope Paul questioned the whole attitude behind war and the arms escalation. He did not hesitate to put his skepticism into blunt, powerful terms:

> If the consciousness of universal brotherhood and sisterhood truly penetrates into the hearts of men and women, will they still need to arm themselves to the point of becoming blind and fanatic killers of others who themselves are innocent, and of perpetrating . . . butchery of untold magnitude, as Hiroshima on August 6, 1945?[12]

In May of 1976, in the report of the Secretary General to the General Assembly of the United Nations, we find this statement of the Holy See:

> The armaments race is to be condemned unreservedly. Even when motivated by a concern for legitimate defense, it is in fact, by virtue of the nature of modern weapons and the situation prevailing on our planet . . . an injustice. For it constitutes . . . a form of theft. The massive budgets allocated to the manufacture and stockpiling

of weapons is tantamount to misappropriations of funds by managers of the large nations or favored blocks.

The obvious contradiction between the waste involved in the overproduction of military devices and the extent of unsatisfied vital needs *is in itself an act of aggression* against those who are victims of it. It is an act of aggression which amounts to a crime for *even when they are not used*, by their cost alone *armaments kill the poor by causing them to starve.*[13]

And what is more, in our own country the Catholic hierarchy has spoken ever more forcefully on military service and nuclear weapons. The National Conference of Catholic Bishops, in a pastoral reflection on the moral life, cautioned us against giving blind obedience to national authority:

> . . . no nation, our own included, may demand blind obedience. No members of the armed forces, above all no Christians who bear arms as "agents of security and freedom," can rightfully carry out orders or policies requiring direct force against noncombatants or the violation of some other moral norm.[14]

And then the bishops, aware of the exceeding danger of nuclear weapons, went on to say:

> With respect to nuclear weapons, at least those with massive destructive capability, the first imperative is to prevent their use. As possessors of a vast nuclear arsenal, we must also be aware that not only is it wrong to attack civilian populations, but that it is also wrong to threaten to attack them as part of a strategy of deterrence. We urge the continued development and implementation of policies which seek to bring these weapons more securely under control, progressively reduce their presence in the world, and ultimately remove them entirely.[15]

In the light of such clear biblical and magisterial teaching can there be any doubt about the role of the peacemaker in this period of our history? Without making judgments on the past, it is unmistakably clear that it is no longer possible for a Catholic peacemaker to continue a quest for peace by seeking military solutions to any human problems, even those of injustice or oppression. Indeed I am compelled to state it even more forcefully. In the present danger in which we all live, peacemakers must go further. Einstein cried, "The unleashed power of the atom has changed everything but our modes of thinking, and thus we drift toward unparalleled catastrophe."[16] The peacemaker must begin to reverse this drift toward catastrophe. The peacemaker is more and more clearly compelled to enter into active resistance to any military "solutions" in our atomic era. Such resistance will require the deep spirituality of a Thomas Merton, the holy courage of a Martin Luther King. It may be the ridiculed and solitary witness of a Franz Jäggerstätter. But to fulfill the role of peacemaker we must be willing to start along the path they have shown us. This is a new path for most of us who have always placed such confidence in the human wisdom of our world leaders. But now we must follow a way that is unfamiliar to most of us. We must be willing to enter into a kind of darkness arising out of the doubt and uncertainty we begin to feel when we move away from the familiar path of *human* wisdom. We must begin to travel a path we would not dare to go alone, believing that the Light which shines in the darkness will show us the way, trusting that the Lord will work through us. And here we come to a most important consideration—the manner of our resistance.

Peace: A Gift Shared Through Nonviolence

My own deepening conviction is that the present, intense insecurity in our world is a result of the failure to this point of many peacemakers simply to be sensitive enough to the will of the Father. Too many of us peacemakers have not truly given birth to the peace of the Lord within our hearts, because to do so requires that we die in a real way to ourselves; it involves pain and inconvenience and certainly a measure of selflessness. And because we have not been willing to do so, we have never really brought to life the peace of Jesus deep within ourselves. We have not learned to appreciate true peace as something precious beyond measure, something that we must nurture with love and constant attention. When Jesus, who is our peace, as St. Paul explains (Eph. 2:14), has come to life in the deep core of our being, we must make peace the only way to peace. There is no other way for the one who lives in him. His words, recorded by Matthew, could hardly be more clear.

> You have learnt how it was said: *Eye for eye and tooth for tooth*. But I say this to you: offer the wicked man no resistance. On the contrary, if anyone hits you on the right cheek, offer him the other as well; if a man takes you to law and would have your tunic, let him have your cloak as well. And if anyone orders you to go one mile, go two miles with him. Give to anyone who asks, and if anyone wants to borrow, do not turn away. You have learnt how it was said: *You must love your neighbour* and hate your enemy. But I say this to you: love your enemies and pray for those who persecute you; in this way you will be sons and daughters of your Father in heaven [Matt. 5:38–45].

His example, emphasized to Peter who tried to defend him with force, backs up his words. Insisting that Peter put away his sword, Jesus follows the way of nonviolence even into the ultimate human darkness that is death. Violence he knew could only beget violence. The way of nonviolence, the way his Father called him, he trusted would lead even through death to life and—to peace! Long hours of prayer in communion with his Father brought him to know that his way was to be the way so beautifully described by the great prophet Isaiah.

> Here is my servant whom I uphold
> my chosen one in whom my soul delights.
> I have endowed him with my spirit
> that he may bring true justice to the nations.
>
> He does not cry out or shout aloud,
> or make his voice heard in the streets.
> He does not break the crushed reed,
> nor quench the wavering flame.
>
> Faithfully he brings true justice [Isa. 42:1–3].

No president, no military commander, not many people at all, given to depend so much on the insights of human wisdom, would agree with him. But "those who believe" as St. Paul declares, join with him in the ever stronger conviction that "God's foolishness is wiser than human wisdom, and God's weakness is stronger than human strength" (1 Cor. 1: 25). This way of nonviolence must be the way of the Christian peacemaker. It is the way in which the peacemaker resists the evil of violence being perpetrated as "an act of aggression against the poor" in the arms race. It is the way of resistance also against that immoral posture of deterrence which is the stated policy of our government.[17]

Will it work? Wrong question. Is it right? Is it the way of Jesus? This can be the only question of the Christian peacemaker.

Resist we must. But only nonviolently. Our resistance must be a witness to the truth, an effort to bring out truth. The work of the Christian peacemaker must start within our own society, to bring about its transformation, to make it a society of peace. Peace will beget peace, as surely as violence begets violence. When we are a peaceful people we will begin to bring peace to other nations and among nations.

But if we do not change our hearts and still harbor most of the old conflicts that have been with us all along, then it will be impossible for us to become peacemakers. What will happen is that we move into constant activity, where, if the interior search for peace becomes tiresome, we can still go through with the exterior motions of pursuing it. It almost seems tempting at times to forget about interior peace because that can prove a hindrance to what we would like to accomplish. And we'd like to accomplish a lot. A nuclear arms protest, for example, can offer a ray of light in a world growing darker with the threat of nuclear war, a war described by Thomas Merton as "a moral evil second only to the Crucifixion." Carried out in a nonviolent way, such a protest should be, as it was for Gandhi, a sign of truth and morality to all who witness the demonstration. But without a genuine commitment to nonviolence such a protest can, in fact, be an attack on those we name enemies.

No one acting in a nonviolent way will provoke anger where it need not be provoked or taunt those against whom a protest is made, or worst of all perhaps, wallow in a kind of proud and condescending self-righteousness that passes for courage and masks the weakness of those who falsely seek to be peacemakers. It becomes tempting to condemn, or at least dismiss as un-Christian and ignorant, anyone not fully appreciative of the demonstrator and all he or she is going through to give witness. To give witness does not mean showing others how wrong they are and letting it go at that. Such a tactic can be received as primarily a personal attack, leaving those responsible for the prevailing situation groping for defense measures or being forced to remain silent, feeling generous just to have put up with the demonstration at all. In fact, such violence will arouse so much antagonism that those enforcing or permitting injustice and violence become more firmly entrenched in what they are doing. This is not to say that ill-will is to be avoided at all cost; at times the price of telling the truth might well arouse terrible antagonism that is also cloaked with justification.

Clearly it is the role of the peacemaker to try to look not for the evil of those threatening the world with violence, with oppression, with nuclear annihilation, but to look for their goodness, their capability, and to begin working with them. Clearly the attitude of the nonviolent peacemaker ought to grow more receptive to possibilities of reconciliation within our own national community. Couldn't our dialogue with those whom we seek to reach express itself in affirmation rather than bitter negation, starting something like this: "Yes, we see eye to eye in that we both want peace, and we both see the need for a strong defense, and we both agree that the military power of the other side is very strong. But then we come to a parting of ways. Maybe your own search for peace, General, Senator, Reverend, would allow you to consider your policy formulations in light of these considerations which have not been taken into account. . . ."

Could we not hope to begin exploring nonviolent ways to achieve national civil defense?[18] Could we not start to put our abundant resources into a Department of Peace rather than continuing to fund a military establishment almost without limit? Could we not start to put forth much more effort into exploring the possible avenues to help reconcile those at odds with one another, finding the ways Einstein pleaded for to change "our modes of thinking?" Could not the Church, the state, the schools, the press, encourage such studies? So many valuable insights could be explored by drawing on the behavioral sciences: psychology, psychiatry, sociology, theology, philosophy, and biology. Could we not begin to disarm now?

Is it too presumptuous, too unrealistic to hope that we might approach a genuine spirit of understanding and reconciliation? I think not. And as we gradually bring this spirit to life and follow entirely new paths to peace in our own country, we could expect our leaders to begin to act in this way with leaders of other nations. Slowly but persistently the true peace of God—which is beyond all understanding—will begin to take firm root in our hearts and the hearts of our brothers and sisters everywhere.

"Blessed are the peacemakers. They shall be called God's children." If any of us wants to be among those called the children of God, our task is clear: nurture that tiny seed of peace within our own hearts. Even die a little to bring it to life. Reach out to a suffering world to bring about human development. *Resist* the immoral demands even of our own government. Challenge ourselves to grow in nonviolence. Seek constantly to find truth and goodness in others—even our "enemies." This is the role, the task, of the peacemaker. This is the call Jesus makes to us in asking us to follow him into the way of peace.

Will I answer this call? Will you? Will we be peacemakers? Our answer might well determine whether the world arrives at the year 2000 in peace or destroys itself before then.

Notes

1. Pope John XXIII, *Pacem in Terris*, ed. William J. Gibbons, S.J. (New York: Paulist Press, 1963), n. 112.
2. Pope Paul VI, *Populorum Progressio* (New York: Paulist Press, 1967), n. 76.
3. Mahatma Gandhi, *All Men Are Brothers*, ed. Krishna Kripalni (Chicago: World Without War Publications, UNESCO, 1958), p. 65.
4. Gordon Zahn, *War, Conscience and Dissent* (New York: Hawthorn, 1967), p. 184.
5. Ibid., p. 181.
6. Thomas Merton, "Nuclear War and Christian Responsibility," *Commonweal* 75 (February 9, 1962): 509. (Quoted by Gordon Zahn in an article entitled "The Peacemaker.")
7. C. Wright Mills, "A Pagan Sermon to the Christian Clergy," in *The Pacifist Conscience*, ed. Peter Mayer (New York: Holt, Rinehart and Winston, 1966), p. 412.
8. Zahn, *War, Conscience and Dissent*, p. 79.
9. Ibid., p. 79
10. Pope John XXIII, *Pacem in Terris* (Washington, D. C.: National Catholic Welfare Conference, 1963), n. 127.
11. "Pastoral Constitution on the Church in the Modern World," in *The Documents of Vatican II*, ed. Walter M. Abbott, S.J. (New York: America Press, 1966), n. 81.
12. Paul VI, Peace Day Statement, January 1976.
13. Statement of the Holy See, in the Report of the Secretary General on "Strengthening of the Role of the United Nations in the Field of Disarmament," to the General Assembly of the United Nations, May 7, 1976. Italics in original.
14. National Conference of Catholic Bishops, *To Live in Christ Jesus* (Washington, D.C.: United States Catholic Conference, 1976), p. 34.
15. Ibid.
16. Otto Nathan and Heinz Norden, eds., *Einstein on Peace* (New York: Simon and Schuster, 1960), p. 376.
17. Cf. *To Live In Christ Jesus*, p. 34.
18. See, for example, Gene Sharp, *The Politics of Non-Violent Action* (Boston: Porter Sargent, 1973).

Afterword

Gordon C. Zahn

When Tom Shannon first disclosed his plans for this book—carefully waiting until he could present it as a *fait accompli*—my immediate reaction was one of surprise and embarrassment. The surprise should need no explanation; it was planned to be one. The embarrassment requires a little explanation lest it be taken as a display of false modesty or that "shyness" the editor so surprisingly credits to me. (Nor, I should add, is it to be read as a reaction against the implications of advancing age necessarily incorporated into "dedicatory" memorials of this nature.) Instead, my objections to being so honored lie in the very strong suspicion that the honor may prove to be misdirected and is, in any event, premature.

However encouraging the increased recognition of what I like to refer to as the pacifist implications of Christianity may be, it is probably too soon to celebrate any individual for whatever contributions he or she may have made to the awakening of that awareness. If I am not above taking satisfaction in the evidence that my books and essays helped open discussions that led to some of these advances (no false humility here, as you can see), I would also insist that too many critical war and peace issues remain unresolved or unaddressed to justify any distribution of laurels at this time. Among the things the fledgling Catholic peace movement does *not* need is the emergence of anything approaching a "cult of the personality." Had I been given the chance, I would have argued against the project. The anticipation of such opposition probably accounts for the amazingly successful "conspiracy of silence" engaging so many close friends and associates while the book was being prepared.

Now, with the completed manuscript in hand, I can frankly confess to being immensely pleased with the results. It is not that my embarrassment and reservations are less. Rather, the significance of the collected essays is such that the reason for bringing them together can be (and probably will be) easily overlooked or ignored by most readers. To have been even an indirect cause of something that should stand by itself as a major contribution to the Christian moral teachings on war and peace is a most gratifying experience.

Personal Reflections

So now I am presented with the task of adding some personal reflections. This is no easy task, especially since I will exclude the most obvious approach to the assignment. I have no intention of treating each individual essay in order. This decision is not dictated solely by any sense of propriety or by the desire to avoid the temptation to return compliment for compliment and, in the process, reduce this most valuable collection to a superficial exercise in mutual admiration. Instead, it is a recognition of a real lack of competence to discuss and evaluate most, if not all, of the separate contributions. How could I hope to meet Deats and Muelder, for instance, on an equal footing? My knowledge of Protestant pacifism is at best peripheral, and even then something derived from personal associations rather than from familiarity with the essential source materials. Much the same can be said for True's extremely interesting review of nonviolence in American literary traditions. The most I could do here would be to raise questions as to why one strain or another was not introduced or developed more fully, knowing all the while that these would be the questions of a literary dilettante to someone with a professional command of the subject.

Those contributions written from the perspective of the just-war ethic offer quite a different challenge. I have had many opportunities to debate certain arguments or interpretations with their authors in a variety of other contexts. To do so here again would be repetitious, so I will try to limit myself to some of my more fundamental disagreements with the just-war tradition itself of specific issues and developments I feel deserve more scholarly exploration or practical application. This should not be interpreted as a lack of appreciation or respect for people like Finn, Hehir, Childress, Lammers, *et al.* Indeed, one of the most striking contributions of these authors is their willingness to test and, in some instances, challenge the more traditional assumptions and implications of the just-war ethic. If nothing else, the willingness to grant the pacifist tradition something approaching equality with the just-war ethic is an important advance over the attitudes characteristic of most of that position's advocates in the past.

As for the remaining contributions, there is little I could offer in the way of response other than to offer entirely predictable agreement and applause. They represent positions so very close to my own that the temptation would be to repeat many of their statements and arguments in what was surely intended to be more than a closing summary. Eileen Egan's discourse upon the Sermon on the Mount and the contrasts presented by war and its ideology reflects her many years spent in the service of peace and international justice. In a slightly different vein, Tom Cornell's historical resumé of the admittedly few, yet surprisingly significant successes registered by the more organizationally-oriented Catholic opposition to war fits in well with David O'Brien's contribution. As for O'Brien's "preliminary assessment," it is impressive as it stands, but it also gives rise to the hope that it is a promise of a future and definitive analysis of the Catholic resistance to the war in Vietnam. Bishop Gumbleton and Joe Fahey, as always, plead the cause of peace education and action most effectively at a time when there is every indication that the need for both will increase dramatically rather than diminish in the years immediately ahead. Finally, and this is particularly difficult to put into words, I am deeply moved by the contribution of Paul Hanly Furfey. Not only do I regard him as a revered teacher and model, but I would be prepared to argue that it is Furfey, not me, to whom a volume like this should be dedicated. I share Patricia McNeal Dolan's judgment that he is the "originator" of the American Catholic peace movement. In a more personal vein, I know that without his support and encouragement, it is most unlikely that this one-time office clerk could ever have gained the academic credentials which opened the way to whatever impact my writings on peace may have had.

The State of the Question: A Review

Almost twenty years have passed since the publication of another book which set out to describe the "state of the question" regarding modern war and morality.[1] Since there is nothing to suggest that the present collection which addresses itself to "old questions" and "new answers" was intended to be a conscious up-dating of that earlier volume, the similarity of purpose must be taken as a happy coincidence. That volume, too, consisted of a series of essays written from a variety of professional perspectives. There were prominent Jesuit theologians (John Courtney Murray, John C. Ford, John R. Connery), distinguished academicians and specialists in military strategy (Thomas E. Murray, James E. Dougherty, William V. O'Brien), and one dissident sociologist expounding the then theologically suspect and generally unfamiliar case for pacifism.

That volume differed from the present collection in that all contributors were Catholic and it was the "Catholic" state of the question with which it was concerned. That the present volume addresses its issues in a broader frame of reference testifies to the gains that have been made in ecumenism. The shift in balance between the just-war and pacifist approaches is no less significant. In a footnote to his Introduction, Nagle made special note of the distribution and wrote, "With regard to the proportion between articulate pacifists and other Catholic writers in the United States, the editor is convinced that *Morality and Modern Warfare* reflects a fair representation."[2] Actually, of course, it was much more than fair. Had "articulate pacifists" constituted one-tenth of all Catholic writers of the time, the subsequent history of the Church in America would have been quite different.

It would be a mistake to deduce from the change in proportion represented here that Catholic opinions concerning war have shifted in the same direction and to a comparable degree. These contributions, after all, were selected for a purpose which was certain to assure a disproportionate representation for the pacifist position. Nevertheless, it will be clear even from those essays written from the just-war perspective that there has been a dramatic shift. In 1960 it would have been difficult, perhaps impossible, for any editor to *find* this number of writers willing to participate in a volume honoring the pacifist perspective—much less ready to defend that perspective themselves. We may be sure there would have been no bishop willing to do so. Although Pax Christi was already active in Europe, few American Catholics knew of it or were interested in learning about this international Catholic peace movement. (I can attest to this from my own experience. In the 1950s I suggested that the Catholic Association for International Peace add a new committee to the multitude already listed on the back of its official stationery, a committee charged with responsibility for keeping up with Catholic peace organizations elsewhere in the world. The response to my letter was negative. As far as the CAIP was concerned, there was no more need for such a committee than there would be for a committee on "Catholic isolationism"!)

In my own contribution to the Nagle volume ("Social Science and the Theology of War"), I raised a number of challenges to Catholic teachings and performance with respect to actual and potential wars that would be repeated in later essays and books. The only justification for strumming the same note all these years lies in the fact that these challenges have retained most of their validity and do so, to a great extent, even today.

This is not to deny that "the state of the question," from the pacifist point of view, has greatly improved over what it was two decades ago. When the Nagle book was published, John XXIII had been pope for slightly more than a year, and the Council he called into being lay two years into the future. *Pacem in Terris,* the watershed document of the modern Catholic peace movement, would be issued the spring following the formal convening of Vatican Council II. We may assume that some progress would have been made toward the "re-discovery" of those pacifist implications of the Christian faith even without the impetus and inspiration provided by John, Paul VI (the "Pilgrim of Peace"), and the Council, but there is no doubting that such *official* sources contributed most to increasing the number of Catholics susceptible to pacifist arguments and appeals.

In this country, of course, the shift of attitude was greatly accelerated by our involvement in the Indochina war. The extensive and effective Catholic opposition to that war described in David O'Brien's essay may have been most immediately related to the Church in America, but its impact was worldwide and contributed to a re-definition of theological teachings on war and peace in prominent European circles which in its turn found its way back into our own theological writings and debates.

The changes have been significant. Twenty years ago no one of Bryan Hehir's stature would have been willing to recognize pacifism as an acceptable, much less equal, option for the Catholic. Very few Catholic writers would have given serious thought to nonviolence as a possible alternative to war, and few of these would have thought favorably of its prospects. Conscientious objection, as both Finn and Hehir note, had been all but condemned by Pius XII in his 1956 Christmas message. Today we cannot only cite supportive passages in the documents of Vatican Council II and in pastoral statements issued by national hierarchies, but the American bishops have gone beyond these to call for recognition of *selective* conscientious objection and, more amazing still, amnesty for the conscientious deserters of the Vietnam era. Individual bishops have appeared before courts and draft boards to plead the cause of conscientious objectors and war resisters. Viewed from the perspective of one of the rare (and studiously ignored!) Catholic conscientious objectors to World War II, this reversal of form borders on the miraculous.

After making full allowance for these improvements, however, I am bound to say that my basic criticism in that earlier article still holds true with, at most, minor modifications:

> The "state of the question" regarding the morality of nuclear war may be simply stated: For all too many Catholics there is no question or, at least, none that falls within the average layman's scope of competence.[3]

If the reason I gave then (". . . we have not realized that the morality of modern war, including *pre-nuclear* war, can or should be a legitimate subject for serious disputation") no longer applies, it would be well not to draw too much comfort from the fact. Vatican and episcopal pronouncements may have corrected that omission, but they no longer carry the weight they once did. It is a tragic fact that, now that spiritual leaders have finally begun to provide the leadership that was lacking before, other postconciliar changes in the Catholic Church have so lessened the authority of bishops and even popes that their words no longer command the attention, not to mention obedience, of the men and women in the pew (of which, as we well know, there are significantly fewer to hear). Let us not exaggerate the implications of this particular change, however. If it can be said that the majority of our Catholic faithful are apathetic or indifferent to the moral dimensions of war and resistive to statements of ecclesiastical officials which might try to change those attitudes, it was probably ever thus—at least since the introduction of the just-war ethic.

Nor should we exaggerate the extent to which ecclesiastical leaders have matched those statements with effective action. Pax Christi U.S.A. takes justifiable pride in having no fewer than three bishops on its governing council and a dozen or more others on its membership rolls. The sad fact remains that these represent an extremely small segment of the American hierarchy. Similarly, even though O'Brien's survey of the Vietnam record shows that we were spared the chauvinistic excesses that marked episcopal behavior in past wars, this should not blind us to the fact that a bishop is much more likely to grace the podium of some "patriotic" function or group than to lend his presence or even his moral support to some community-wide peace activity or disarmament rally.

In the Nagle volume, as in many subsequent writings, I have tried to stress the irrelevance of the just-war ethic to the grim actuality of modern war. I see little reason to change my mind on this. However, in developing this theme I have usually stressed the inability to fit the actuality into the carefully defined conditions which are supposed to determine whether a given war is just or unjust. There is another sense in which the just-war ethic is "irrelevant" which has been generally overlooked. Simply stated, it is that there is too great a gulf between those who develop and discuss the ethic and its implications and those who fight the wars.

To consider just the present volume, for example, one may admire and respect the careful and detailed scholarly analyses, the clarity of the arguments and their logical consistency, which characterize the contributions of those who accept the just-war ethic. At the same time, however, one should recognize that the appreciation of these virtues is restricted to an audience of ethical specialists who will have little or no opportunity to affect the course of an actual war or, for that matter, the behavior of those engaged in that war. Most of the latter are either unaware of these analyses or indifferent to them, except to the extent that they can be made to serve the interests of military and political leaders.

Certainly the careful distinctions and definitions will be lost upon the great mass of Catholic faithful, most of whom (with pastoral and episcopal encouragement) pride themselves on their patriotic loyalty and who really believe it is not for them to question their government's acts and policies in time of war. Even were it possible for theologians or spiritual leaders to raise the appropriate doubts of the justice of a given war or specific acts of war, the price of not "going along" would be too great for most to contemplate or accept. The ethicians, then, can continue to lavish time and intellectual energy upon their search for the perfect balance between "military necessity" and "moral obligation," and it will make little or no difference. Most Catholics ordered to report for service will report. Most Catholic soldiers ordered to perform a certain act (Dresden? Hiroshima? My Lai? Doomsday?) will still obey.

So, too, with the delusion that the results of all this scholarly effort will be taken into account by the "magistrates" and even govern the behavior of the men who issue the orders. This expectation ignores the teaching of history that "military necessity" is an infinitely flexible concept and one which will always come into play once a situation is defined as sufficiently critical to threaten the loss of the war, a major battle, or even a limited action and the lives of those involved. The military commander who is prepared to ask his computers to weigh the "good effect" of a proposed campaign against the "evil" and then proceed only if the "proportionality" is favorable (all the time "willing" only the good, of course) is a figment of the imagination. He may be found in ethical handbooks or theological journals, but he is certainly not likely to have an office in the Pentagon.

As stimulating intellectual exercises, the just-war ethician's efforts do little harm in themselves. Unfortunately, again as history makes tragically clear, there are side effects that cannot be ignored. Those same individuals or agencies which are the least likely to be influenced by the limits the ethician would impose upon military decisions will always be ready and eager to exploit every ethical loophole or exception (even, one might suggest, the very implications of a concept like "just" war) as justification for some new escalation of war's inhumanity. It is not unfair to say that the contributions of the just-war thinking to the proliferating theories of deterrence have helped make it possible for what was once "unthinkable" to become not only "thinkable" but "do-able" as well.

This was a major concern of mine in 1960, and it has not diminished. If we are forced to make a choice between risks, I, as a pacifist, would prefer risking the evils we might have to endure as a result of too rigid an exclusion of war to the evils we would certainly be called upon to commit as the result of too easy an acceptance of actions deemed "necessary" by some military leader, thereby meeting the test of the "just" war. This has a direct bearing upon the function and responsibility of the religious community, a question to which I shall return at a later point.

The broader scope of its title notwithstanding, the Nagle volume and my contribution to it focused mainly on the nature and moral implications of nuclear war. This, too, remains a contemporary issue despite the fact that prominent ecclesiastical leaders have publicly gone on record against the use and even the *threat* to use the murderous weapons we are continuing to produce despite the fact that current stockpiles could destroy the world and its inhabitants several times over. Rare, I am happy to say, is the cleric—or, for that matter, the professional theologian—who is willing to voice approval of these weapons. There are some who may counsel restraint in condemning all, arguing instead for sparing some (the "petite" bombs) for possible use in a limited battlefield situation; but this permissiveness can usually be traced to some present or past involvement on the part of such priest or bishop with the military and commitment to its values and interests. Given the fact that Vatican Council II reserved one of its two condemnations for weapons designed to destroy whole areas and their populations, describing such acts of war as an offense against God and humankind, this particular issue seems fairly well settled, at least at the theoretical level.

When we turn from theory to practice, however, little effort has been made to translate this opposition into effective action. One cannot but wonder what the effect would be were the American bishops to mount and fund a campaign for nuclear disarmament on a scale comparable to their nationwide campaign against abortion. Surely, it must not have missed their notice that the escalation of ecclesiastical denunciations of the modern military arsenal has been matched and exceeded by the escalation of those armaments themselves. Nor is this just a matter of escalation in quantity; the introduction, or impending introduction, of new and more sophisticated weapons systems (Trident, the MX missile, etc.) opens new prospects of world destruction—yet this escalation in quality proceeds unhampered by any significant action on the part of the Church.

One example: in 1967 when it was only a remote possibility, the American hierarchy publicly denounced the neutron bomb as the most dramatic expression of "the anti-life direction of technological warfare" and a depressing "symbol of our civilization." "It would be perverse indeed," the bishops continued, "if the Christian conscience were to be unconcerned or mute in the face of the multiple moral aspects of these awesome prospects."[4] It is more than a decade later. The President is on the verge of giving final authorization for the production and deployment of these weapons. The bishops and the overwhelming majority of their flock stand mute. It is perverse indeed.

What is usually taken to be apathy or indifference is more likely resignation to a situation mistakenly defined as inevitable. In discussions with service personnel or war veterans I have regularly encountered agreement that war and the killing required in war are contrary to their Christian ideals—but, as they see it, once the country "calls," there is nothing for the individual to do but serve. It is true that the past twenty years have witnessed significant advances in the rediscovery of the rights and obligations of the private conscience, but even the concerted opposition to the Vietnam War described by O'Brien, Furfey and Cornell should not blind us to the fact that, at its peak, the resistance movement involved a relatively small segment of the total Catholic community. Those welcome and encouraging episcopal statements in support of conscientious objection are always carefully hedged so as not to be mistaken for *recommendations* that draft-eligible Catholics refuse military service.

Bishop Gumbleton's exposition of the case for nonviolent alternatives and Eileen Egan's meditation upon the Beatitudes and works of mercy offer other and better answers than the generally accepted notion that "national security" must be equated with the capacity, and the intention, to annihilate all potential enemies. The problem is that such alternatives have little or no access to the broader Catholic population, most of which remains ready to support and fight even the kind of war that is forbidden. The threatened revival of peacetime conscription can only make the situation worse. Eighteen-year-old men (and possibly women too?)—even those who have experienced Catholic education—have not been exposed to the kind of moral preparation which would make it possible for them to make a mature judgment about war and military service. Once they are subjected to military indoctrination and discipline, their capacity to make a later judgment about a given war in which they are ordered to serve, or a given act they are ordered to perform, will be severely limited if not destroyed altogether.

All things considered, the differences between "the state of the question" described in the Nagle book and the situation in which we find ourselves today justify a measure of cautious optimism. Memorial Day speakers may still proclaim that "war has its place," but they are less likely to find these sentiments echoed in the official pronouncements and documents of the Roman Catholic Church. And on the behavioral level, more (though certainly not most!) members of what has justly been viewed as one of the more hyperpatriotic religious communities are becoming aware of the need and the right to question, and even refuse, the nation's call to arms.

On the other hand, there is little immediate prospect of the Catholic Church becoming a fourth "peace church," however much the convinced pacifist might regard that as a desirable or ultimate objective. Those questions that are being asked and the moral alternatives that are being studied and advanced are restricted for the most part to a theologically conscious or concerned "elite" and have not reached the bulk of the Catholic faithful. If war, even a war that all our authors would agree was unjust, were to break out tomorrow, it is a safe bet that most Catholics would respond to the call to service and sacrifice as they always have. It is almost as certain that they would find support and encouragement in the public statements and actions of the Church's leaders. Vatican Council II refused to incorporate a reaffirmation of the "presumption of justice" principle (accepted by Childress) when it came to the final version of "The Constitution on the Church in the Modern World." At the time "the pacifist lobby" claimed that as a major victory, which, of course, it was. Unfortunately that victory is likely to have little impact upon Catholic behavior in time of war. Then, as always, that "presumption" will be made in practice (assuming a question or doubt is even raised) simply as a matter of course.

Advances in the Debate

One conclusion that follows is that any "new answers" to the "old questions" in our search for peace must somehow reach beyond the usual arena of academic or ecclesiastical debate. More attention must be given to the "thrust" of the Christian message than to the already over-argued niceties of substance. The faithful must be alerted to the urgency of the need to translate intellectual and ethical judgments into moral imperatives and effective action.

This is not to say, of course, that there is no further need for clarification of thought and concepts. Even the essays included here reveal a continuing need for consensus on some of the more crucial terms involved: "force," "power," "coercion," "violence," even a term like "pacifism" itself. The Deats contribution is extremely valuable in this respect, but much more must be done. Too many people have an overly simple understanding of what pacifism involves and are quite unaware that a pacifist does not necessarily deny the role of "power" in human affairs and accepts the use of certain types of "force" (persuasion, example, "soul force," etc.) and even, at times, "coercion" (boycott, fasting) to achieve legitimate objectives.

If I were to choose a single most important contribution made by this collection of essays, it would be the one mentioned earlier: the willingness to recognize pacifism as a legitimate Catholic option and one deserving at least equal status with the more traditional just-war teachings. In making this choice I am influenced, of course, by my own past (and not always happy) experience on this score. It is not too long since individual Catholics who were clearly "pacifist" in their orientation and acts—Thomas Merton is one who comes to mind—took pains to dissociate themselves from the term and the position. Even within our small group of Catholic conscientious objectors to World War II, those who openly identified themselves as pacifists opposed to all war and violence were likely to be warned by their fellow COs that such a stand had more in common with the Quakers and other "heretical sects" than with the "orthodox" teachings of the Catholic Church.

Given this significant advance in the essays of Finn, Hehir, and others, it may seem ungracious for me to suggest that this is really not enough. Hehir rightly notes that the Church has not moved to the point of endorsing pacifism as the only valid, or even preferred, option; and he raises the "question of coherence" (i.e., whether there can be pacifist and just-war Christians in the same community of faith) in terms which clearly imply an affirmative answer. As a pacifist, I am not so sure that the Church can rest easily with two essentially contrary interpretations of Christian belief and mission. *Objectively*, or so it would seem, only one interpretation can be right: either it is always wrong to wage war *or* under certain conditions it can be permitted, or even obligatory, to do so.

Subjectively, needless to say, there is less of a problem. Allowance must always be made for those who act under a sincere, but erroneous, conscience. It is my impression, however, that this is not what Hehir has in mind. Besides, even if it were, it would still be the Church's obligation to perform its teaching function in such a way as to reduce the likelihood of such "erroneous consciences" being formed and to correct them when they are.

The argument for a more complete reversal of teachings that have dominated the morality of war for centuries requires more extended development than space permits. As the many generous citations indicate, I have attempted to do this in other publications, and there is little need for me to repeat those arguments here because other contributors have already made the case for the pacifist approach. The most telling indictment of the just-war ethic is its dismal failure to fulfill the purposes claimed for it. It is obviously true, as Childress notes, that the criteria were not designed to determine whether wars can ever be justified; at some point, however, we must come to terms with the fact that they have also failed to determine whether a *particular* war is just or unjust. Similarly, those who would define war as a "rule-governed activity" have a distinct obligation to demonstrate that the "rules" actually do "govern" and are not simply ignored, suspended, or abandoned at the discretion of those responsible for its conduct whenever "military necessity" is claimed.

The real problems with the just-war ethic, however, are more basic and of older origin and relate to what might be called the appropriate "stance" of the Christian churches and the thrust of the Christian belief and value system. Before Ambrose and Augustine gave legitimacy to the concept of a "just" war, the Christian community was unmistakably "against" war and required the believer to avoid participation in war. Those Christians who acted contrary to what Windass has described as "the only stream of thought"[5] in the primitive Church may not have been excluded from the religious fellowship, but they were often subjected to special penances and otherwise set apart as not fulfilling the obligations of their religious calling.

This anti-war, anti-violence thrust was reversed as the just-war ethic made it possible (later obligatory) for Christians to rationalize their departure from the literal application of Scriptural injunctions and commandments in order to take up arms in the service of the secular ruler. Over the centuries the various accretions and extensions of the developing just-war ethic has followed essentially the same pattern: as war and the political order changed, the conditions have been revised or re-interpreted in whatever fashion was needed to permit Christian participation in the killing and destruction. It is not just a Paul Ramsey, then, who may be incapable of making a negative judgment concerning his country's military policy of strength; the same can be said of most, if not all, of the just-war theorists since the time of Augustine. That a John Courtney Murray could make the scandalous statement cited by Finn ("Since nuclear war may be a necessity, it must be made a possibility.") stands as a judgment against the just-war ethic and the claims made for it.

In the symposium mentioned by Childress, I presented a recommendation which merits being included here. Instead of continuing to seek and create new justifications for war and participation in war, I believe that any church professing to be committed to the New Testament and its teachings must adopt a public stance under which it would *never* encourage, support, approve, or condone war. Having done this, it must then use all appropriate means at its command to persuade its members to oppose, reject, and, where necessary, refuse participation in war.

The verb, please note, is "persuade." Allowance must always be made for two unfortunate, but probably unavoidable, facts: (1) Christianity does not now have, and is unlikely to ever have, sufficient influence over the affairs of nations to eliminate the possibility of international conflict; and

(2) not all members of the Christian community will be sufficiently responsive to its guidance to assure that all, or even most, will reject war and participation in war. Because of this, the Church, in keeping with its sacred mission, will be called upon to continue to perform its pastoral functions even for these errant members and provide whatever moral guidance and support it can within the limitations imposed by a war that it cannot endorse or approve.

The Pacifist and Statecraft

As for the criteria developed under the just-war ethic, they could still have a useful part to play in the context of this essentially pacifist stance and thrust. Now, however, instead of providing the mechanism for the justification of some wars and some practices, they would be used to define conditions and actions so clearly unjust that they would "merit unequivocal and unhesitating condemnation."[6] Only in such cases would participation in a war defined and condemned as unjust—or open violation of the rules of conduct *in bello*—be cause for formally excluding the guilty (a Hitler, for example) from the Christian fellowship and sacraments until suitable amends are made.

Since these proposals would represent a restoration of the direction and thrust of Christian teachings and obligations of its earliest years, they do not represent "new answers" to the "old problems" of war and peace. In this sense, too, it is not the "entirely new attitude" called for by Vatican Council II. Nevertheless, it *would* be a more authentic Christian witness than that provided under the just-war ethic across the centuries. One possible objection is that adopting so "negative" a stance would remove or neutralize any influence Christianity and Christians might have upon "statecraft" and might even benefit the forces of evil and oppression in situations where the common good or a nation's survival might be at stake.

Two answers might be offered to this objection. On the spiritual level there are the Beatitudes and the Sermon on the Mount and their implications as discussed by Eileen Egan. These, taken in context with the workings of grace and the power of God (which, as Scripture tells us, is made perfect in infirmity), combine to produce an "otherworldly" perspective in which the practice of statecraft becomes at best a secondary consideration. After all, if it avails us not to gain the whole world at the cost of our immortal souls, it might follow that the salvation of our souls could require us to be prepared to suffer the loss of the political and spiritual freedoms we prize where the only alternative is to commit sin.

The most urgent task of Catholic statecraft is to oppose measures and policies which would lock us into a situation that is likely to force that awful choice upon us. If modern war has reached the point of development where its weapons and strategies threaten the continuation of the human race, it is evident (or should be) that it is no longer an instrument for serving or protecting the common good. Once a nation's "survival" is equated with assuring little more than a functioning remnant after the populations of the contending parties (and "innocent bystander" nations as well) have been destroyed, the threat and uses of war become themselves the most immediate threat to human survival.

There must be no further delay in creating and developing other means of defense that are compatible with Christian values, means which will permit believers to join the struggles for justice and oppose oppression without being obliged to injure or kill another human being, even the *enemy* they are commanded to love. Nonviolent alternatives to war are the answer, but until now we have devoted far too little effort to discovering ways to make them effective. The hesitant first steps that have been taken in the last twenty years or so are no more than a beginning. Until nonviolence and its techniques can be brought to the attention of the masses in terms that will persuade them of its promise and win them away from their present commitment to violence and threats of violence as the only "realistic" hope for advancing and defending the higher values we profess, there is little justification for even speaking of a "Christian statecraft."

The virtues of nonviolence are not limited solely to defense. It can also serve as the instrument of the "pacifism of resistance" of which Lammers speaks. To achieve this, however, a true conversion is needed and this, as always, is preeminently the task of those religious communities which claim both the delegated authority and the special resources of grace through which the world is to be won for Christ and his way. In this we return to the very critical issue of the "public policy" of the Church discussed by Hehir, especially as it relates to defining the individual Christian's proper role, privileges, and obligations in the secular order. I have already indicated several points of disagreement with his interpretation, but a few added comments are in order here with particular reference to what I regard as a dangerous tendency in contemporary politico-theological thinking.

A Critique of "Moral Man" and "Immoral Society"

Too many of our discussions of war and pacifism are conducted almost entirely within the frame of reference defined by Reinhold Niebuhr and his followers. It is never easy to challenge a position associated with so eminent an authority in his field, and the difficulty is magnified when, as in this instance, the challenge is posed by someone outside that field who can claim at most a peripheral, second-hand familiarity with his principal works. I have already confessed my lack of "expertise" in the area of Protestant theology (and it extends as well to Catholic theology, I might add), a subject I am more than willing to leave to Deats and Muelder to explore.

At the same time there are certain aspects of what I might call "the Niebuhr Dilemma" which trouble me *as a sociologist*. Since these have had a demonstrable impact upon the formation—or at least the justification—of social and military policies I deplore, I feel my objections deserve to be put on the record in a volume like this.

To begin, there are the uses made by political and strategic theorists of the famous distinction between "moral man" and "immoral society." The implied division of human behavior into what appear to be two separate and distinct planes of activity, the one subject to moral regulations and the other less so, could create a situation in which the individual actor is susceptible to a kind of moral schizophrenia. More disturbing still, this division seems to derive from a reification of that intricate network of individual human interactions we call society into something more tangible, a hypothetically empirical entity capable of being "immoral" (or, for that matter, moral). Even if the distinction is presented as a literary flourish or heuristic device, we must be wary of the sociologistic fallacy which would attribute to "society" a real existence apart from its constituent members or the intellectual and volitional capacities upon which any judgment of morality or immorality must be based. It is not "society" (or, for that matter, even the abstraction we call the "state") which makes war or participates in war; it is always and only the human actors involved in that network of interactions who do so.

Given my professional perspective, I would be the last to deny that participation in this network of interactions exerts an influence, often enough approaching a determining influence, upon the behavior of the individual. "Social controls" can define the meaning of a given situation and operate to restrict the range of available choices (or, more correctly, the actor's *awareness* of the range of available choices) of action. Even this does not justify according "society" existence in its own right, apart from *and superior to*, the flesh-and-blood actors who constitute its "members."

To reject this conceptualization of society as an entity capable of acting in a moral or immoral fashion is not to close one's eyes to the inescapable historical fact that these networks of interaction induce patterns of thinking and acting in the individuals engaged in them, which actions can be described and evaluated in moral terms. But, here again, such patterns (racism, genocide, war, etc.) are not to be attributed to "society" as such except as a verbal convenience. The immorality of an action must always and ultimately rest with the individual (or group of individuals) responsible for committing it. If, as is so often the case, that individual's moral perceptions are confused or his will weakened by involvement in a particular network of interactions, allowances can always be made in assessing personal guilt and imposing punishments.

As pure conceptualization, of course, the Niebuhr distinction would pose no grave danger. In its application, however, it has had a serious and harmful effect upon our thinking about war and peace. By seeming to establish separate and only remotely related spheres of activity, it has served to introduce an arbitrary division between "private" and "public" behavior. This is most in evidence with respect to individuals in positions of public responsibility—Paul Ramsey's "magistrates"—but it carries over as well to the behavior of the ordinary individual who is both "believer" and "citizen." In the process, individuals who represent a multiplicity of roles to be played in a wide range of social interactions (and who, as autonomous persons, should bear primary responsibility for determining the order of priority among those roles) discover to their confusion that their behavior is subject to different and, in certain important respects, inconsistent normative expectations.

A recent article begins with a socio-psychological truism, "Human beings find their dignity and honor in their identities," and then continues, "In the modern world, for various reasons, the most powerful form of identity has become national or ethnic identity."[7] Much as I regret the fact, I tend to agree. Furthermore, I would include the popularity of the Niebuhrian formulation among those "various reasons" to the extent that it seems to imply a dissociation of moral responsibility for acts performed in the public sphere, in effect giving them the position of priority over the narrower, more personal, elements in one's "identities." Those magistrates faced with the choice of surrendering "national identity" or commanding an act that has been defined as "an offence against God and man himself" would feel fully justified, even obligated, by their public position to choose the latter. Nuremberg justice notwithstanding, the same would hold true for those who obey that command all the way down the line.

Pacifists, however much they may agree with the quotation, are more likely to see the concentration on national identity as the root cause of the chauvinism out of which grow the evil flowers of modern war. One can recognize the difference between the "public" and "private" roles which, taken together, make up our total identities and provide us with dignity and honor; one can even acknowledge the special and more demanding obligations those public roles may place upon us. What one is not permitted, I would argue, is to apply different moral standards in meeting them.

It might be well for our churches and their responsible leaders to be a little less concerned about their competence with regard to issues of "statecraft" and more intent upon restoring the religious identity to the position of first priority among the individual's many identities. This may require, as I have suggested elsewhere, a return to the attitudes and teachings that dominated the earliest years of Christianity's existence—not, I hasten to add, in any sense of narrow evangelical fundamentalism but, rather, in the full commitment to the Spirit that breathes through the Gospels. A society composed of truly "in-spirited" men and women, a network of interactions governed by a dedication to love and nonviolence even at the cost of humiliation and martyrdom, might yet convert the world. As it once did.

That a group of writers as gifted and committed as the contributors to this volume could join their efforts, despite admitted differences on some very critical points, in a search for "new answers" to "old questions" is a sign of hope. Perhaps twenty years from now when some enterprising editor takes it upon himself to survey the "state of the question" concerning Christians and peace, humankind will have achieved something much closer to that ideal world. If humankind survives.

Notes

1. William J. Nagle, ed., *Morality and Modern Warfare: The State of the Question* (Baltimore: Helicon, 1960).
2. Ibid., p. 6.
3. Ibid., p. 104.
4. In "Human Life in Our Day" (n. 103), in David J. O'Brien and Thomas A. Shannon, eds., *Renewing the Earth: Catholic Documents on Peace, Justice and Liberation* (New York: Doubleday Image Books, 1977), p. 454.
5. Stanley Windass, *Christianity Versus Violence* (London: Sheed & Ward, 1964), p. 12.
6. "Constitution on the Church in the Modern World," (n. 80). In Walter M. Abbot, S.J., ed., *The Documents of Vatican II* (New York: America Press, 1966), p. 294.
7. Ninian Smart, "Nationalism, Identity, and a More Secure World Order," *Worldview* 22 (June 1979): 9.

INDEX

Shannon, Thomas A. editor

WAR OR PEACE? THE SEARCH FOR
NEW ANSWERS

DATE DUE

MAY 08 2003			
NOV 28 2007			